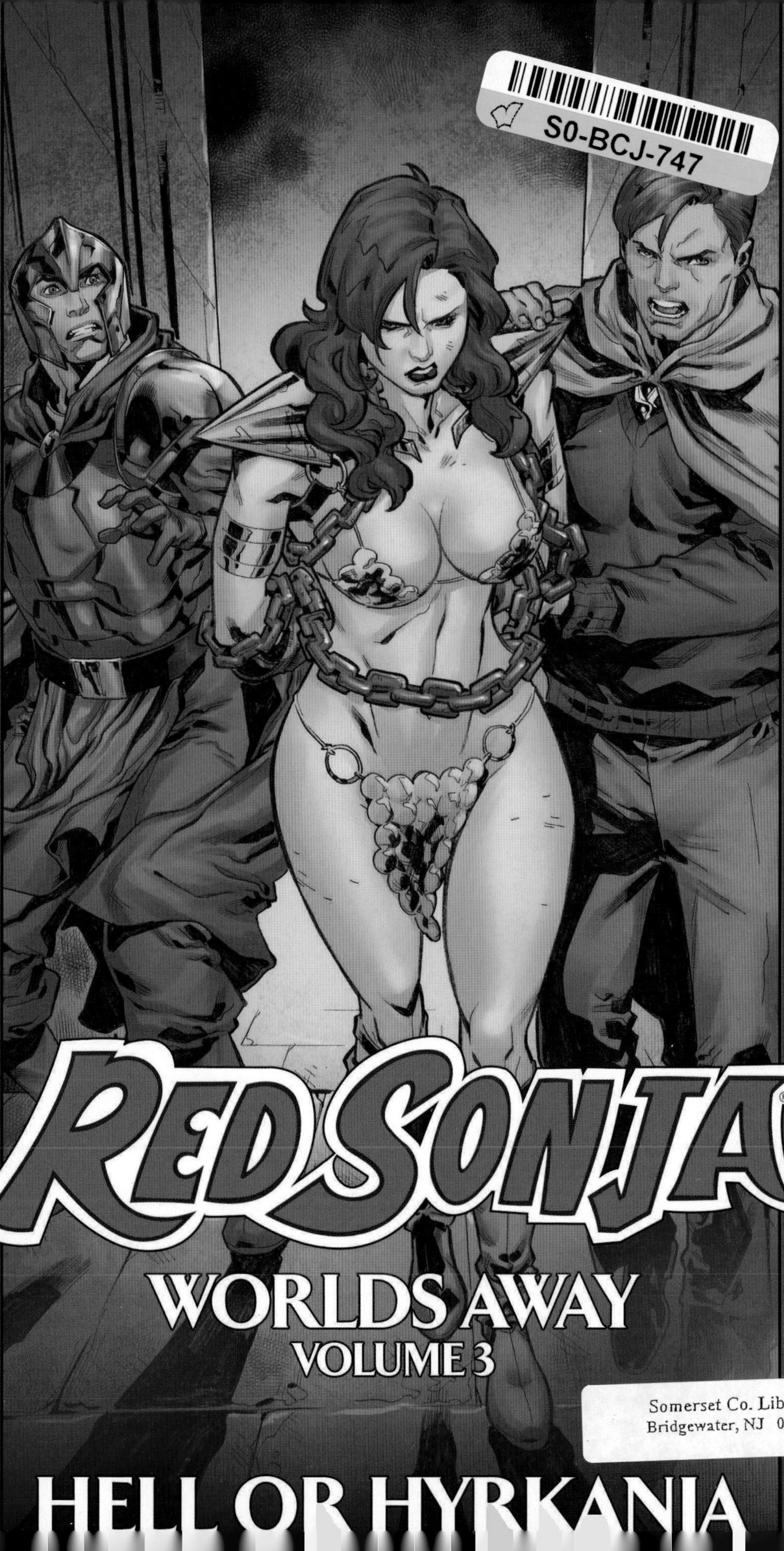

RED SONJA®

WORLDS AWAY
VOLUME 3

HELL OR HYRKANIA

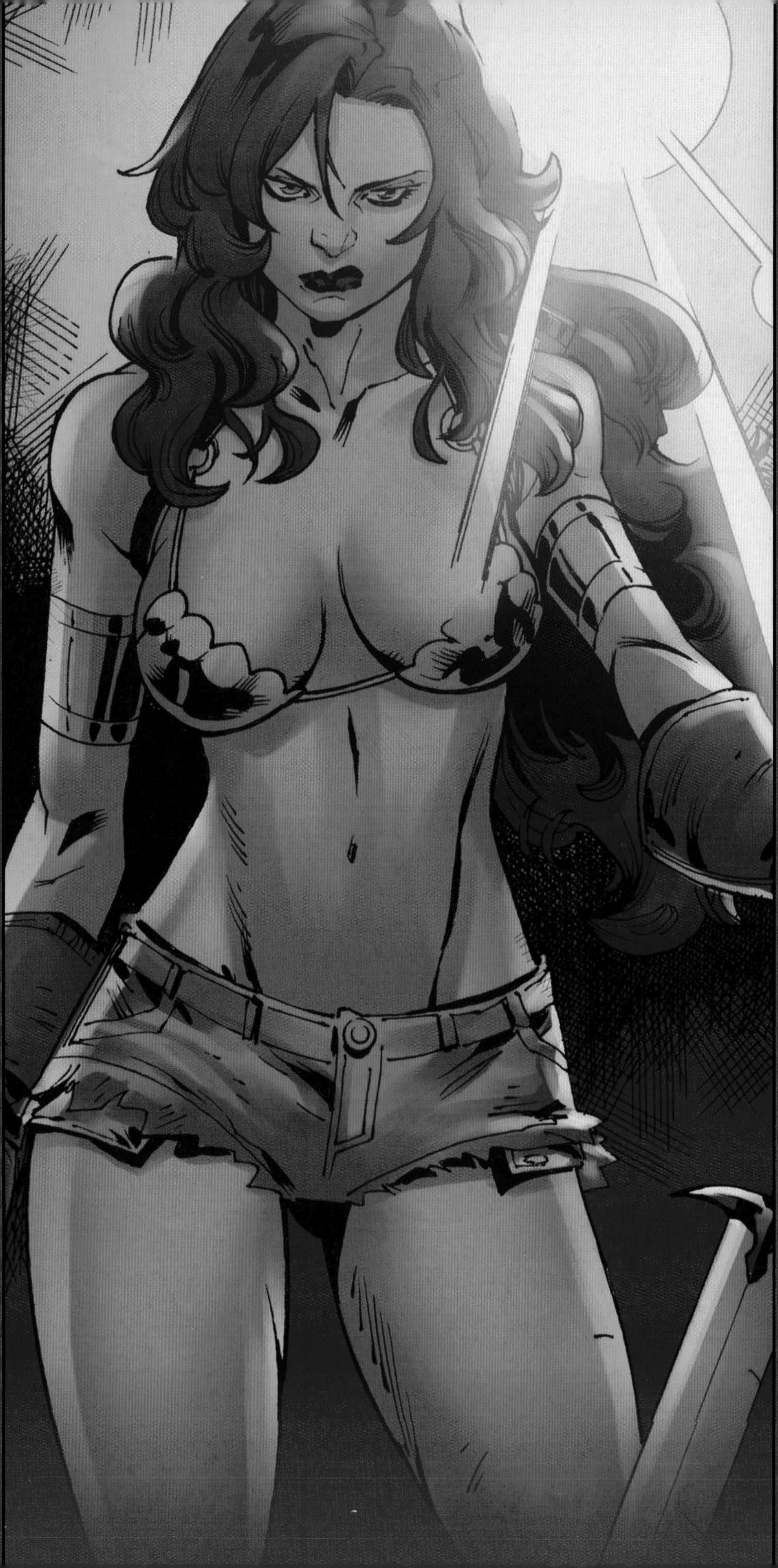

written by
AMY CHU & ERIK BURNHAM

illustrated by
CARLOS GOMEZ

colored by
MOHAN

lettered by
SIMON BOWLAND

collection cover art by
MIKE McKONE

co-executive editors **JOSEPH RYBANDT & LUKE LIEBERMAN**
associate editor **ANTHONY MARQUES**
book design by **CATHLEEN HEARD**

based on the heroine created by
ROBERT E. HOWARD

in memory of
ARTHUR LIEBERMAN

special thanks to
SHANNON KINGSTON

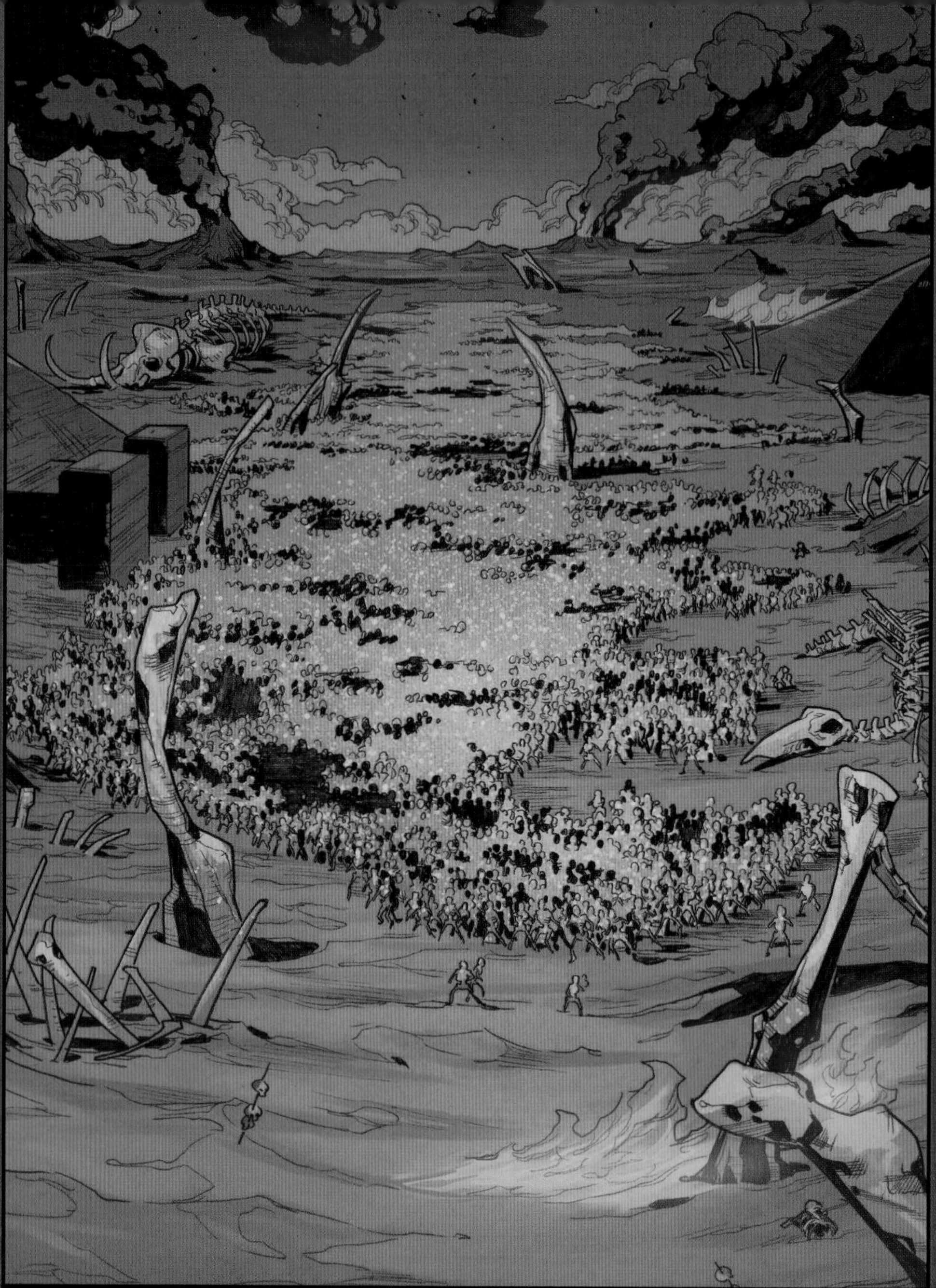

DYNAMITE®

Online at **www.DYNAMITE.com**
On Facebook **/Dynamitecomics**
On Instagram **/Dynamitecomics**
On Tumblr **dynamitecomics.tumblr.com**
On Twitter **@dynamitecomics**
On YouTube **/Dynamitecomics**

Nick Barrucci, CEO / Publisher
Juan Collado, President / COO
Brandon Dante Primavera, V.P. of IT and Operations
Rich Young, Director of Business Development

Joe Rybandt, Executive Editor
Matt Idelson, Senior Editor
Anthony Marques, Associate Editor
Kevin Ketner, Associate Editor

Geoff Harkins, Creative Director
Jason Ullmeyer, Art Director
Cathleen Heard, Senior Graphic Designer
Alexis Persson, Graphic Designer
Rachel Kilbury, Digital Multimedia Associate

Alan Payne, V.P. of Sales and Marketing
Pat O'Connell, Sales Manager

Amy Jackson, Administrative Coordinator

For media rights, foreign rights, promotions, licensing, and advertising: marketing@dynamite.com.

ISBN13: 978-1-5241-0714-7
First Printing 10 9 8 7 6 5 4 3 2 1

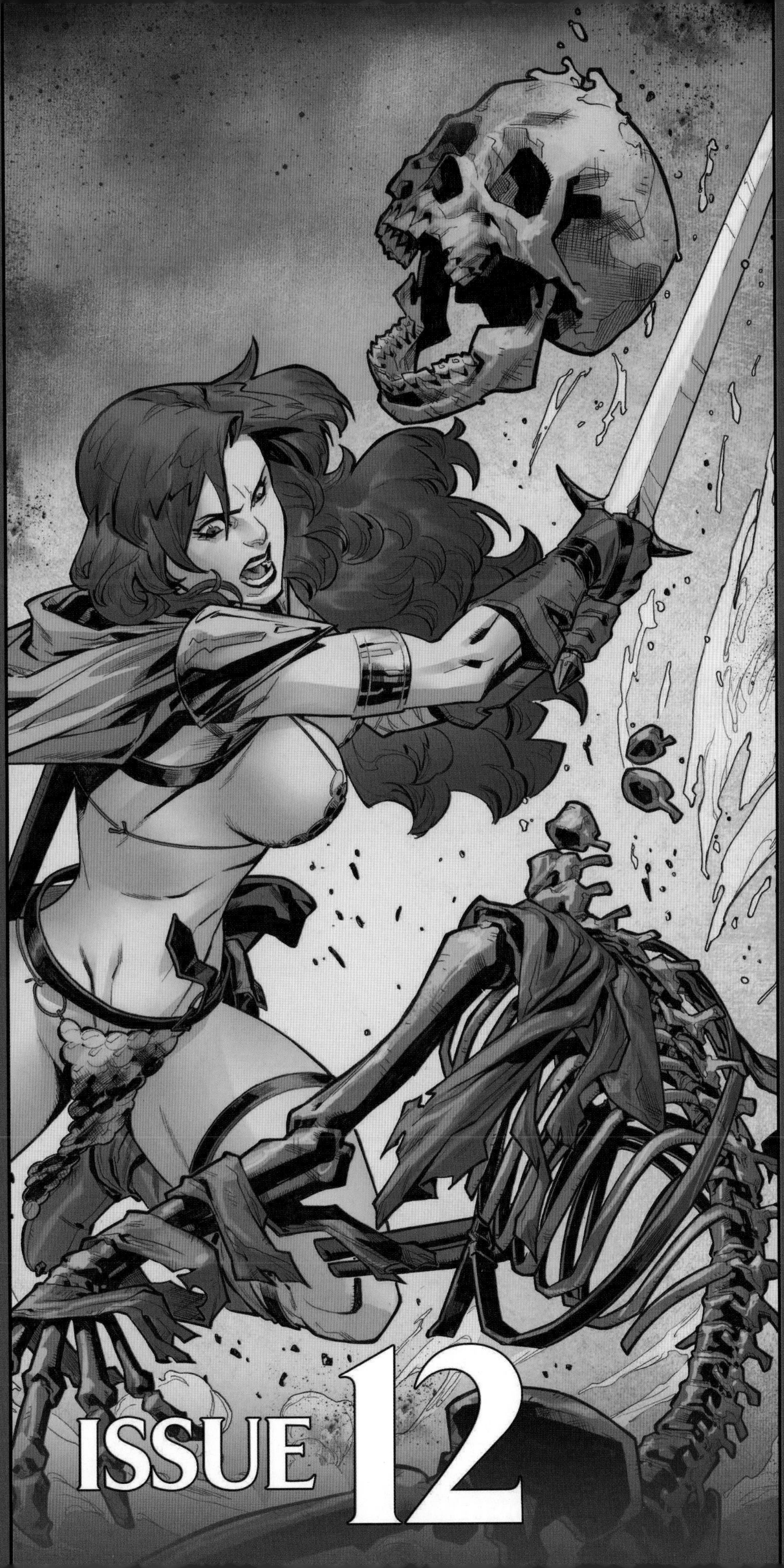
ISSUE 12

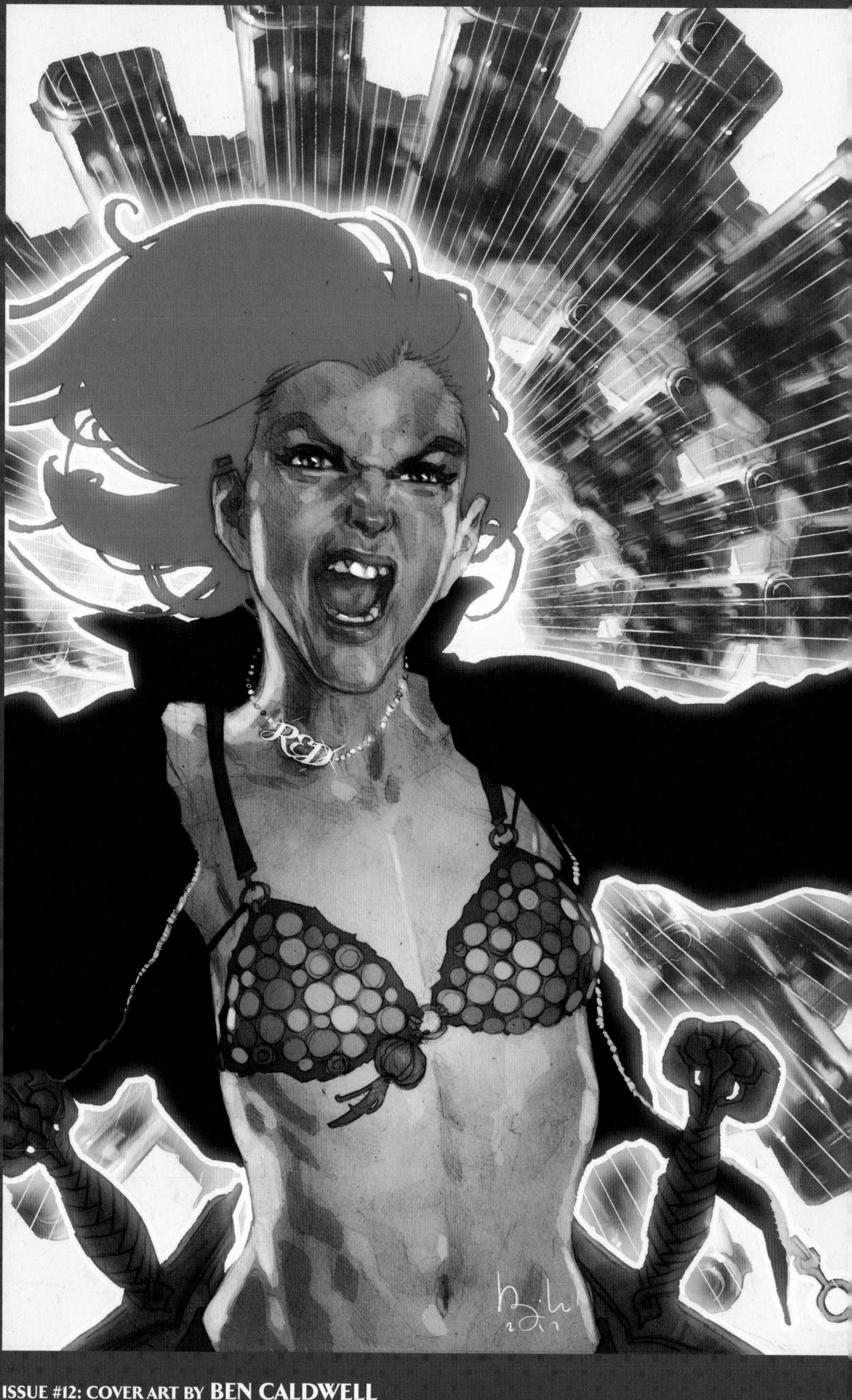

RED

ISSUE #12: COVER ART BY BEN CALDWELL

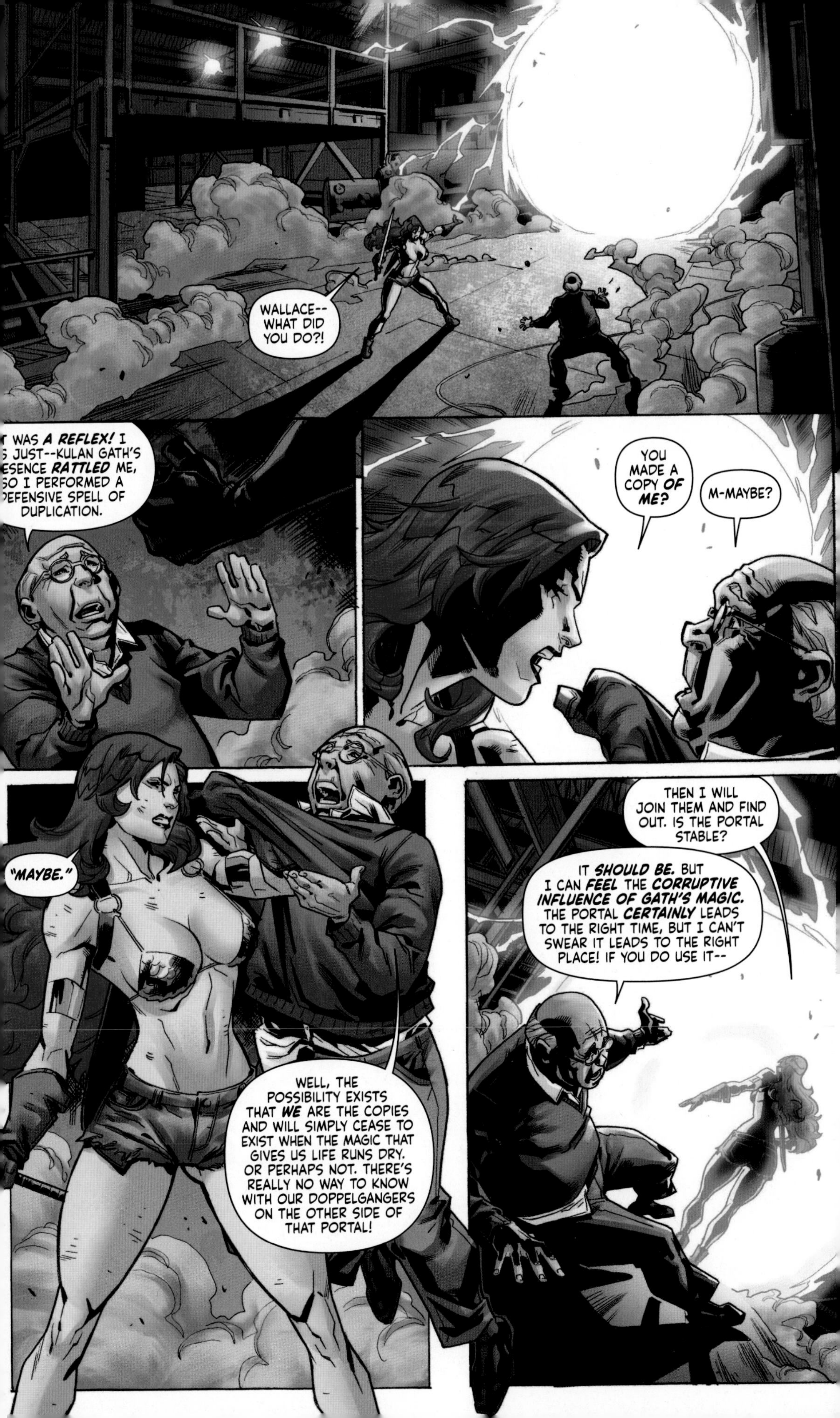

WALLACE-- WHAT DID YOU DO?!
T WAS *A REFLEX!* I S JUST--KULAN GATH'S ESENCE *RATTLED* ME, SO I PERFORMED A DEFENSIVE SPELL OF DUPLICATION.
YOU MADE A COPY *OF ME?*
M-MAYBE?
"MAYBE."
WELL, THE POSSIBILITY EXISTS THAT *WE* ARE THE COPIES AND WILL SIMPLY CEASE TO EXIST WHEN THE MAGIC THAT GIVES US LIFE RUNS DRY. OR PERHAPS NOT. THERE'S REALLY NO WAY TO KNOW WITH OUR DOPPELGANGERS ON THE OTHER SIDE OF THAT PORTAL!
THEN I WILL JOIN THEM AND FIND OUT. IS THE PORTAL STABLE?
IT *SHOULD BE.* BUT I CAN *FEEL* THE *CORRUPTIVE INFLUENCE OF GATH'S MAGIC.* THE PORTAL *CERTAINLY* LEADS TO THE RIGHT TIME, BUT I CAN'T SWEAR IT LEADS TO THE RIGHT PLACE! IF YOU DO USE IT--

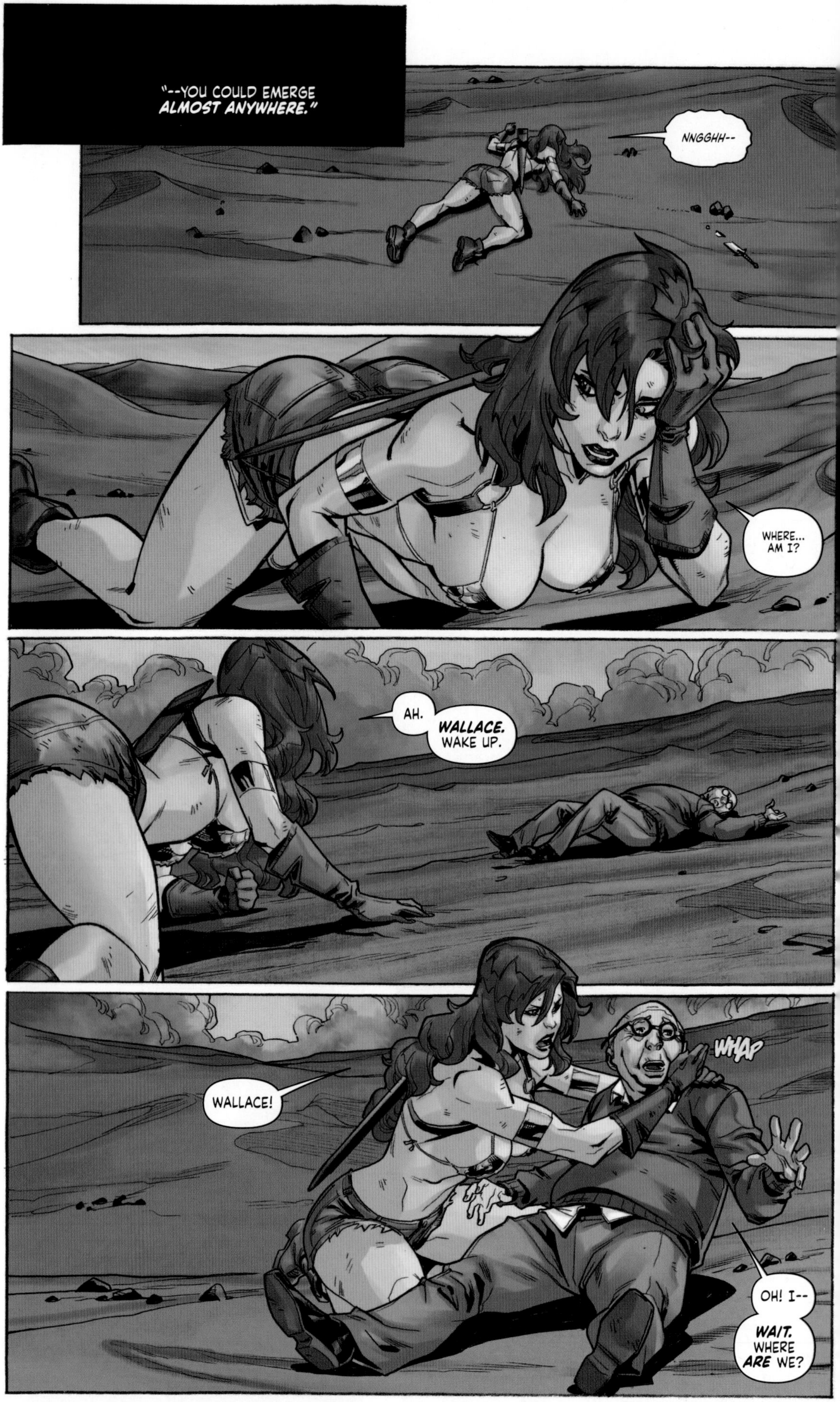
"--YOU COULD EMERGE ALMOST ANYWHERE."
NNGGHH--
WHERE... AM I?
AH. WALLACE. WAKE UP.
WHAP
WALLACE!
OH! I--
WAIT. WHERE ARE WE?

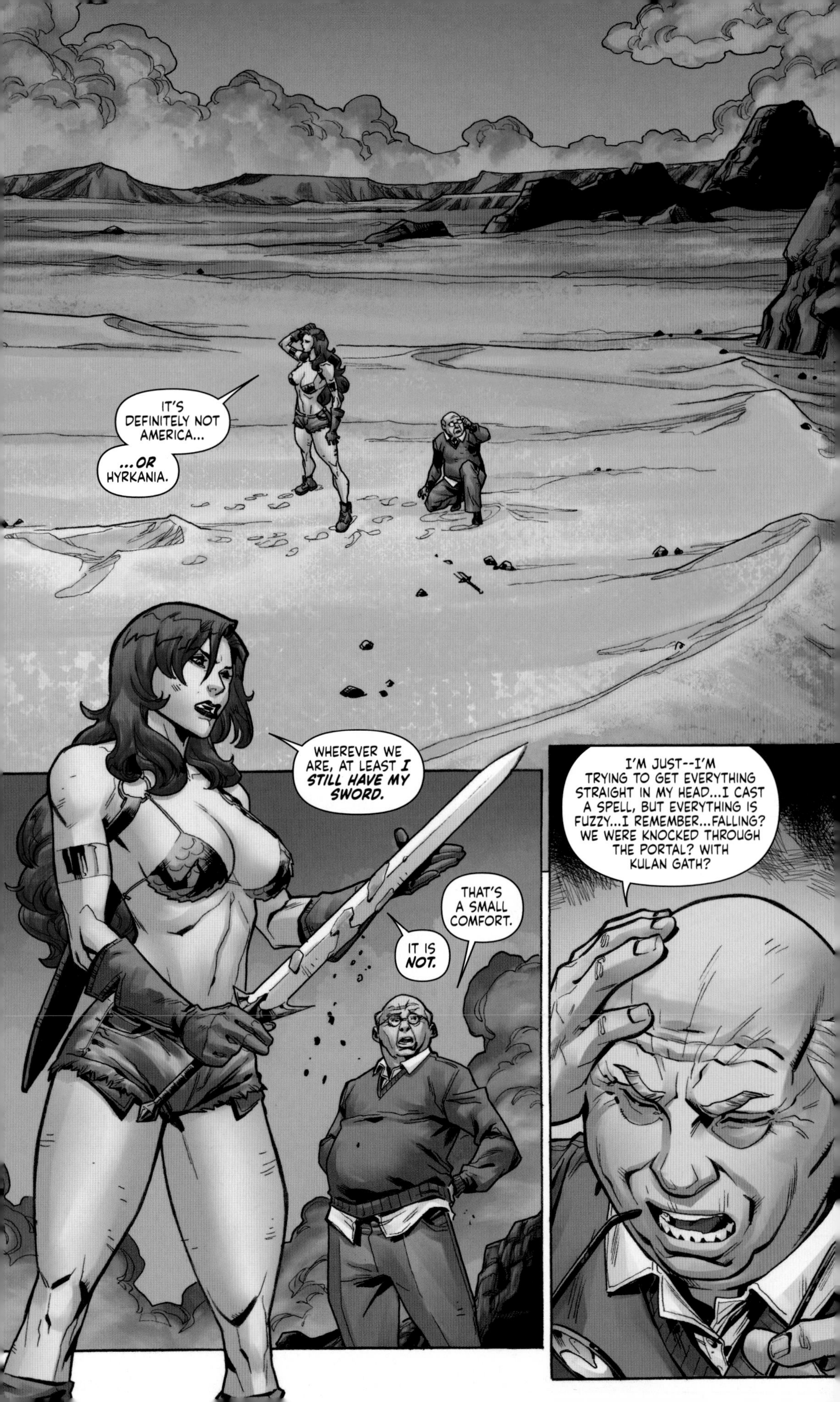

IT'S DEFINITELY NOT AMERICA...
...OR HYRKANIA.
WHEREVER WE ARE, AT LEAST I STILL HAVE MY SWORD.
IT IS NOT.
THAT'S A SMALL COMFORT.
I'M JUST--I'M TRYING TO GET EVERYTHING STRAIGHT IN MY HEAD...I CAST A SPELL, BUT EVERYTHING IS FUZZY...I REMEMBER...FALLING? WE WERE KNOCKED THROUGH THE PORTAL? WITH KULAN GATH?

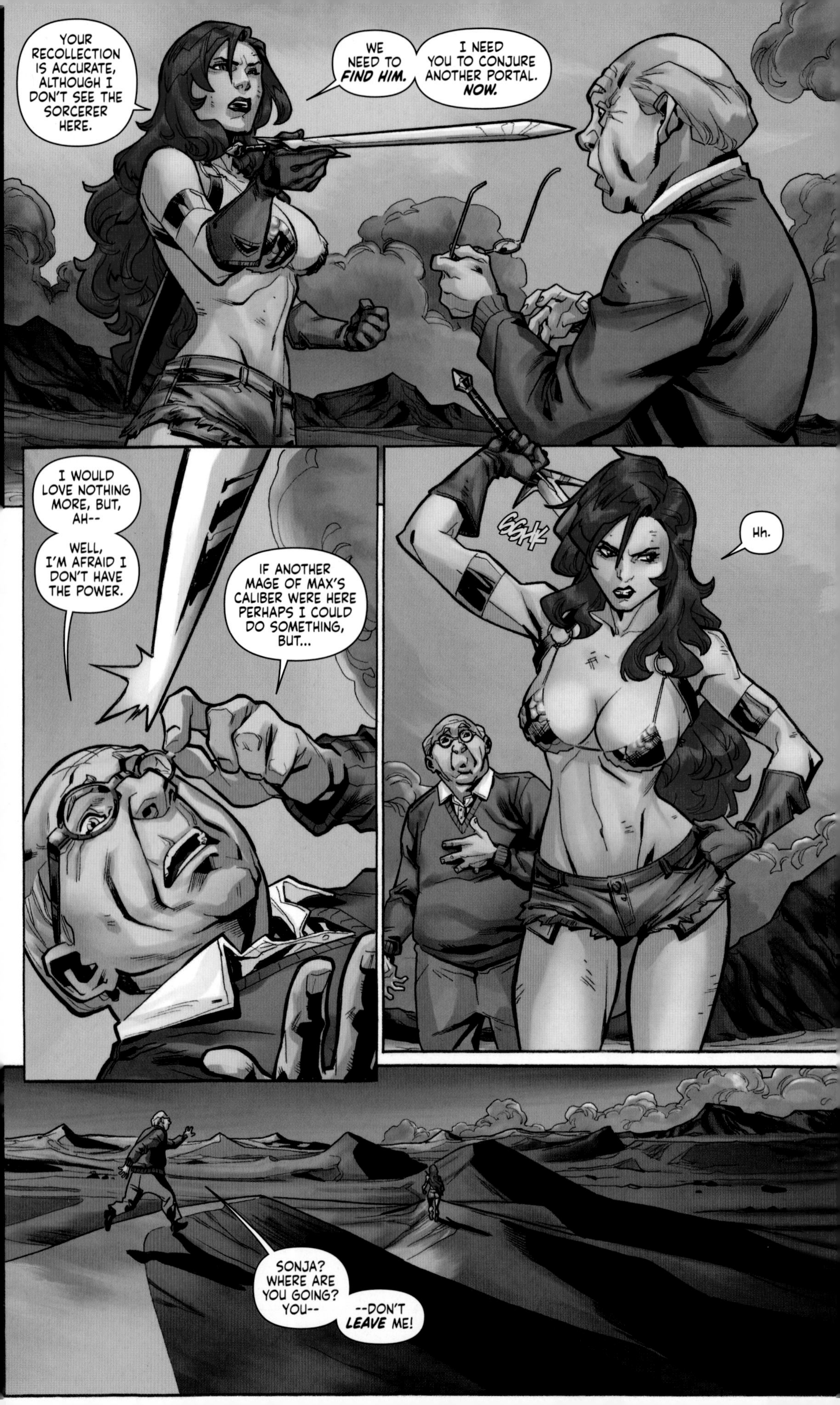
YOUR RECOLLECTION IS ACCURATE, ALTHOUGH I DON'T SEE THE SORCERER HERE.
WE NEED TO *FIND HIM.*
I NEED YOU TO CONJURE ANOTHER PORTAL. *NOW.*
I WOULD LOVE NOTHING MORE, BUT, AH--
WELL, I'M AFRAID I DON'T HAVE THE POWER.
IF ANOTHER MAGE OF MAX'S CALIBER WERE HERE PERHAPS I COULD DO SOMETHING, BUT...
SSHK
Hh.
SONJA? WHERE ARE YOU GOING? YOU--
--DON'T *LEAVE* ME!

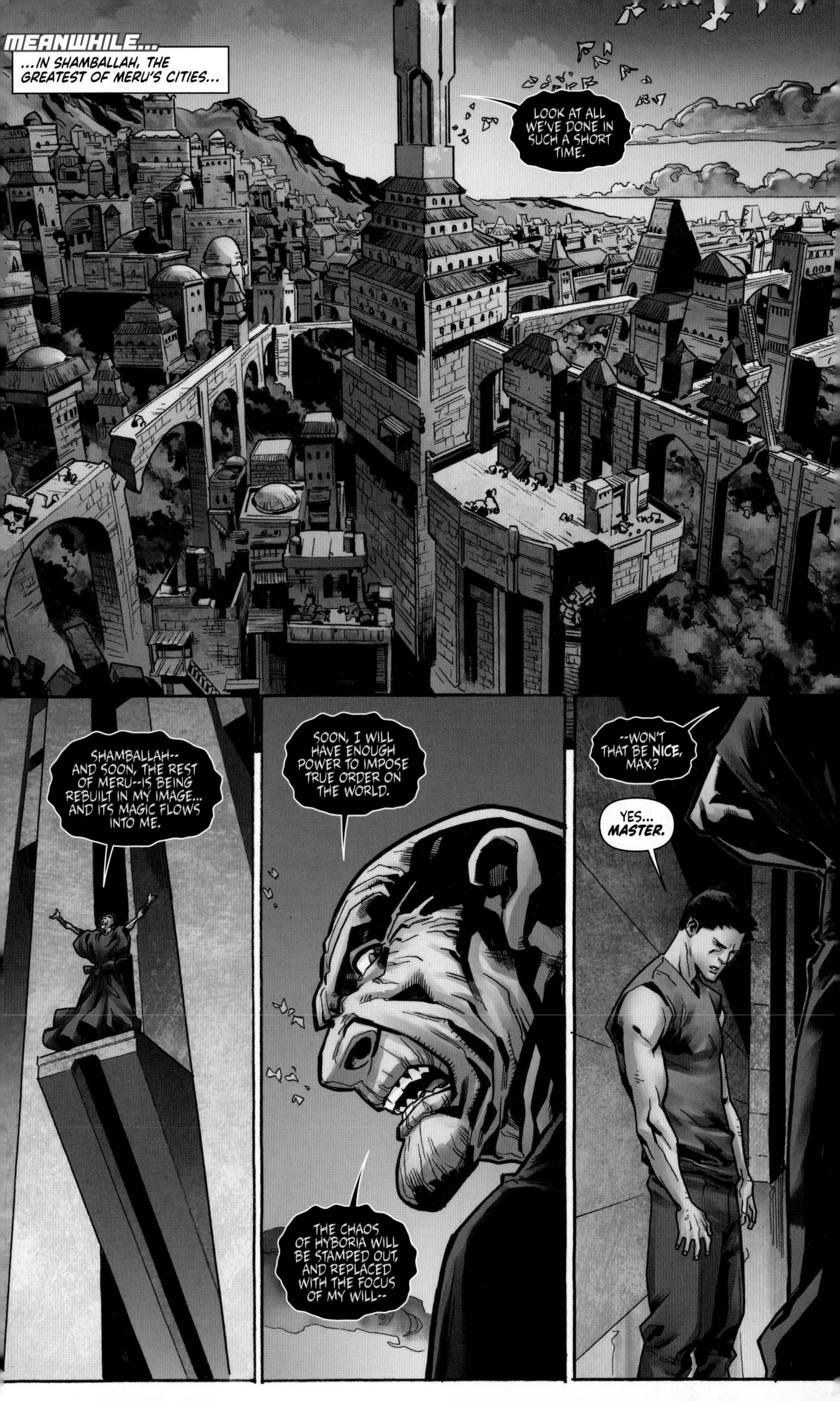

MEANWHILE...
...IN SHAMBALLAH, THE GREATEST OF MERU'S CITIES...
LOOK AT ALL WE'VE DONE IN SUCH A SHORT TIME.
SHAMBALLAH-- AND SOON, THE REST OF MERU--IS BEING REBUILT IN MY IMAGE... AND ITS MAGIC FLOWS INTO ME.
SOON, I WILL HAVE ENOUGH POWER TO IMPOSE TRUE ORDER ON THE WORLD.
THE CHAOS OF HYBORIA WILL BE STAMPED OUT, AND REPLACED WITH THE FOCUS OF MY WILL--
--WON'T THAT BE NICE, MAX?
YES... MASTER.

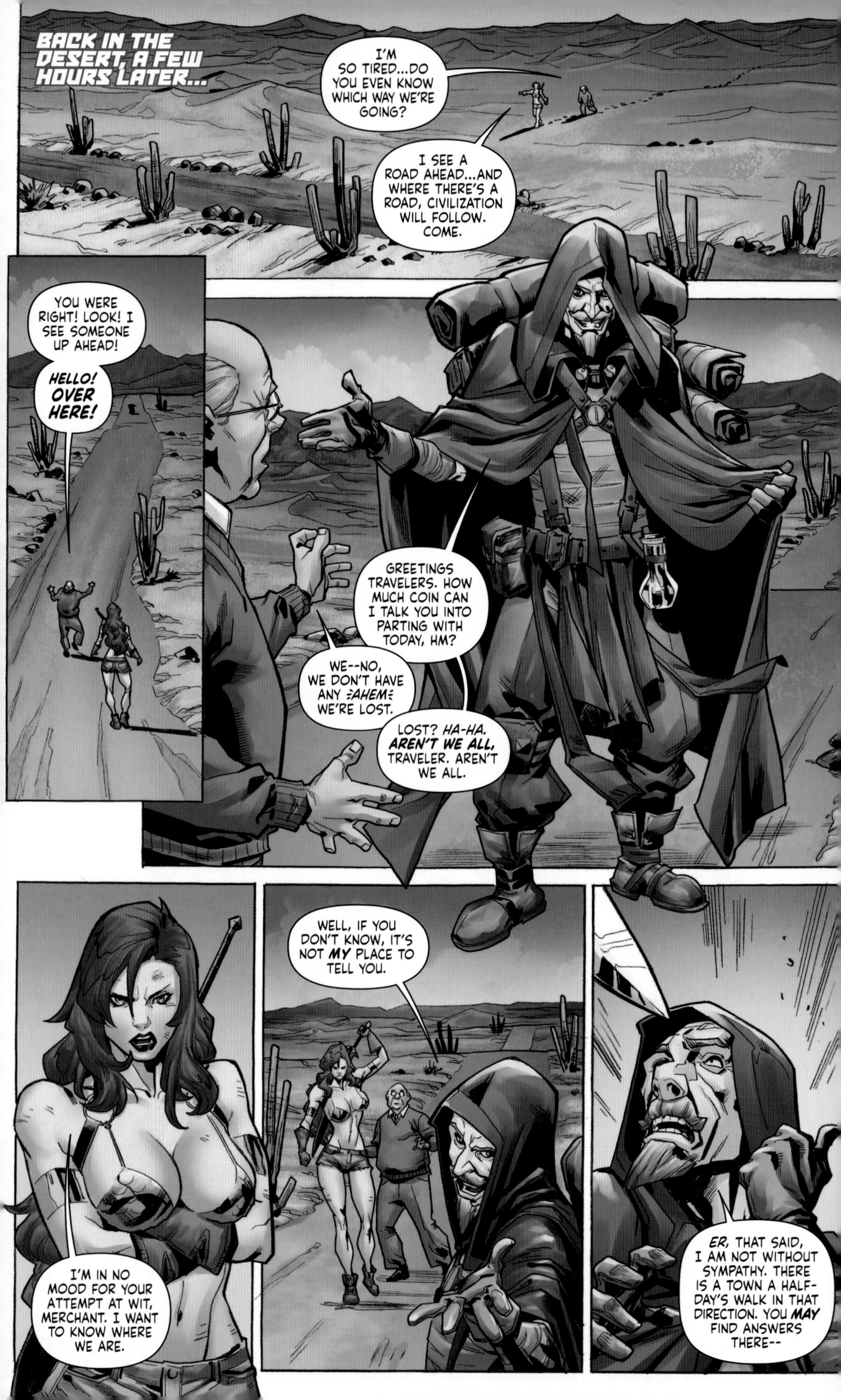
BACK IN THE DESERT, A FEW HOURS LATER...
I'M SO TIRED...DO YOU EVEN KNOW WHICH WAY WE'RE GOING?
I SEE A ROAD AHEAD...AND WHERE THERE'S A ROAD, CIVILIZATION WILL FOLLOW. COME.
YOU WERE RIGHT! LOOK! I SEE SOMEONE UP AHEAD!
HELLO! OVER HERE!
GREETINGS TRAVELERS. HOW MUCH COIN CAN I TALK YOU INTO PARTING WITH TODAY, HM?
WE--NO, WE DON'T HAVE ANY :AHEM: WE'RE LOST.
LOST? HA-HA. AREN'T WE ALL, TRAVELER. AREN'T WE ALL.
I'M IN NO MOOD FOR YOUR ATTEMPT AT WIT, MERCHANT. I WANT TO KNOW WHERE WE ARE.
WELL, IF YOU DON'T KNOW, IT'S NOT MY PLACE TO TELL YOU.
ER, THAT SAID, I AM NOT WITHOUT SYMPATHY. THERE IS A TOWN A HALF-DAY'S WALK IN THAT DIRECTION. YOU MAY FIND ANSWERS THERE--

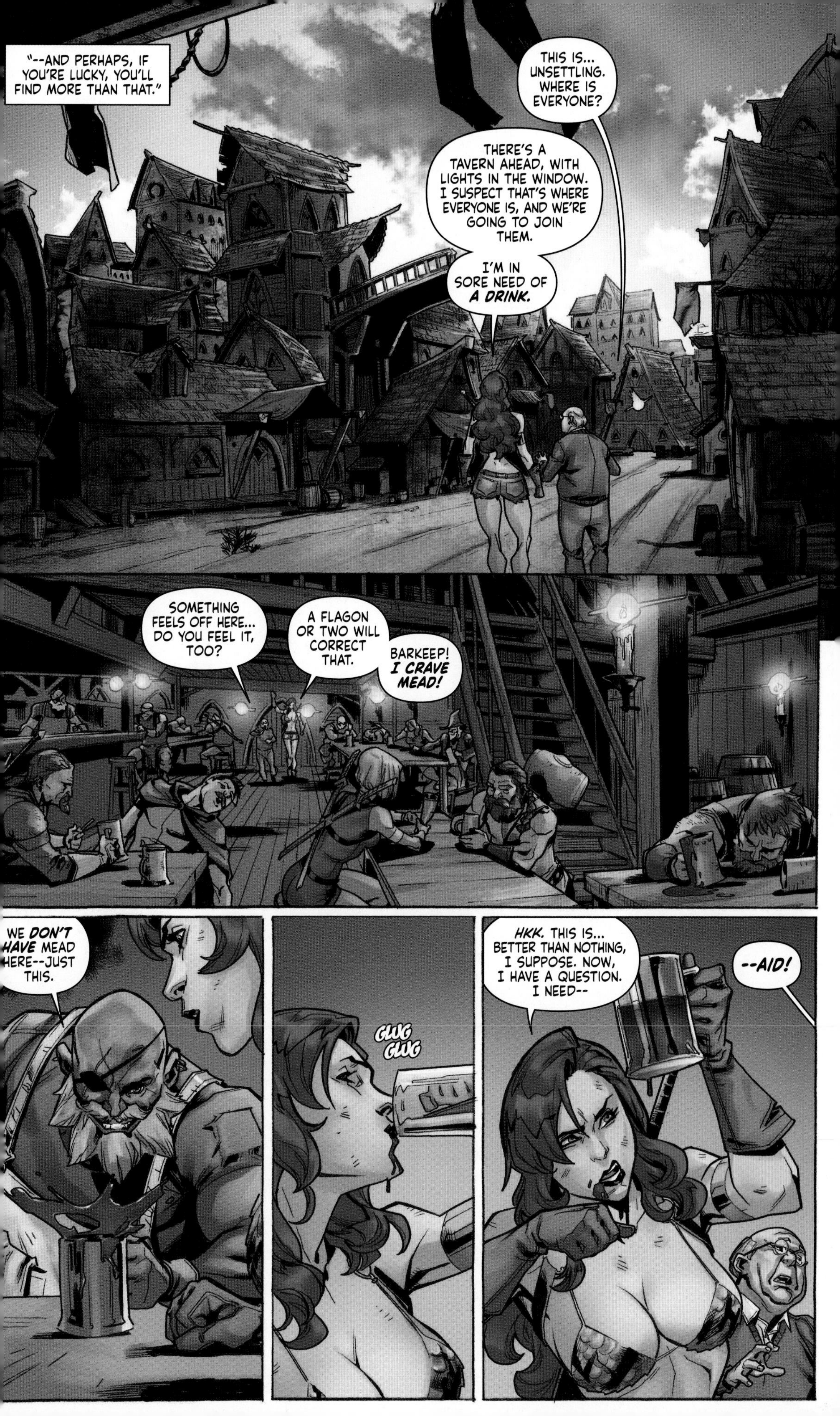
"--AND PERHAPS, IF YOU'RE LUCKY, YOU'LL FIND MORE THAN THAT."
THIS IS... UNSETTLING. WHERE IS EVERYONE?
THERE'S A TAVERN AHEAD, WITH LIGHTS IN THE WINDOW. I SUSPECT THAT'S WHERE EVERYONE IS, AND WE'RE GOING TO JOIN THEM.
I'M IN SORE NEED OF **A DRINK.**
SOMETHING FEELS OFF HERE... DO YOU FEEL IT, TOO?
A FLAGON OR TWO WILL CORRECT THAT.
BARKEEP! ***I CRAVE MEAD!***
WE ***DON'T HAVE*** MEAD HERE--JUST THIS.
GLUG GLUG
HKK. THIS IS... BETTER THAN NOTHING, I SUPPOSE. NOW, I HAVE A QUESTION. I NEED--
--AID!

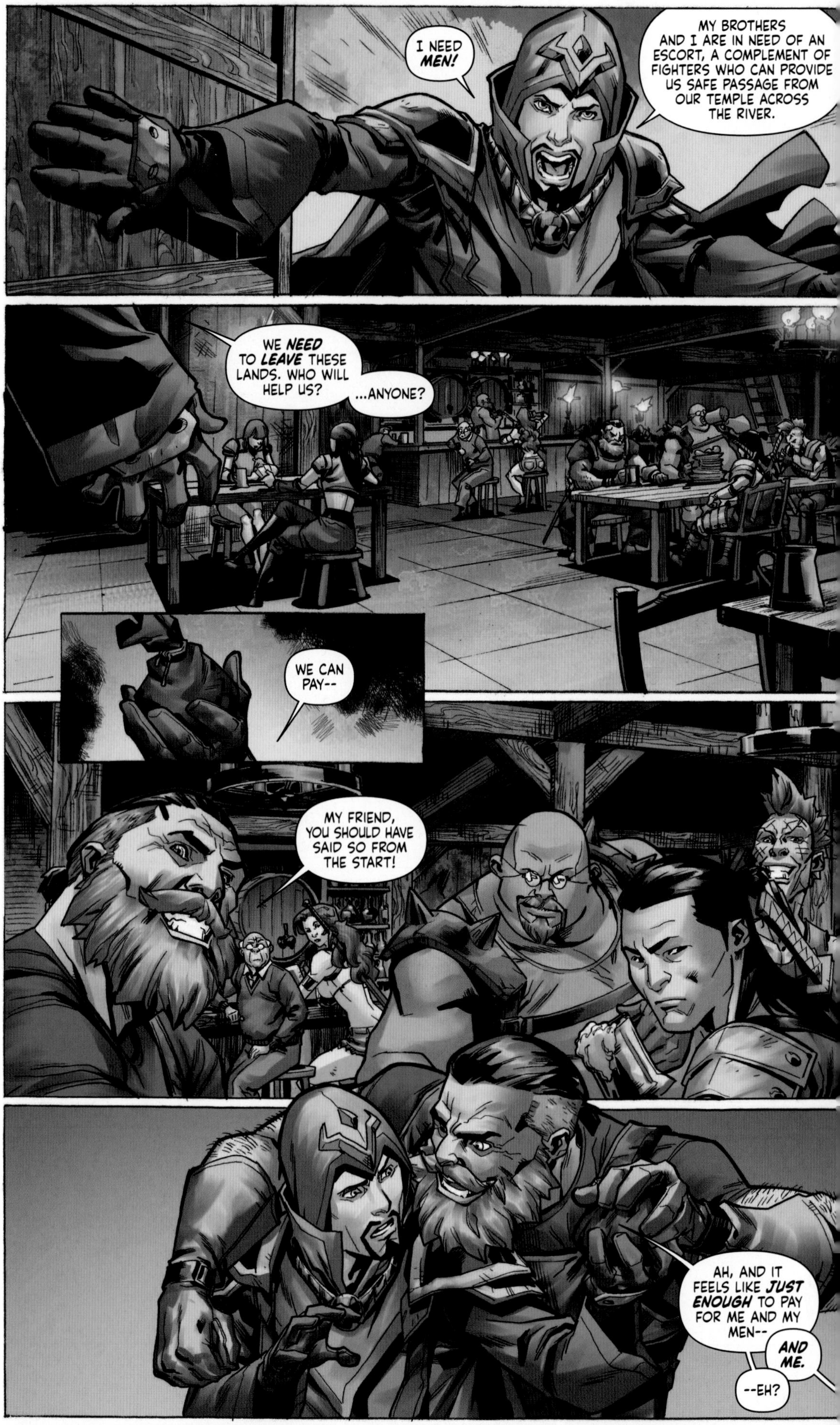
I NEED *MEN!*
MY BROTHERS AND I ARE IN NEED OF AN ESCORT, A COMPLEMENT OF FIGHTERS WHO CAN PROVIDE US SAFE PASSAGE FROM OUR TEMPLE ACROSS THE RIVER.
WE *NEED* TO *LEAVE* THESE LANDS. WHO WILL HELP US?
...ANYONE?
WE CAN PAY--
MY FRIEND, YOU SHOULD HAVE SAID SO FROM THE START!
AH, AND IT FEELS LIKE *JUST ENOUGH* TO PAY FOR ME AND MY MEN--
AND ME.
--EH?

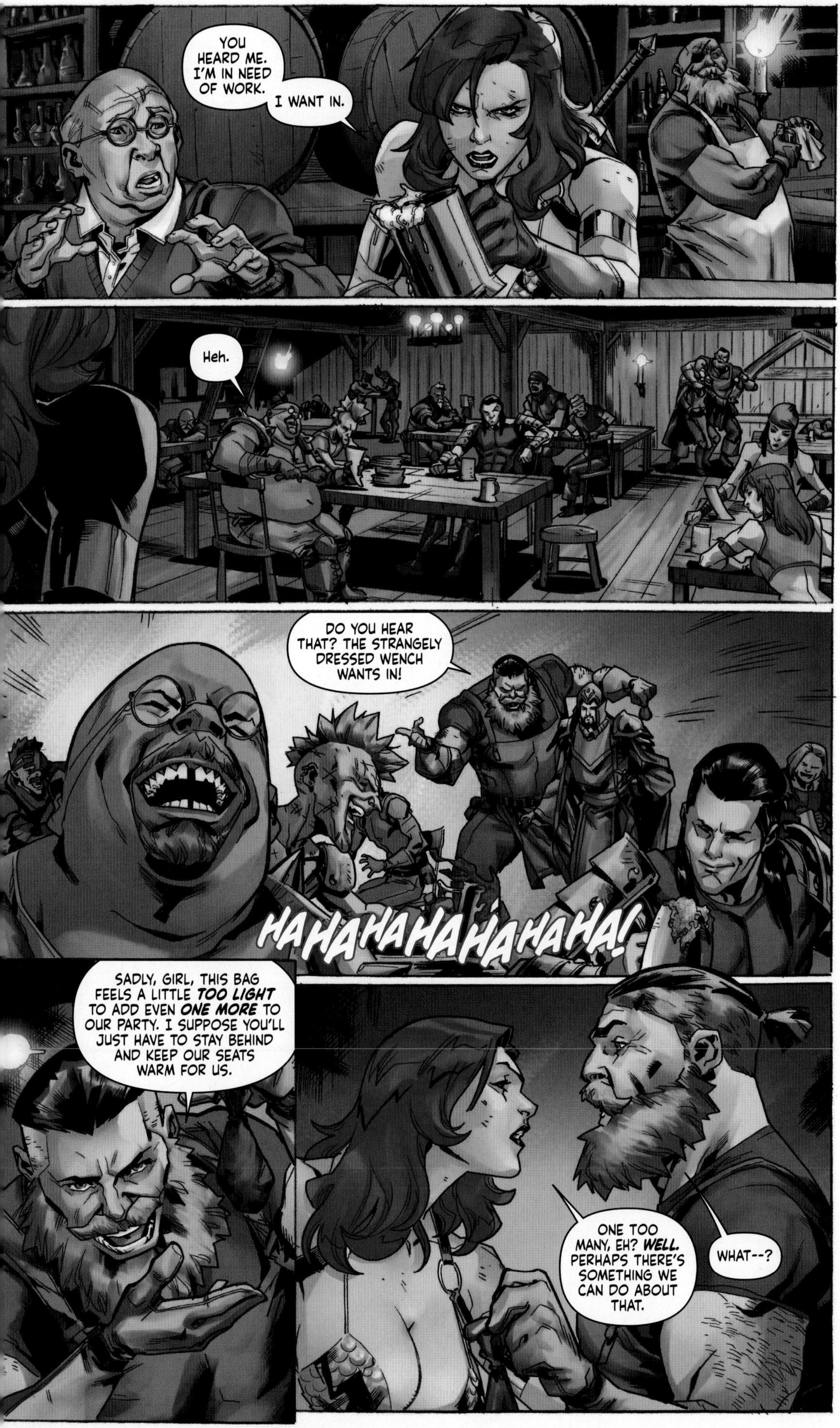
YOU HEARD ME. I'M IN NEED OF WORK.
I WANT IN.
Heh.
DO YOU HEAR THAT? THE STRANGELY DRESSED WENCH WANTS IN!
HAHAHAHAHAHAHAHAHA!
SADLY, GIRL, THIS BAG FEELS A LITTLE TOO LIGHT TO ADD EVEN ONE MORE TO OUR PARTY. I SUPPOSE YOU'LL JUST HAVE TO STAY BEHIND AND KEEP OUR SEATS WARM FOR US.
ONE TOO MANY, EH? WELL. PERHAPS THERE'S SOMETHING WE CAN DO ABOUT THAT.
WHAT--?

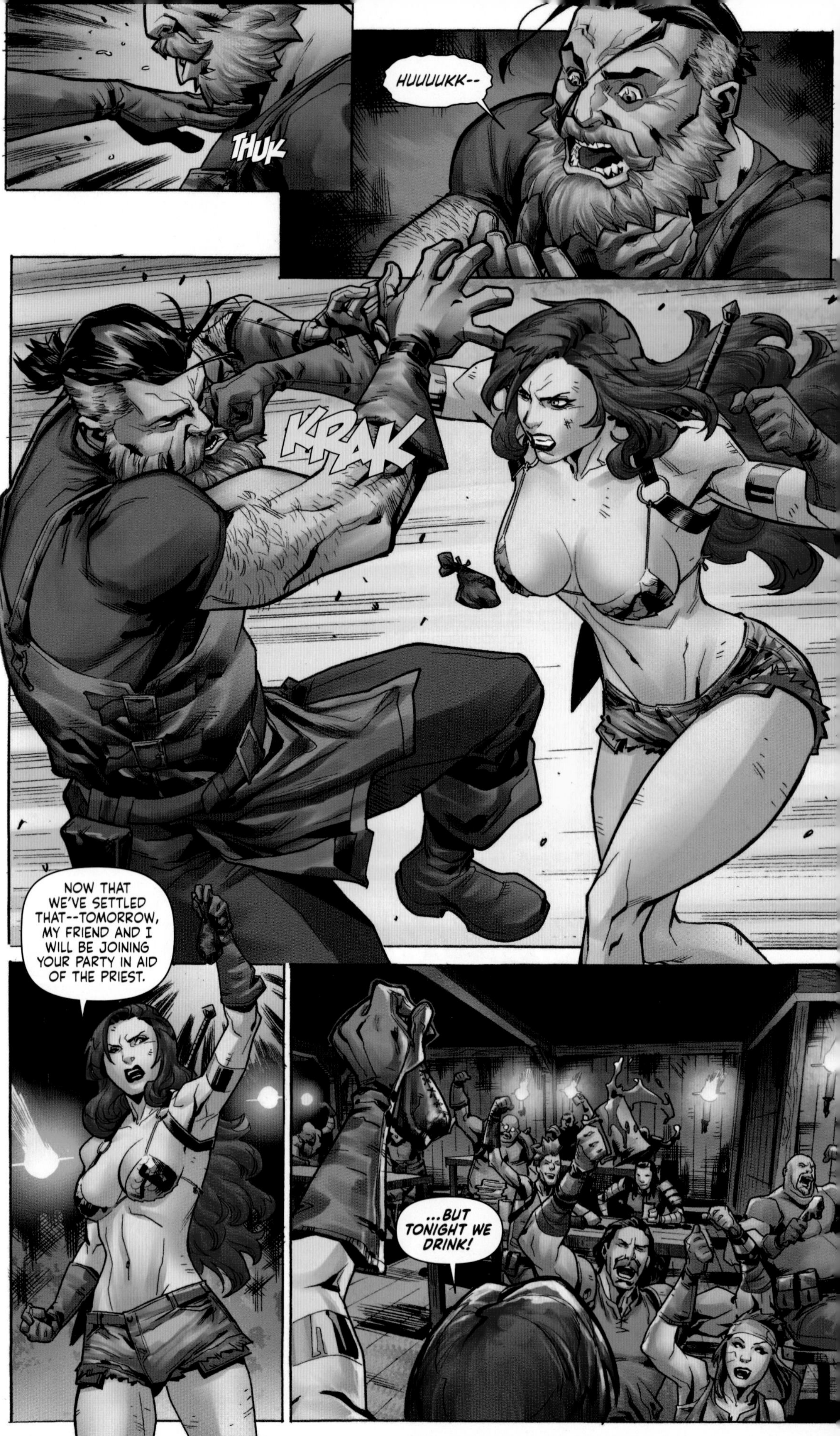
THUK
HUUUUKK--
KRAK
NOW THAT WE'VE SETTLED THAT--TOMORROW, MY FRIEND AND I WILL BE JOINING YOUR PARTY IN AID OF THE PRIEST.
...BUT TONIGHT WE DRINK!

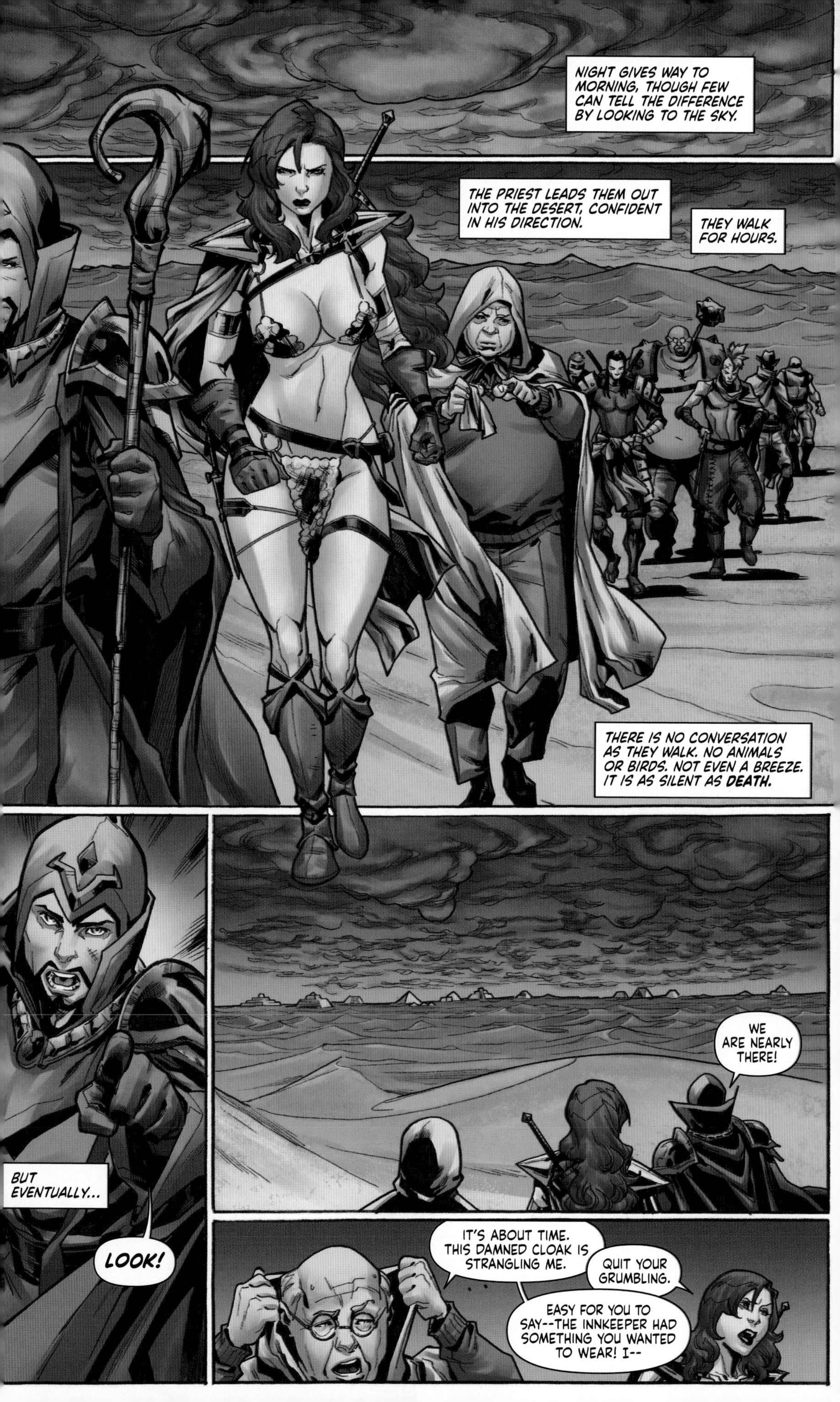
NIGHT GIVES WAY TO MORNING, THOUGH FEW CAN TELL THE DIFFERENCE BY LOOKING TO THE SKY.
THE PRIEST LEADS THEM OUT INTO THE DESERT, CONFIDENT IN HIS DIRECTION.
THEY WALK FOR HOURS.
THERE IS NO CONVERSATION AS THEY WALK. NO ANIMALS OR BIRDS. NOT EVEN A BREEZE. IT IS AS SILENT AS DEATH.
BUT EVENTUALLY...
LOOK!
WE ARE NEARLY THERE!
IT'S ABOUT TIME. THIS DAMNED CLOAK IS STRANGLING ME.
QUIT YOUR GRUMBLING.
EASY FOR YOU TO SAY--THE INNKEEPER HAD SOMETHING YOU WANTED TO WEAR! I--

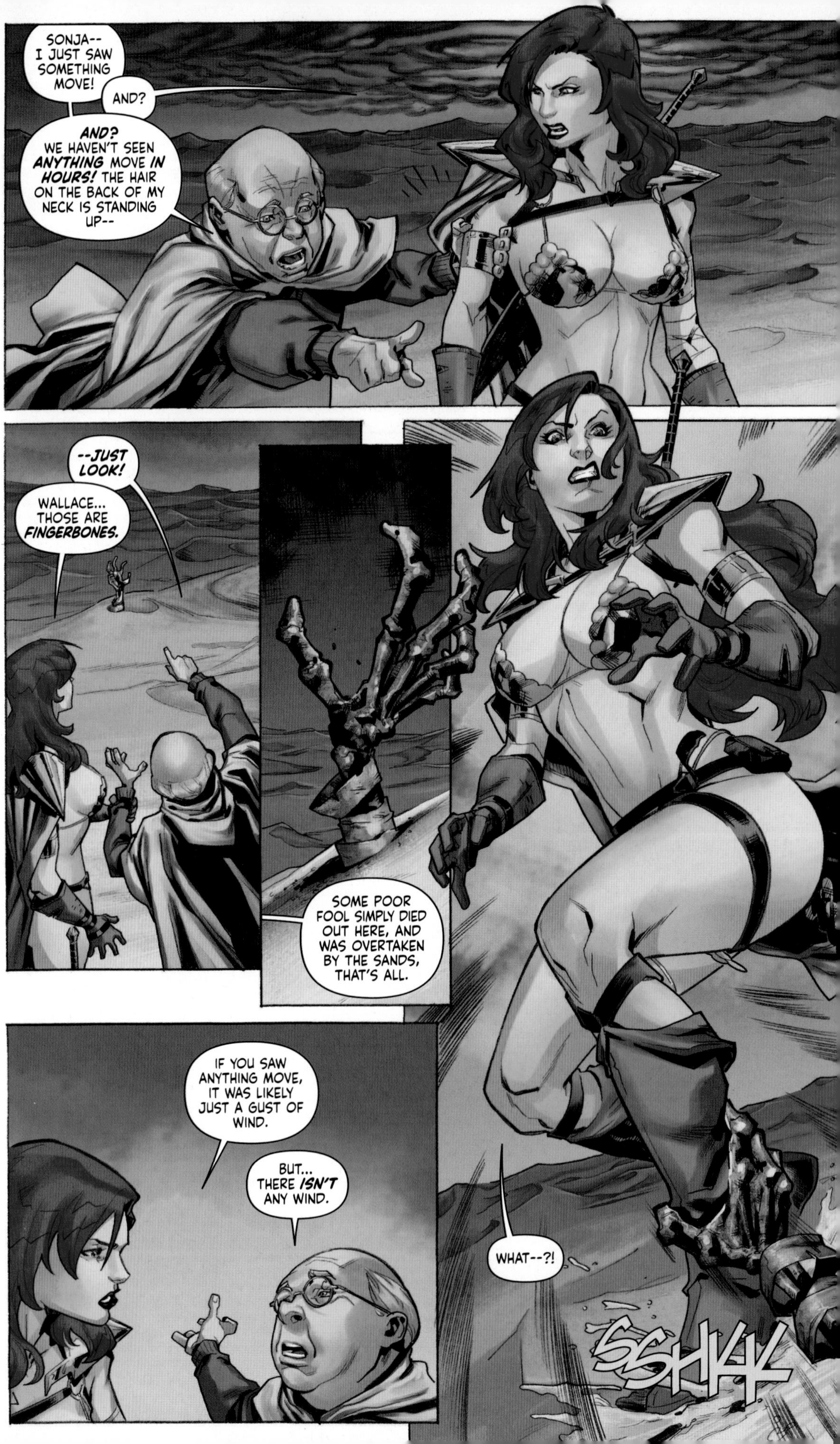
SONJA-- I JUST SAW SOMETHING MOVE!
AND?
AND? WE HAVEN'T SEEN ***ANYTHING*** MOVE ***IN HOURS!*** THE HAIR ON THE BACK OF MY NECK IS STANDING UP--
--JUST LOOK!
WALLACE... THOSE ARE ***FINGERBONES.***
SOME POOR FOOL SIMPLY DIED OUT HERE, AND WAS OVERTAKEN BY THE SANDS, THAT'S ALL.
IF YOU SAW ANYTHING MOVE, IT WAS LIKELY JUST A GUST OF WIND.
BUT... THERE ***ISN'T*** ANY WIND.
WHAT--?!
SSHKK

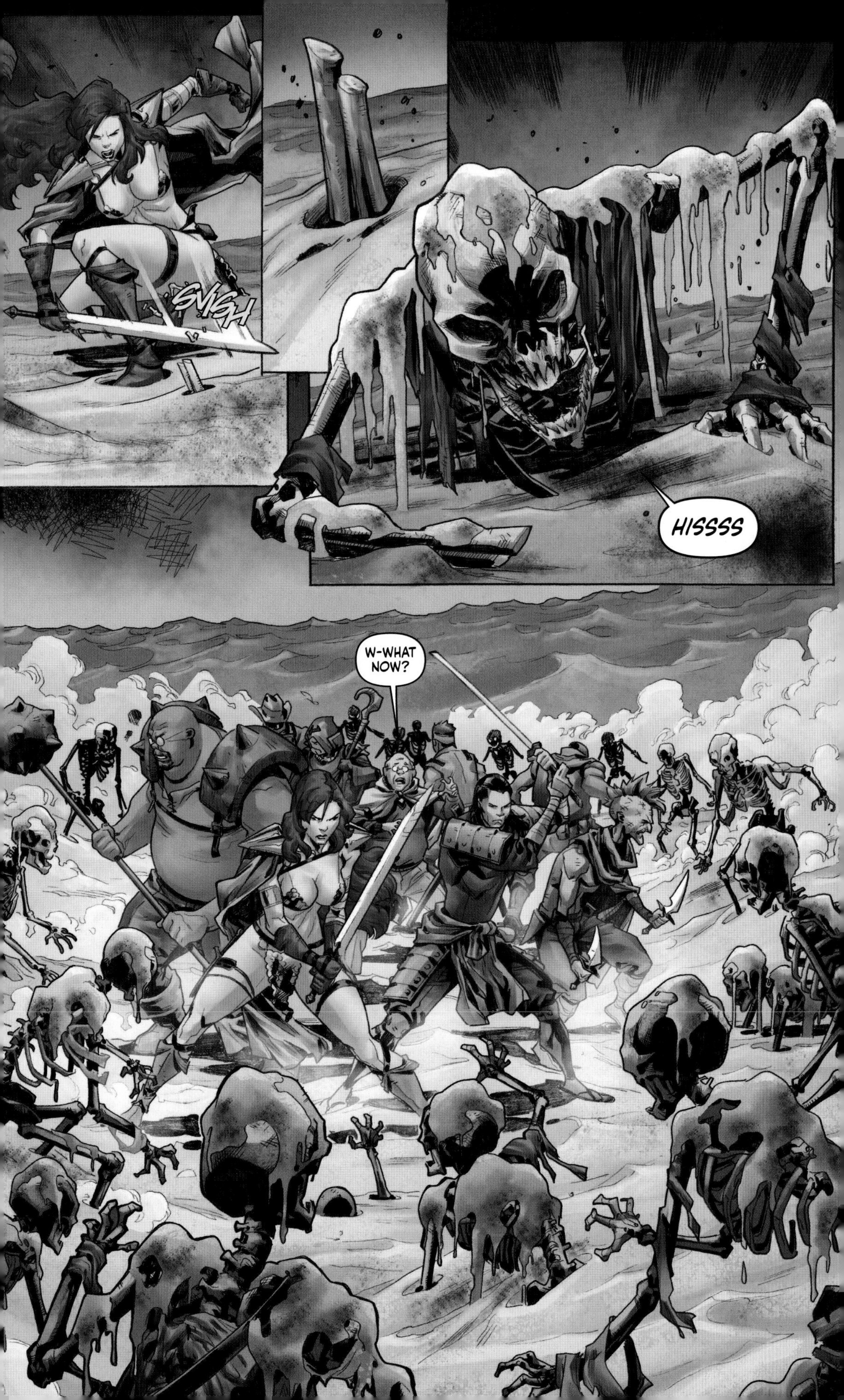
SWISH
HISSSS
W-WHAT NOW?

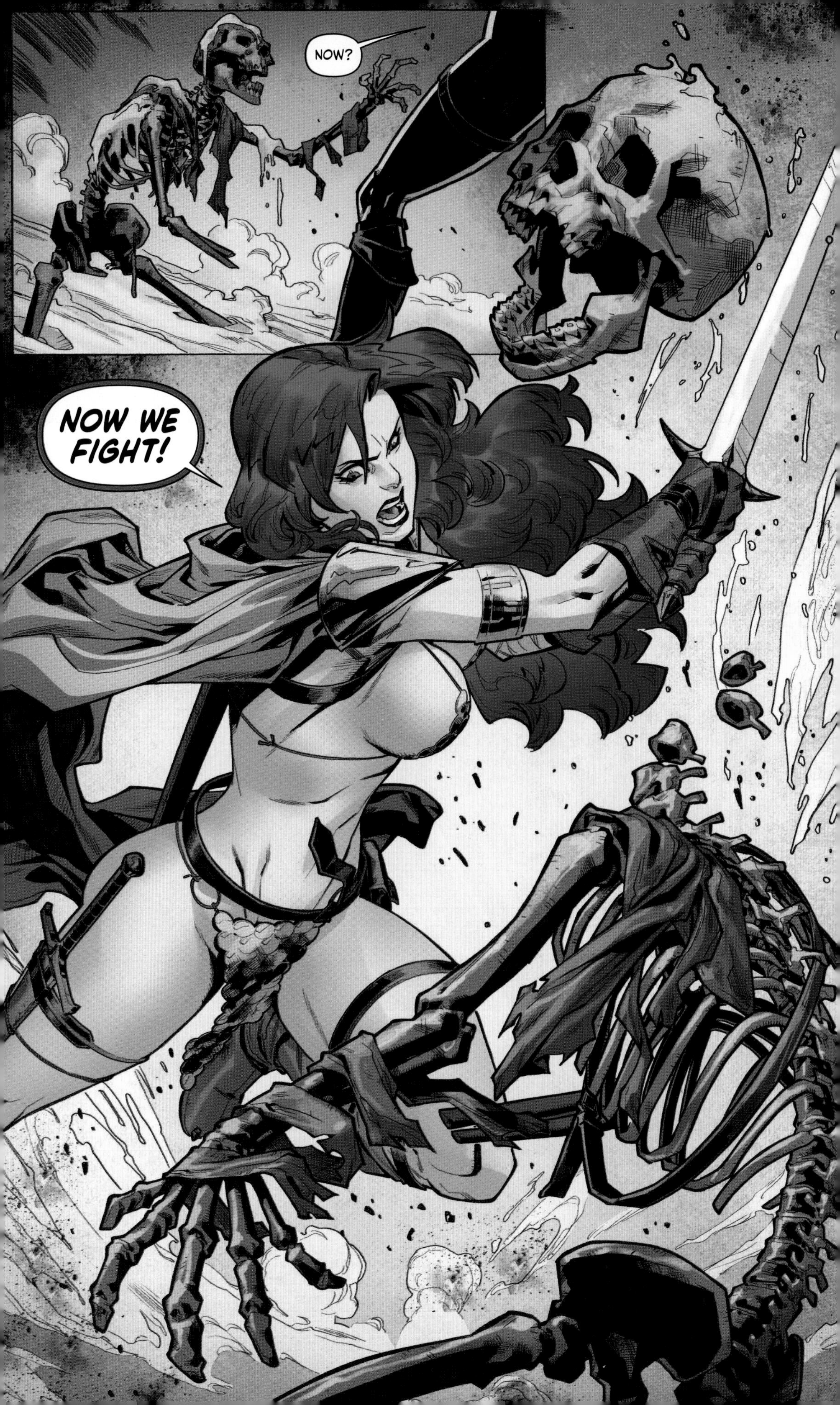
NOW?
NOW WE FIGHT!

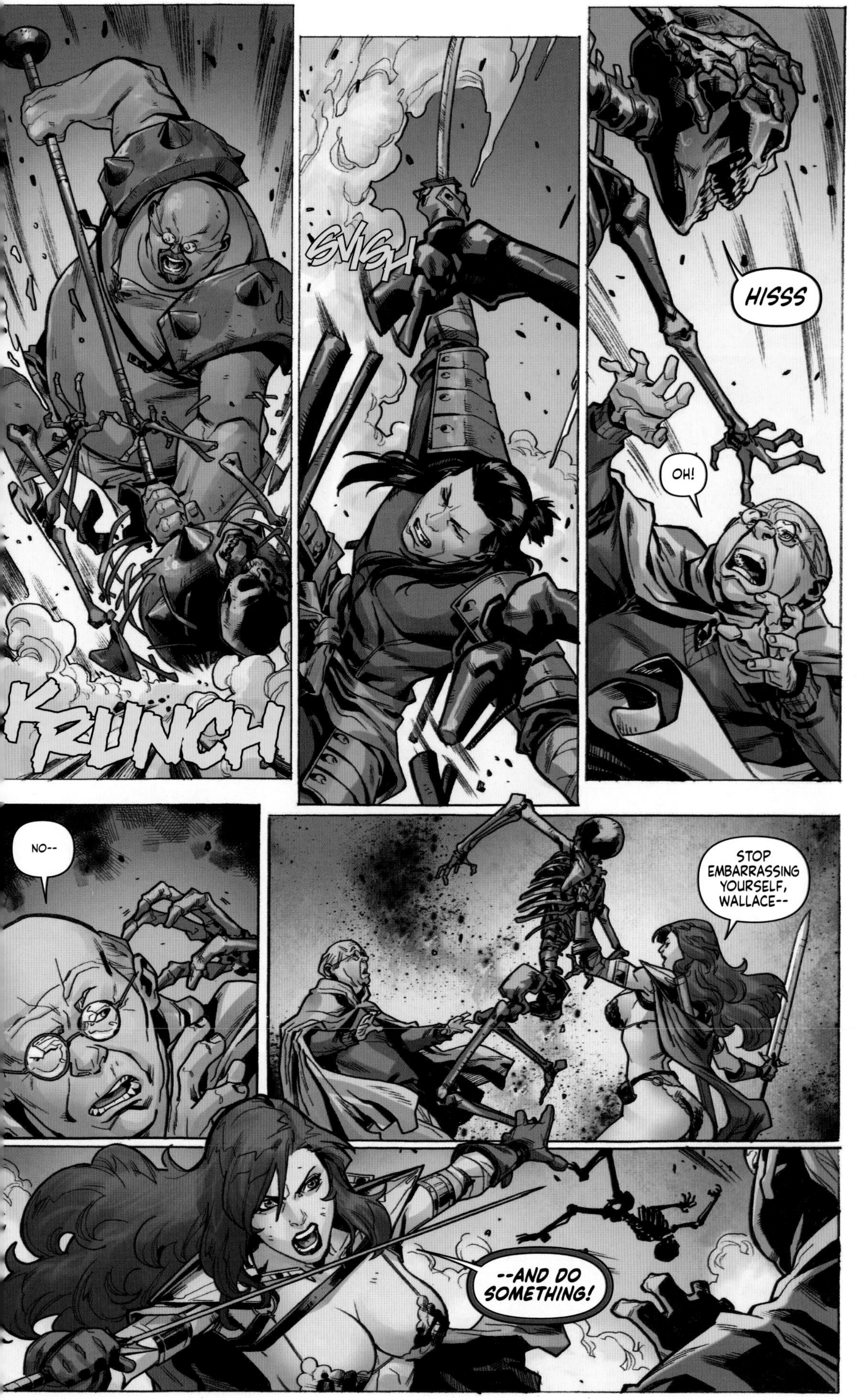
KRUNCH
SVISH
HISSS
OH!
NO--
STOP EMBARRASSING YOURSELF, WALLACE--
--AND DO SOMETHING!

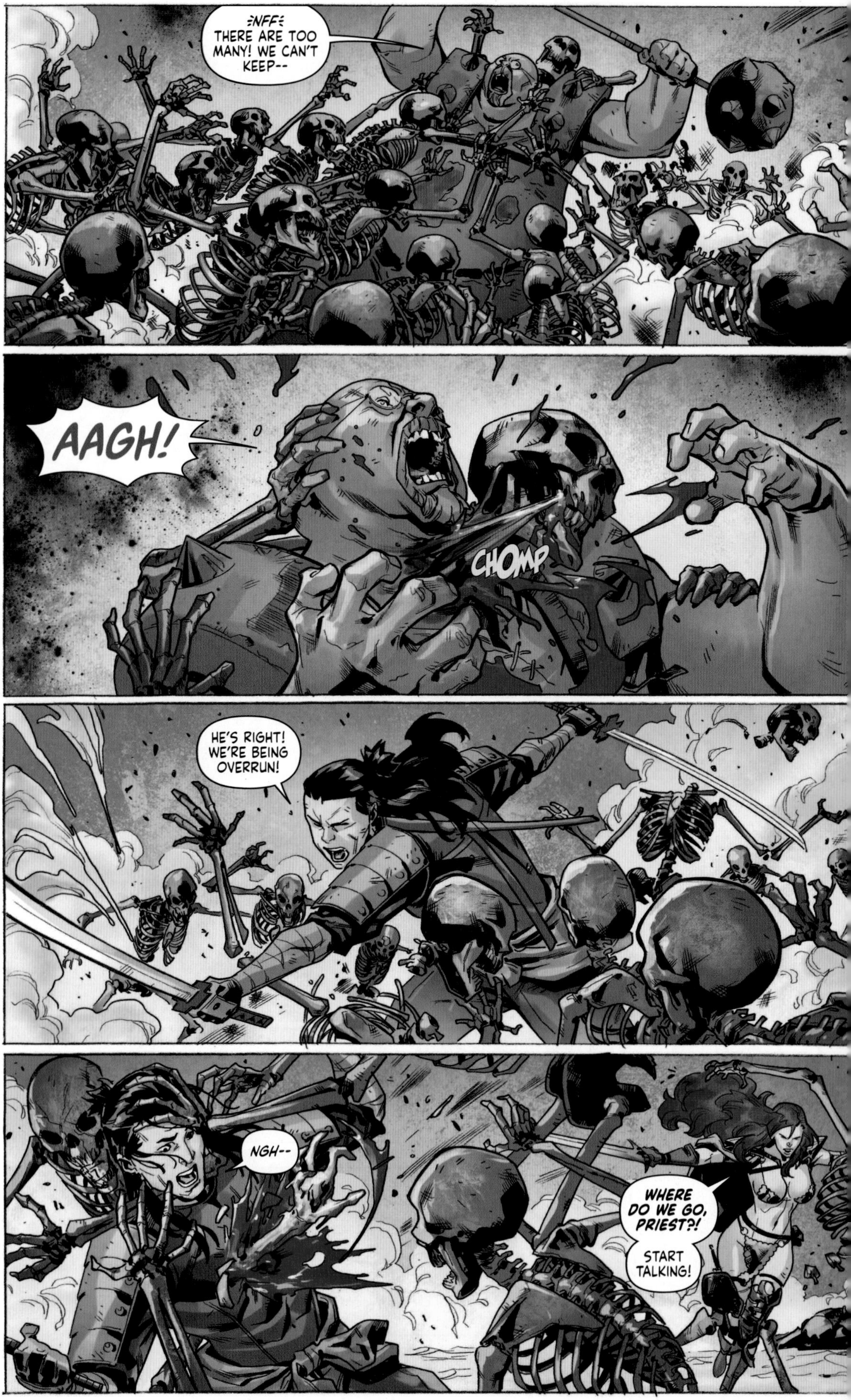
≈NFF≈
THERE ARE TOO MANY! WE CAN'T KEEP--
AAGH!
CHOMP
HE'S RIGHT! WE'RE BEING OVERRUN!
NGH--
WHERE DO WE GO, PRIEST?!
START TALKING!

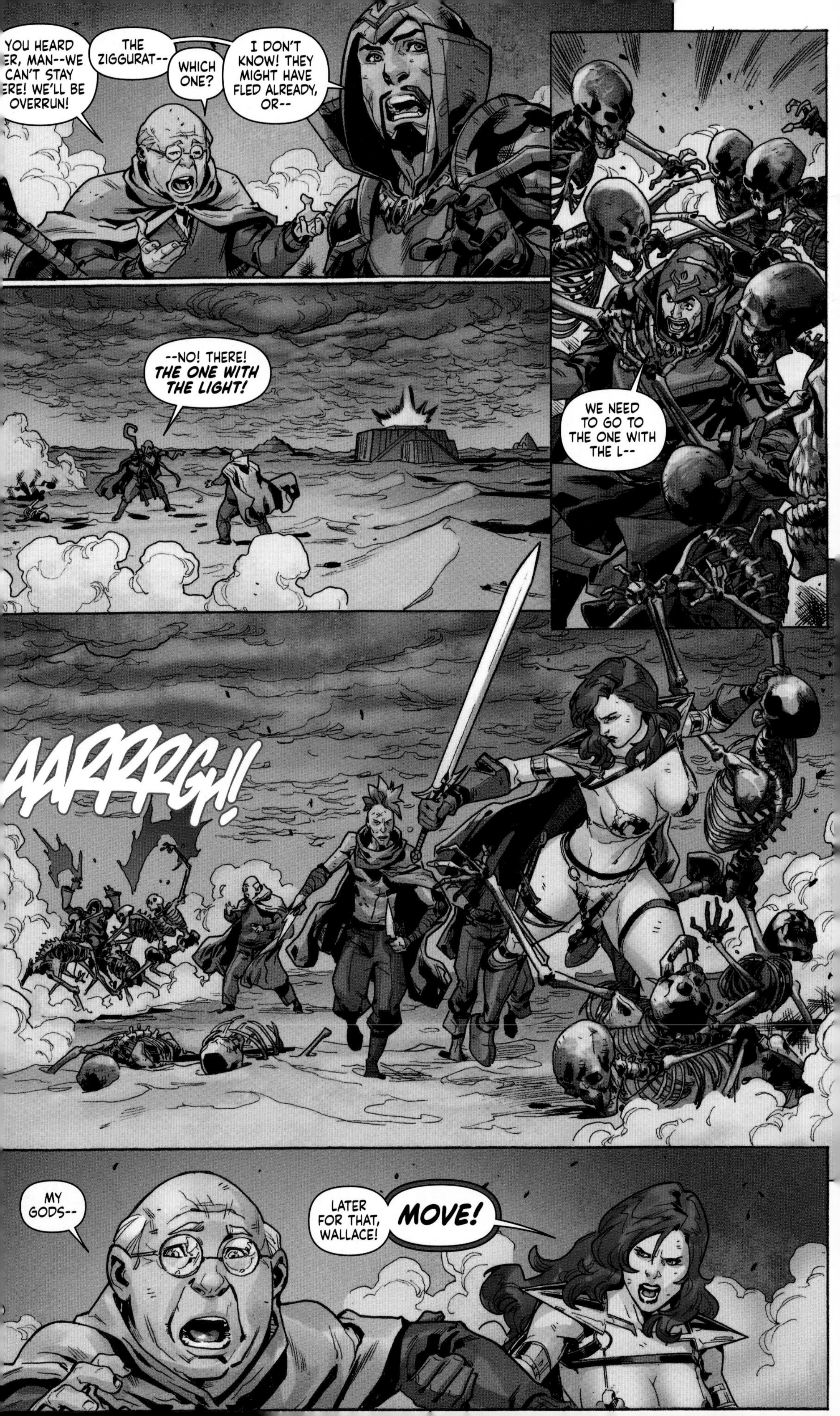
YOU HEARD ER, MAN--WE CAN'T STAY ERE! WE'LL BE OVERRUN!
THE ZIGGURAT--
WHICH ONE?
I DON'T KNOW! THEY MIGHT HAVE FLED ALREADY, OR--
--NO! THERE! *THE ONE WITH THE LIGHT!*
WE NEED TO GO TO THE ONE WITH THE L--
AARRRGH!
MY GODS--
LATER FOR THAT, WALLACE!
MOVE!

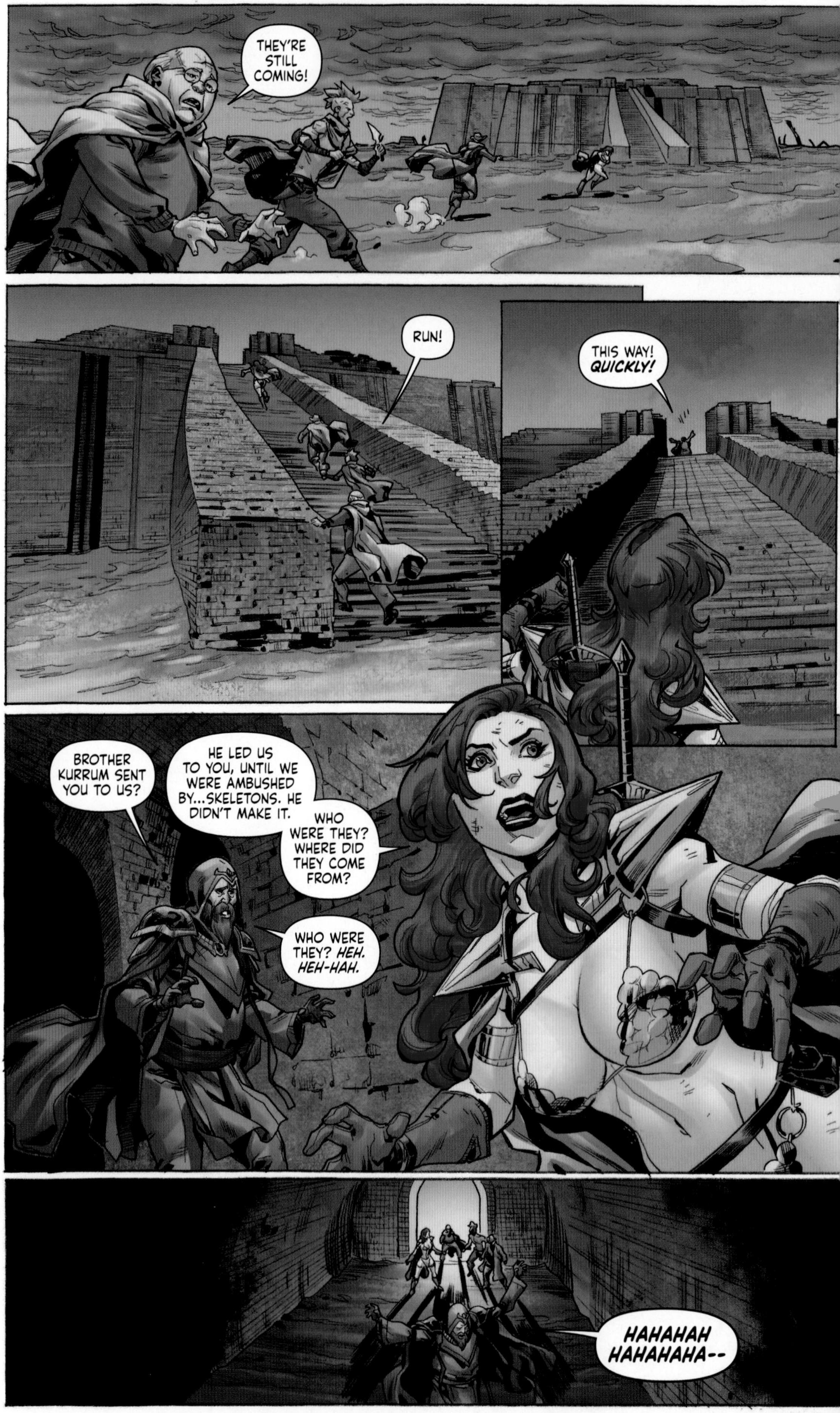
THEY'RE STILL COMING!
RUN!
THIS WAY! *QUICKLY!*
BROTHER KURRUM SENT YOU TO US?
HE LED US TO YOU, UNTIL WE WERE AMBUSHED BY...SKELETONS. HE DIDN'T MAKE IT.
WHO WERE THEY? WHERE DID THEY COME FROM?
WHO WERE THEY? *HEH. HEH-HAH.*
HAHAHAH HAHAHAHA--

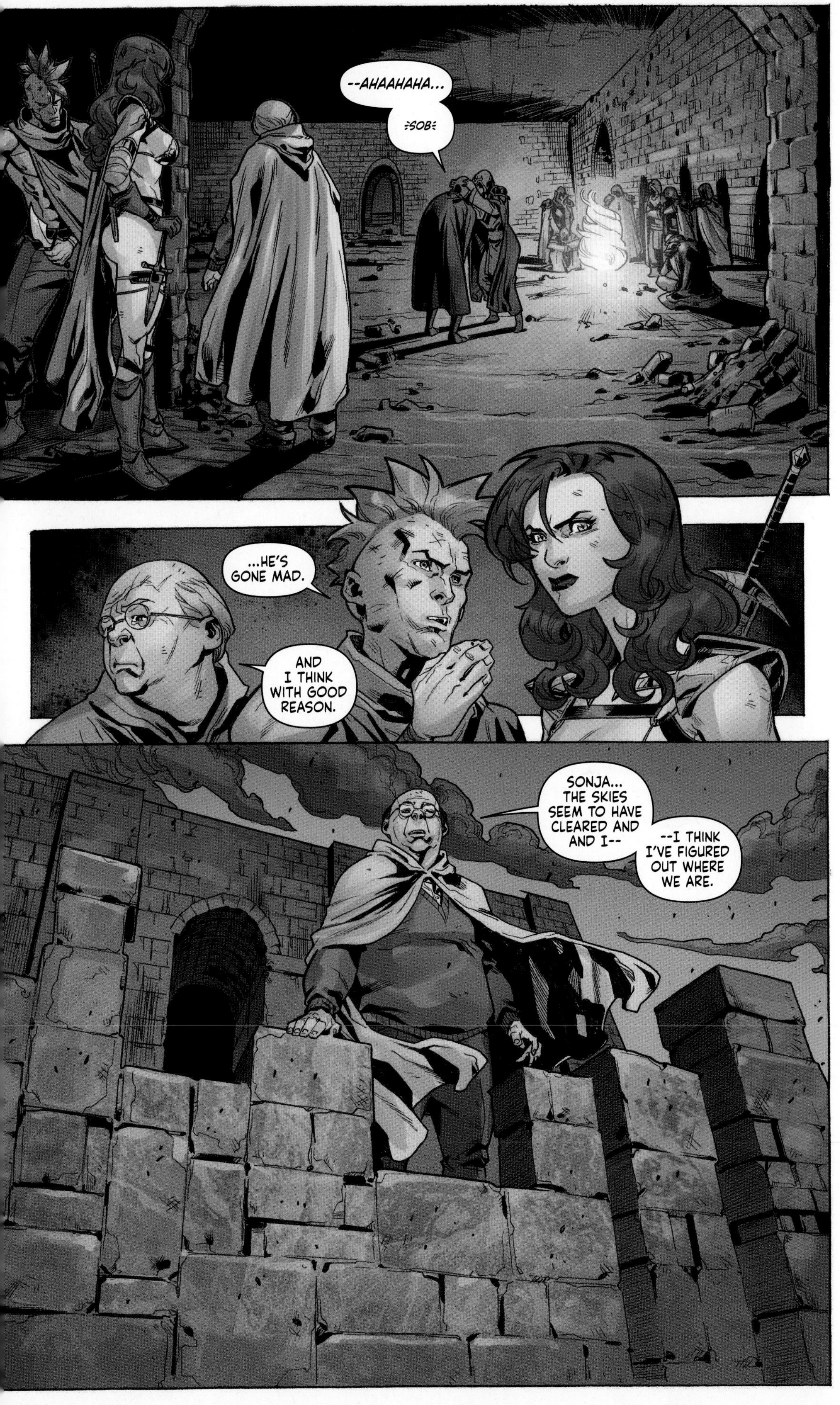
--AHAAHAHA...
SOB
...HE'S GONE MAD.
AND I THINK WITH GOOD REASON.
SONJA... THE SKIES SEEM TO HAVE CLEARED AND AND I--
--I THINK I'VE FIGURED OUT WHERE WE ARE.

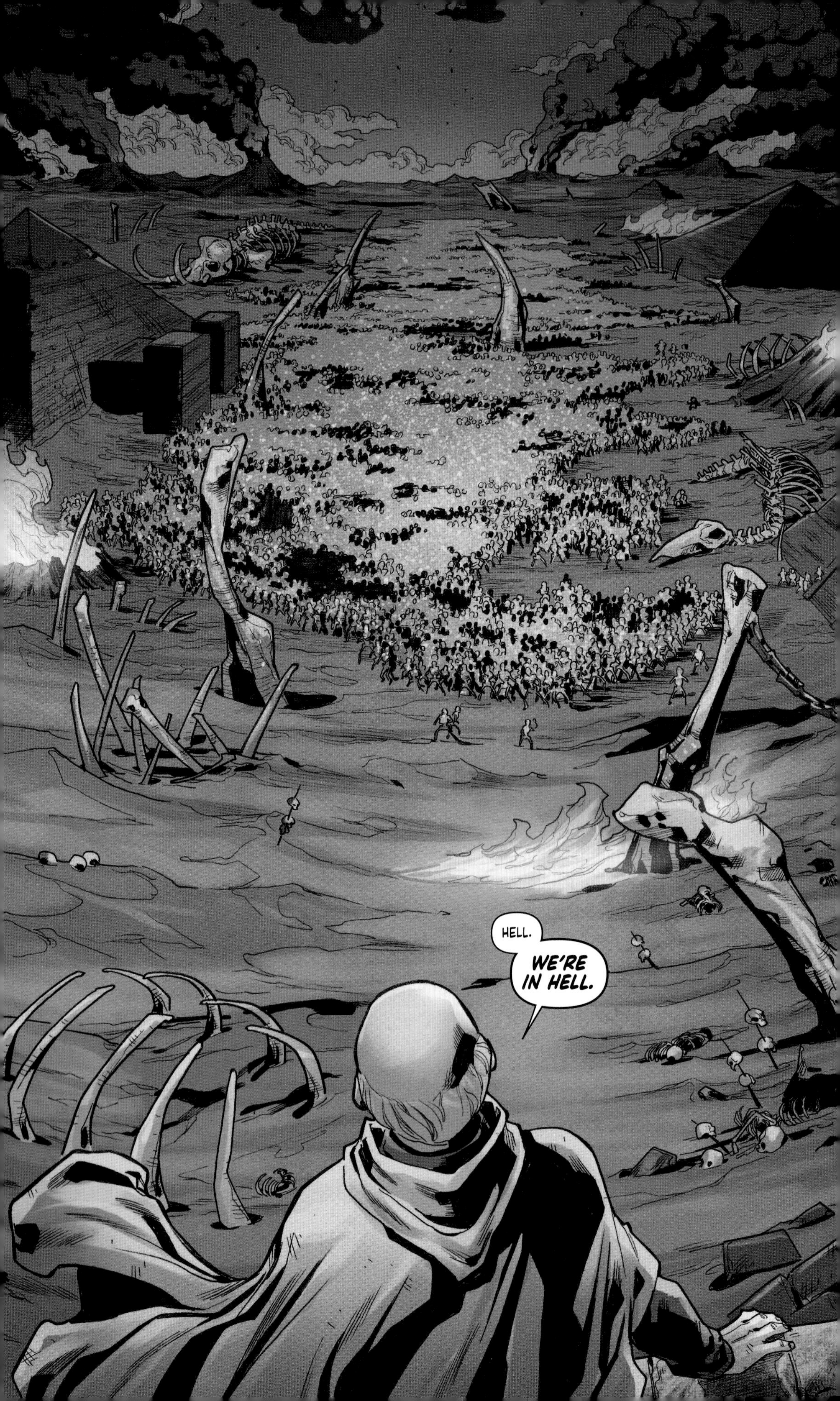
HELL.
WE'RE IN HELL.

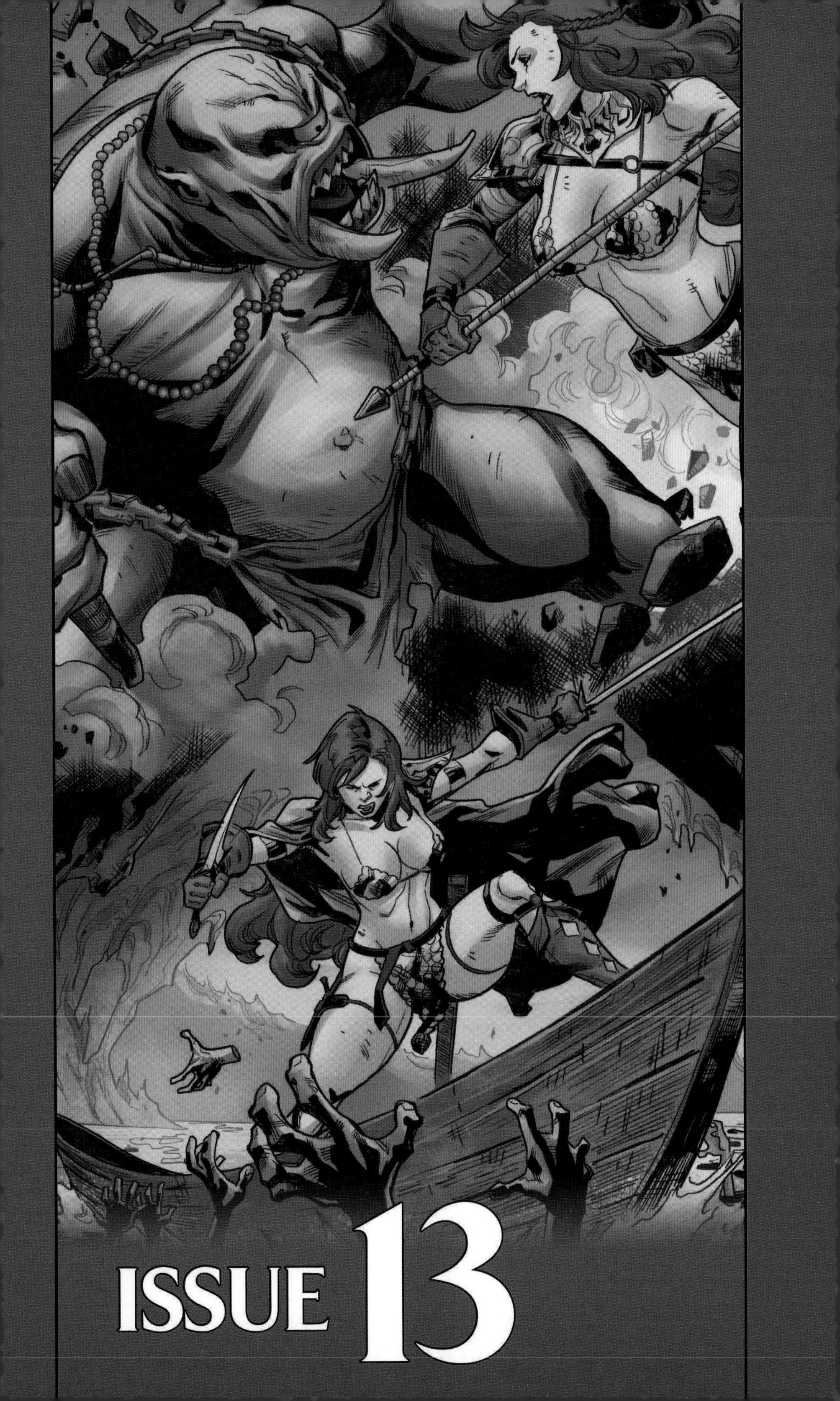

ISSUE 13

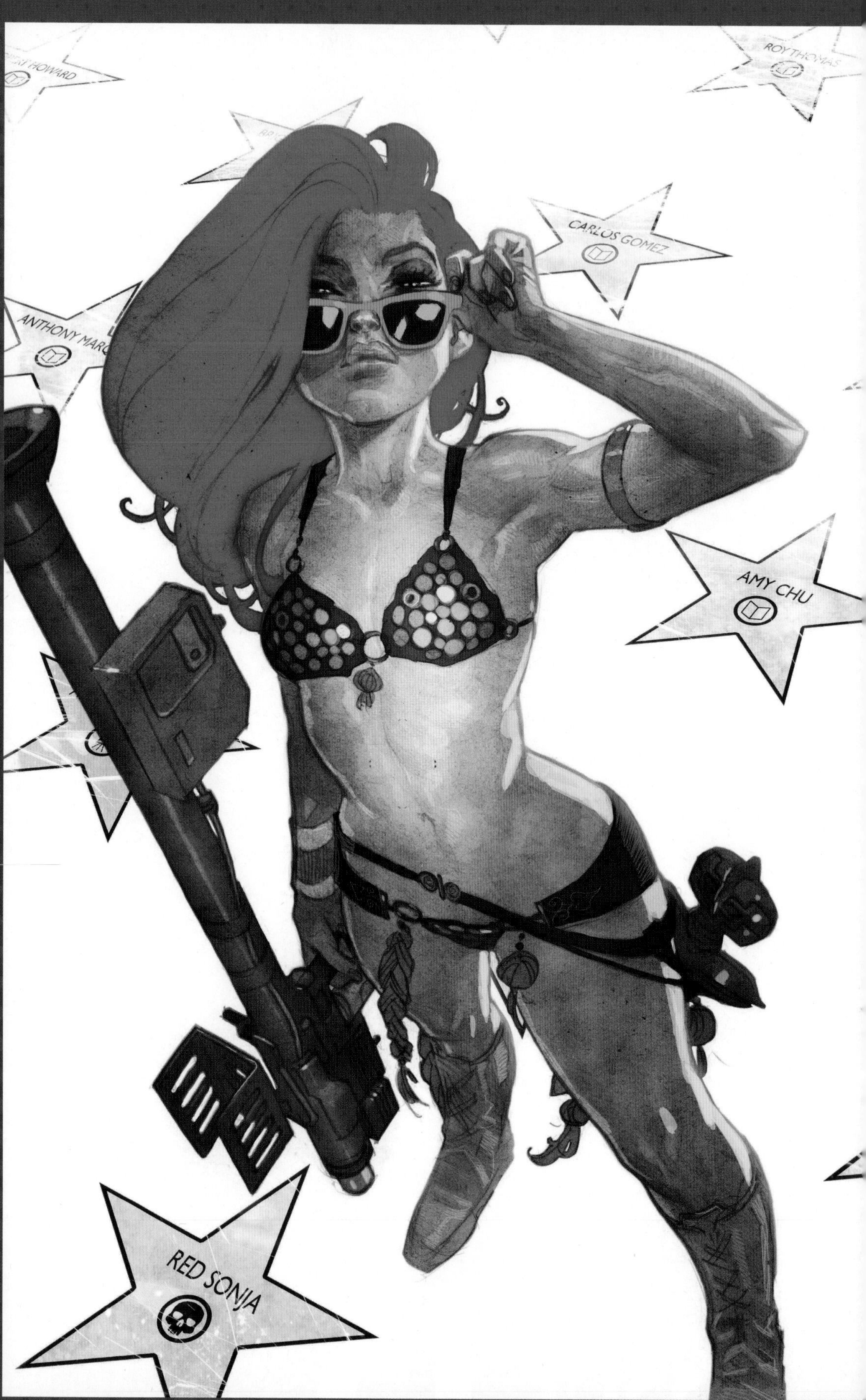
ROY THOMAS
CARLOS GOMEZ
AMY CHU
RED SONJA

ISSUE #13: COVER ART BY **BEN CALDWELL**

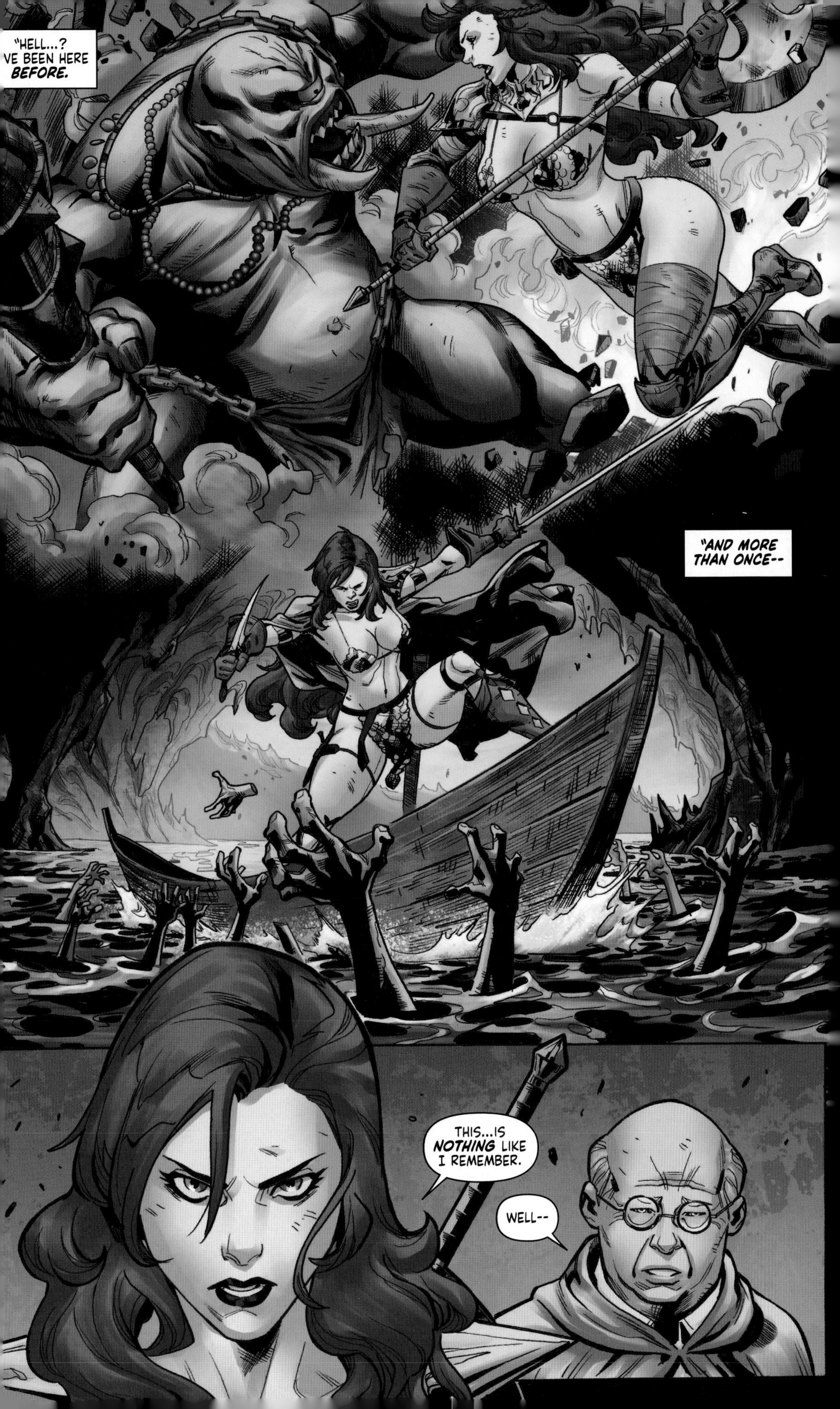

"HELL...? VE BEEN HERE BEFORE.
"AND MORE THAN ONCE--
THIS...IS NOTHING LIKE I REMEMBER.
WELL--

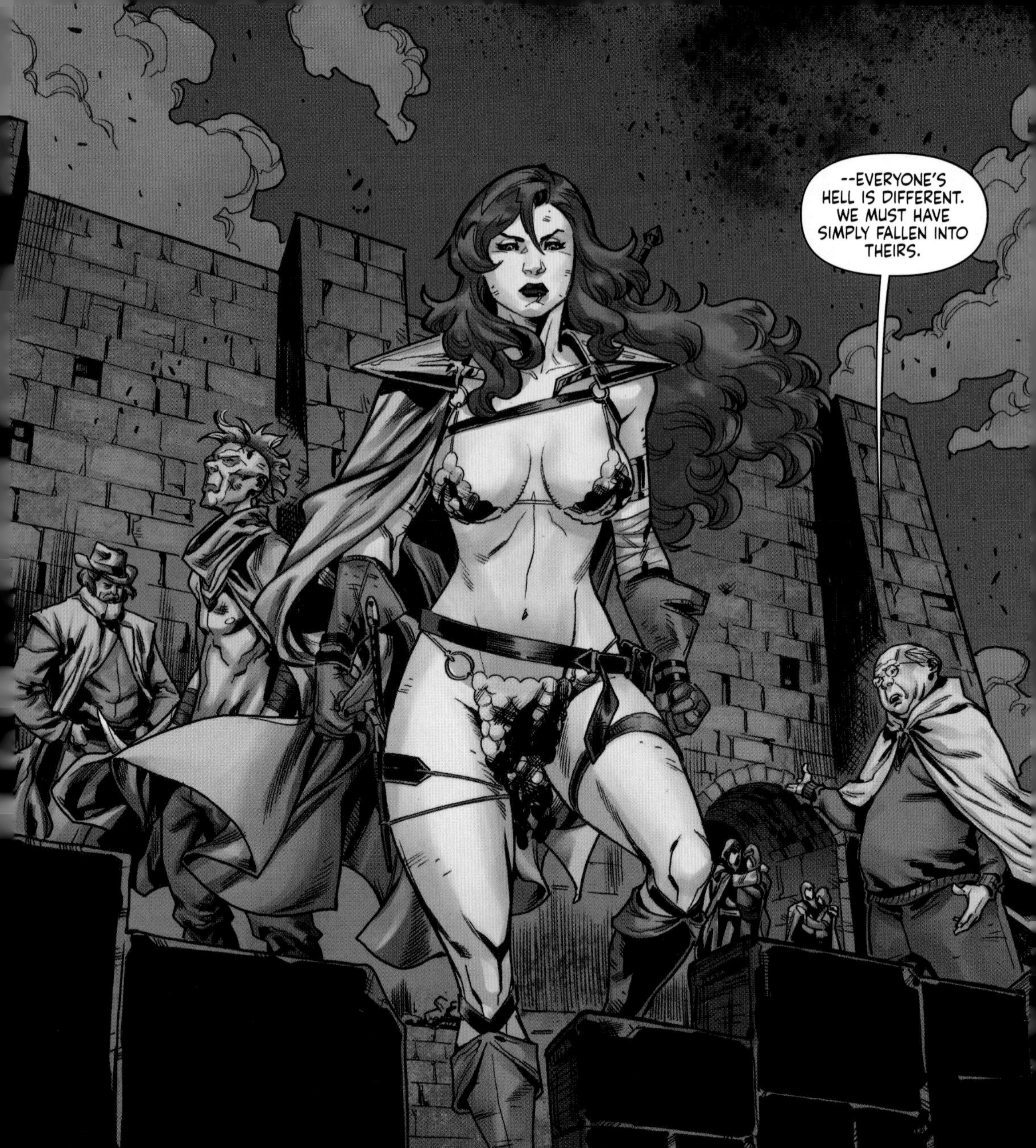
--EVERYONE'S HELL IS DIFFERENT. WE MUST HAVE SIMPLY FALLEN INTO THEIRS.

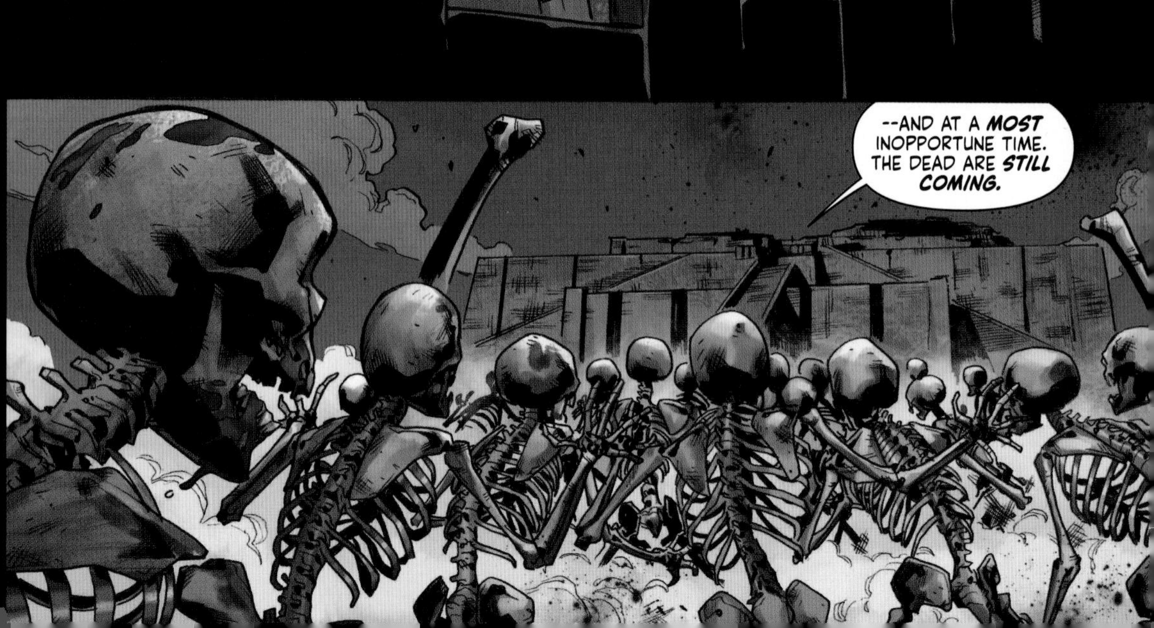
--AND AT A ***MOST*** INOPPORTUNE TIME. THE DEAD ARE ***STILL COMING.***

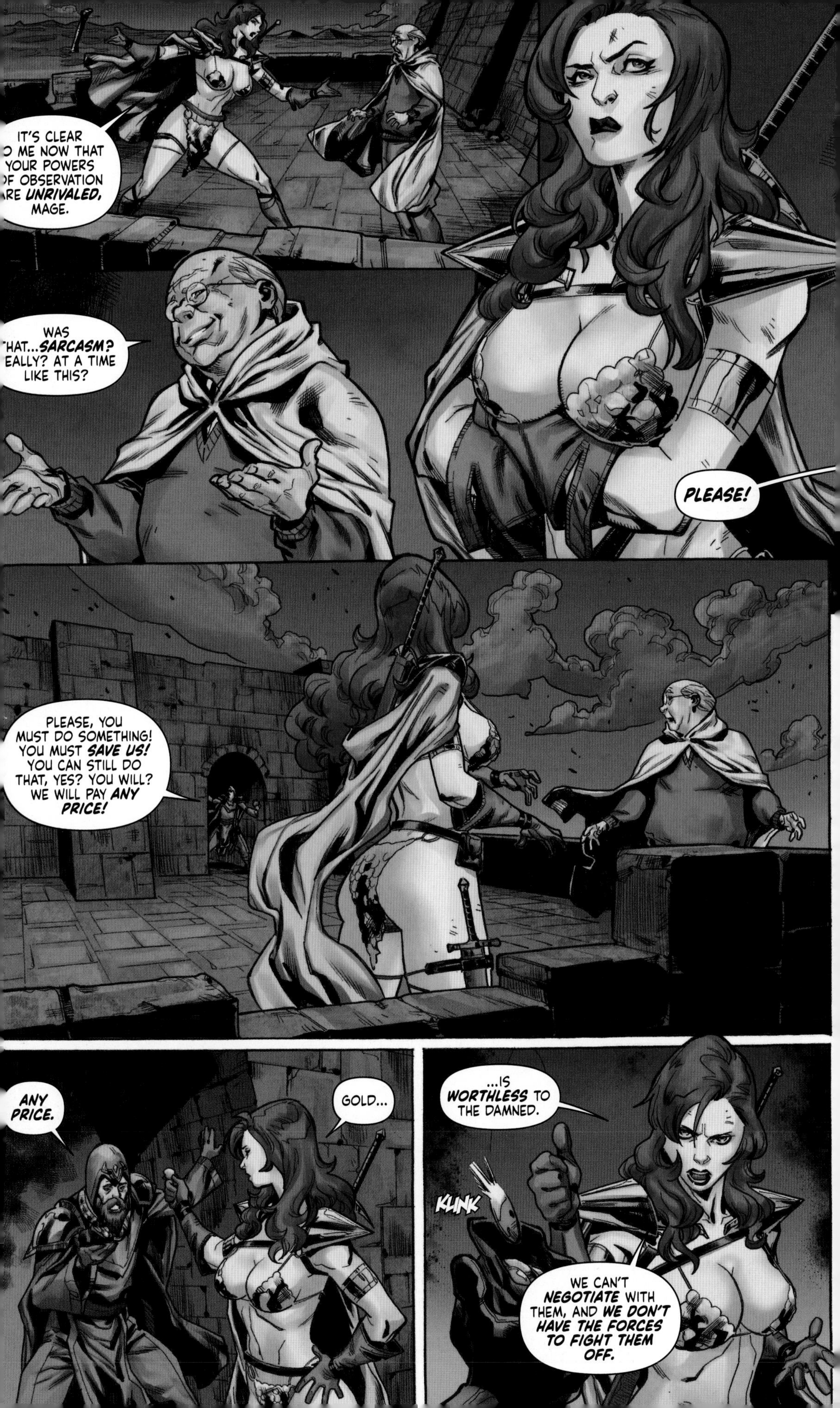

IT'S CLEAR O ME NOW THAT YOUR POWERS F OBSERVATION RE UNRIVALED, MAGE.
WAS HAT...SARCASM? EALLY? AT A TIME LIKE THIS?
PLEASE!
PLEASE, YOU MUST DO SOMETHING! YOU MUST SAVE US! YOU CAN STILL DO THAT, YES? YOU WILL? WE WILL PAY ANY PRICE!
ANY PRICE.
GOLD...
...IS WORTHLESS TO THE DAMNED.
KLINK
WE CAN'T NEGOTIATE WITH THEM, AND WE DON'T HAVE THE FORCES TO FIGHT THEM OFF.

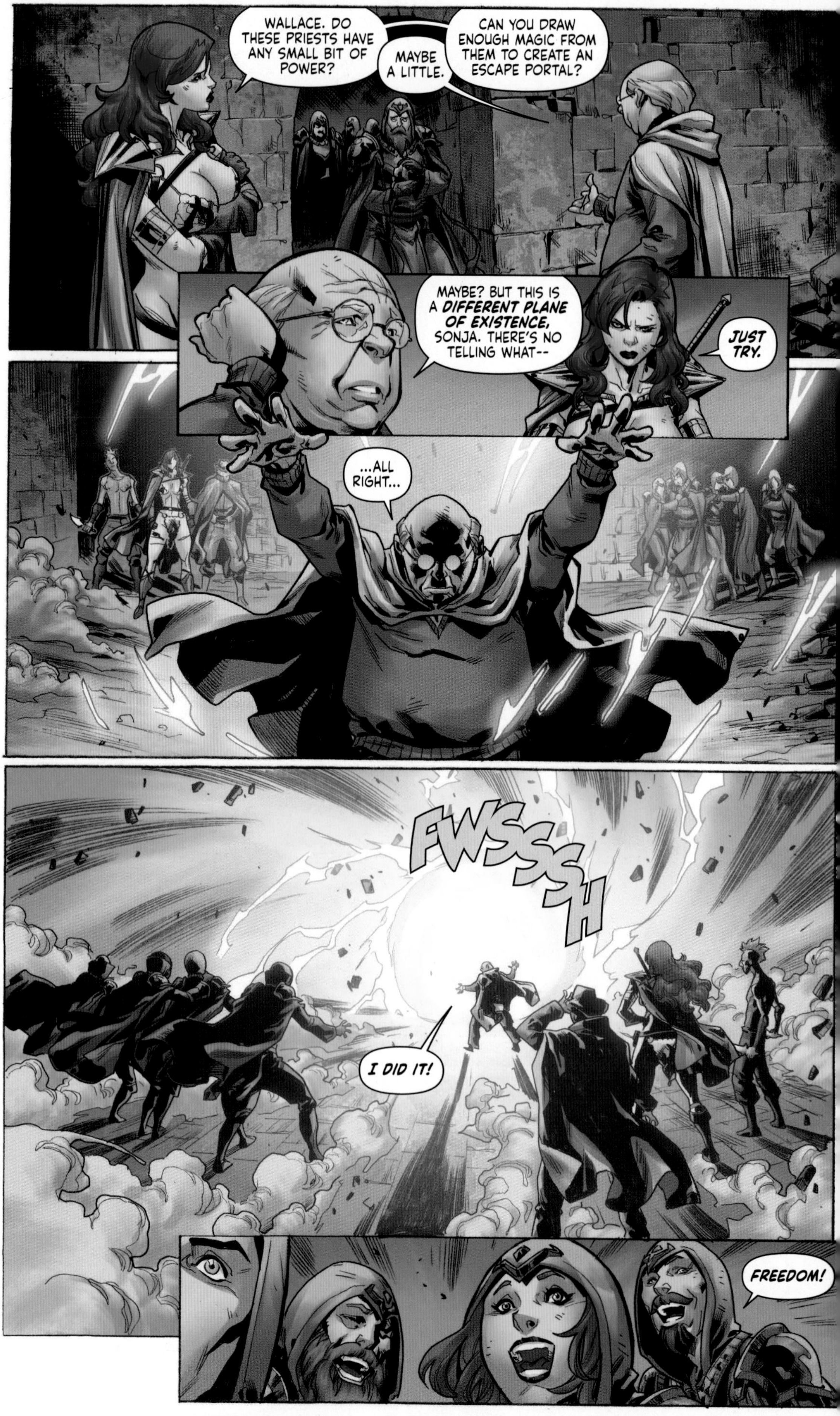
WALLACE. DO THESE PRIESTS HAVE ANY SMALL BIT OF POWER?
MAYBE A LITTLE.
CAN YOU DRAW ENOUGH MAGIC FROM THEM TO CREATE AN ESCAPE PORTAL?
MAYBE? BUT THIS IS A ***DIFFERENT PLANE OF EXISTENCE,*** SONJA. THERE'S NO TELLING WHAT--
JUST TRY.
...ALL RIGHT...
FWSSSH
I DID IT!
FREEDOM!

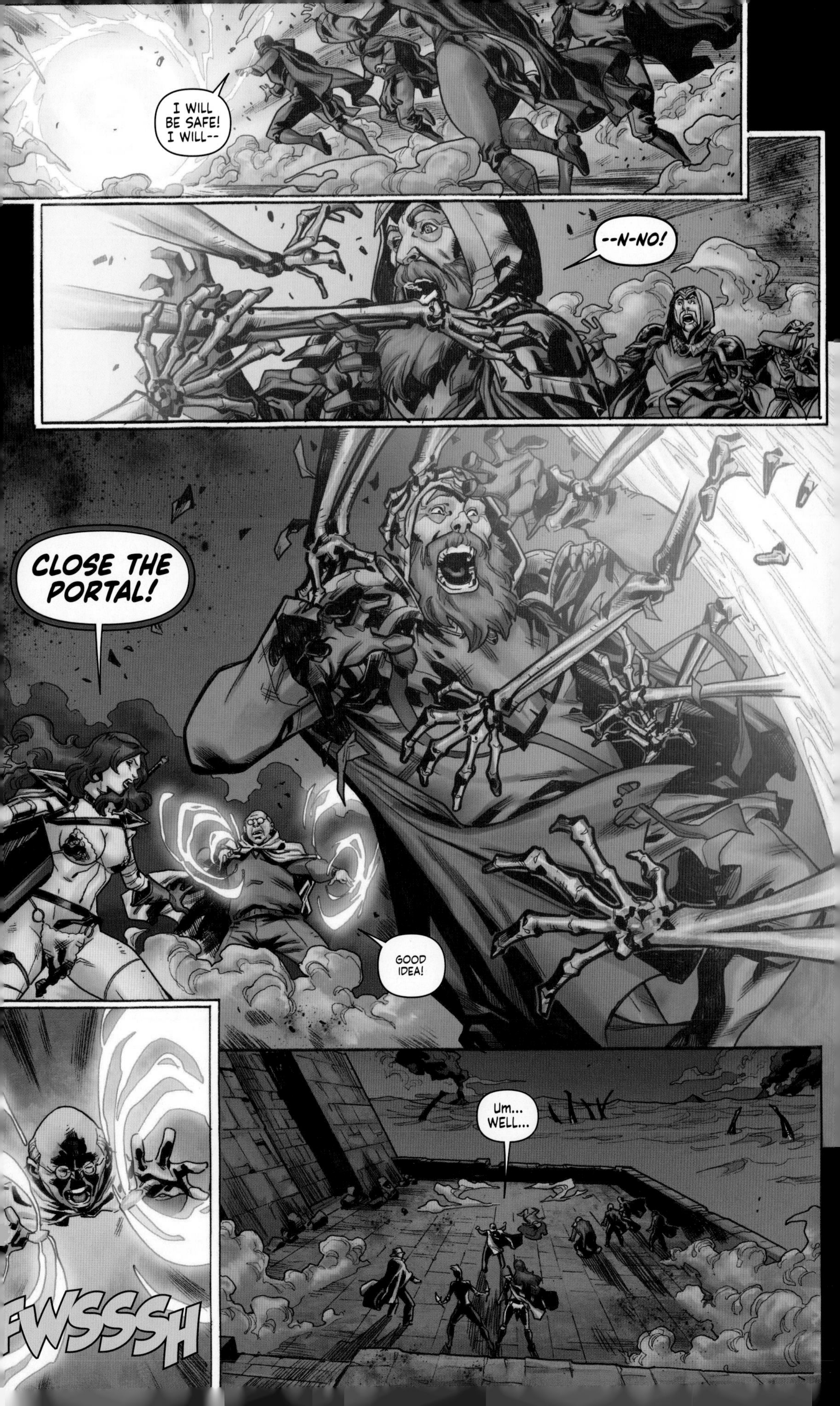

I WILL BE SAFE! I WILL--
--N-NO!
CLOSE THE PORTAL!
GOOD IDEA!
FWSSSH
Um... WELL...

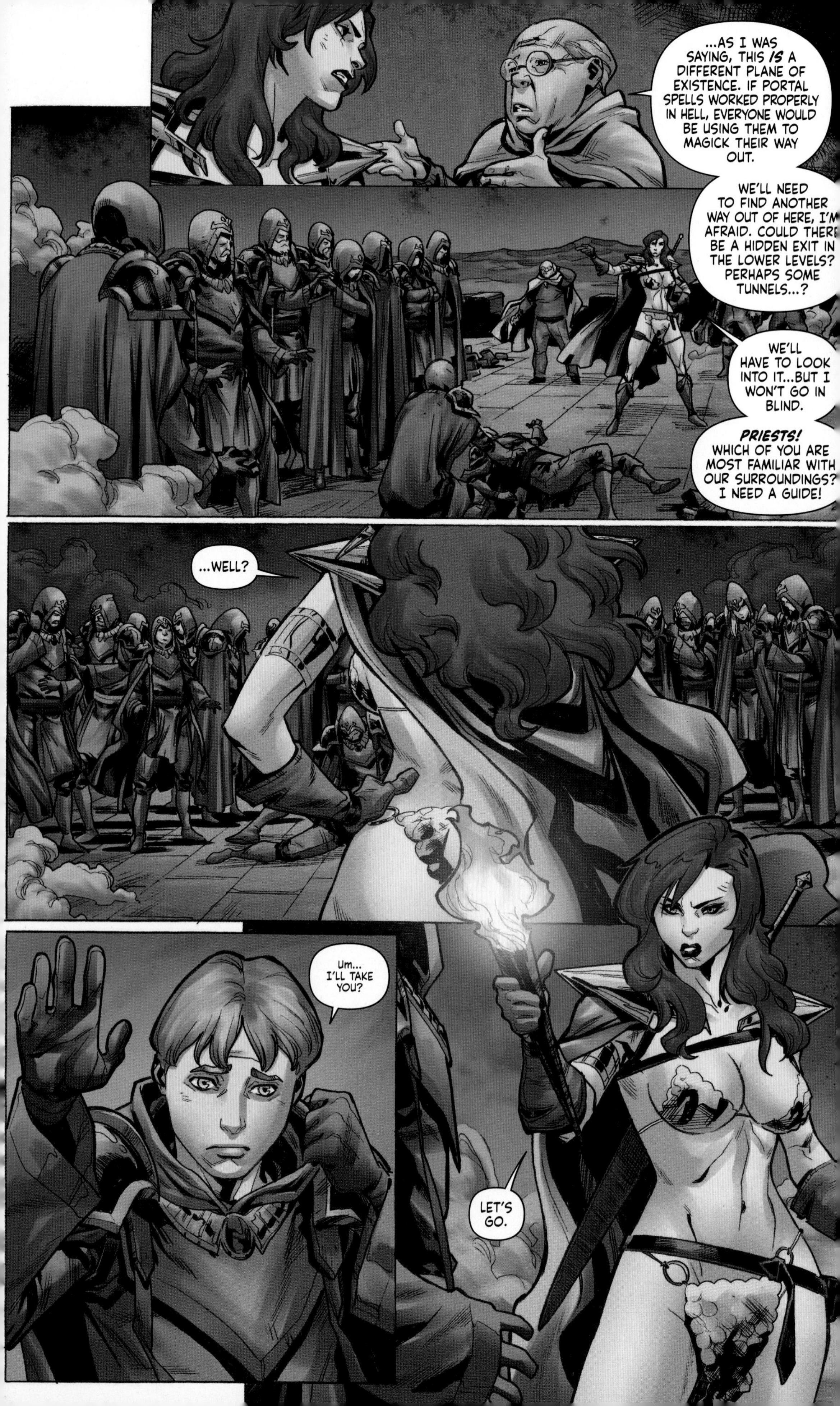
...AS I WAS SAYING, THIS IS A DIFFERENT PLANE OF EXISTENCE. IF PORTAL SPELLS WORKED PROPERLY IN HELL, EVERYONE WOULD BE USING THEM TO MAGICK THEIR WAY OUT.
WE'LL NEED TO FIND ANOTHER WAY OUT OF HERE, I'M AFRAID. COULD THERE BE A HIDDEN EXIT IN THE LOWER LEVELS? PERHAPS SOME TUNNELS...?
WE'LL HAVE TO LOOK INTO IT...BUT I WON'T GO IN BLIND.
PRIESTS! WHICH OF YOU ARE MOST FAMILIAR WITH OUR SURROUNDINGS? I NEED A GUIDE!
...WELL?
Um... I'LL TAKE YOU?
LET'S GO.

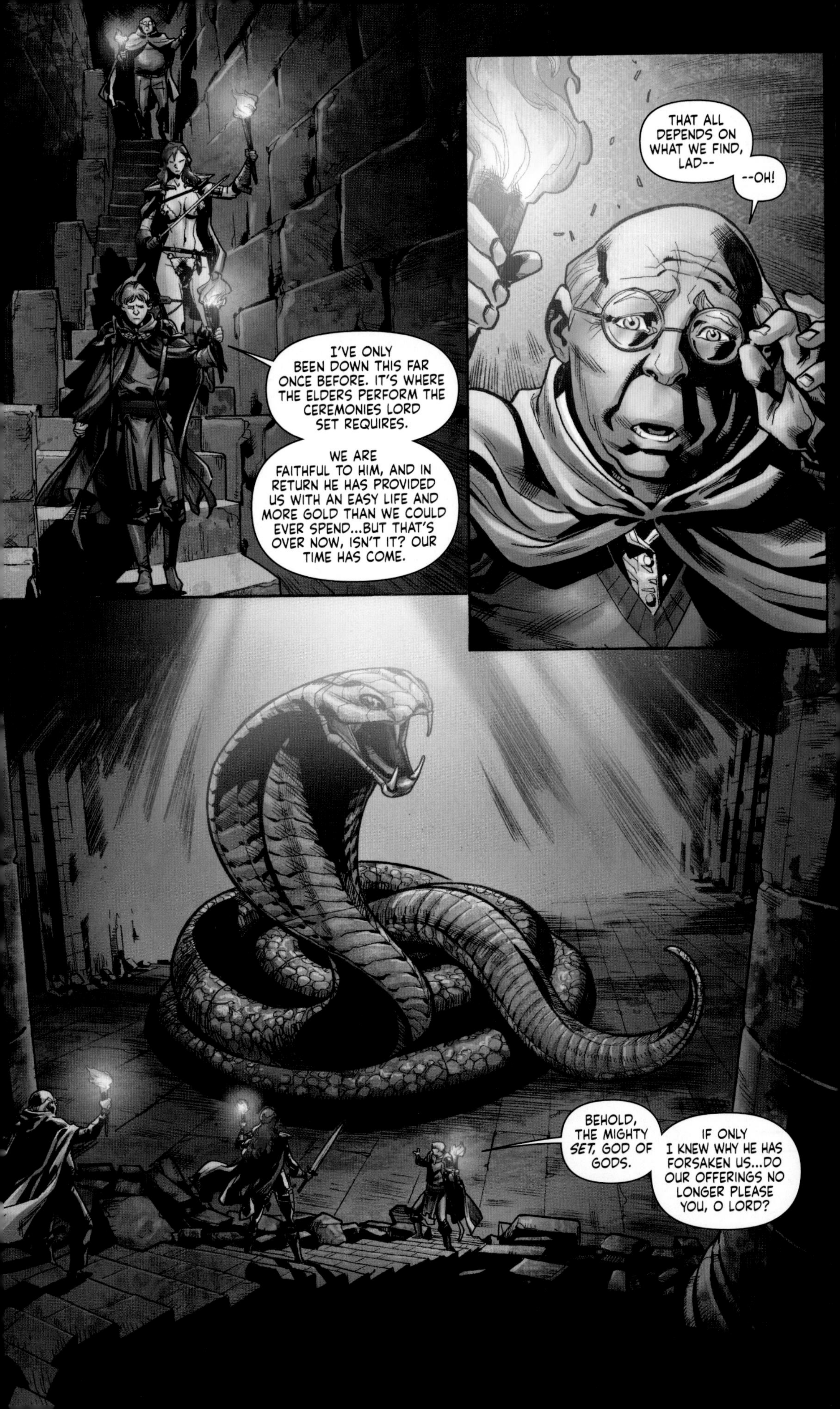
I'VE ONLY BEEN DOWN THIS FAR ONCE BEFORE. IT'S WHERE THE ELDERS PERFORM THE CEREMONIES LORD SET REQUIRES.
WE ARE FAITHFUL TO HIM, AND IN RETURN HE HAS PROVIDED US WITH AN EASY LIFE AND MORE GOLD THAN WE COULD EVER SPEND...BUT THAT'S OVER NOW, ISN'T IT? OUR TIME HAS COME.
THAT ALL DEPENDS ON WHAT WE FIND, LAD--
--OH!
BEHOLD, THE MIGHTY *SET*, GOD OF GODS.
IF ONLY I KNEW WHY HE HAS FORSAKEN US...DO OUR OFFERINGS NO LONGER PLEASE YOU, O LORD?

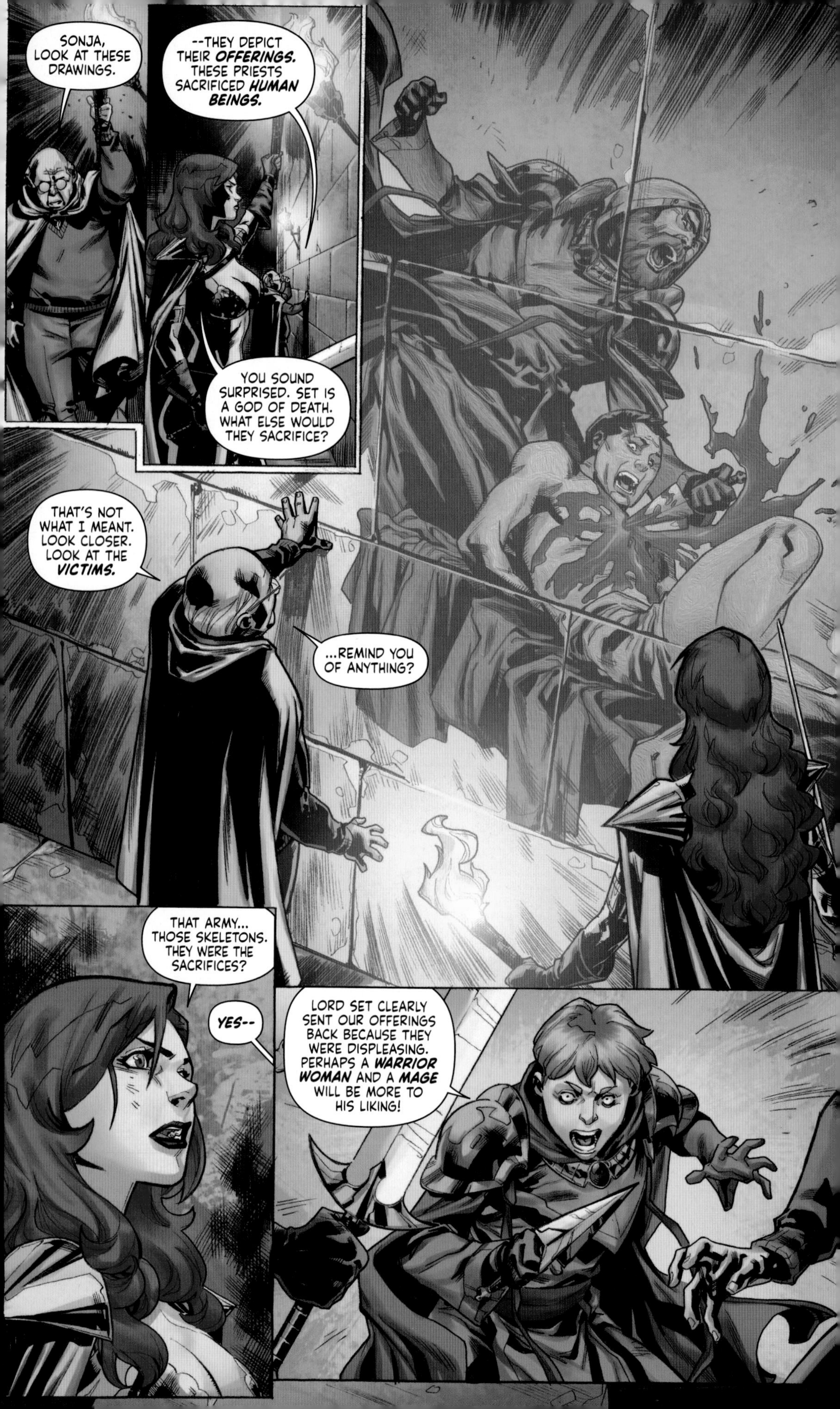
SONJA, LOOK AT THESE DRAWINGS.
--THEY DEPICT THEIR **OFFERINGS.** THESE PRIESTS SACRIFICED **HUMAN BEINGS.**
YOU SOUND SURPRISED. SET IS A GOD OF DEATH. WHAT ELSE WOULD THEY SACRIFICE?
THAT'S NOT WHAT I MEANT. LOOK CLOSER. LOOK AT THE **VICTIMS.**
...REMIND YOU OF ANYTHING?
THAT ARMY... THOSE SKELETONS. THEY WERE THE SACRIFICES?
YES--
LORD SET CLEARLY SENT OUR OFFERINGS BACK BECAUSE THEY WERE DISPLEASING. PERHAPS A **WARRIOR WOMAN** AND A **MAGE** WILL BE MORE TO HIS LIKING!

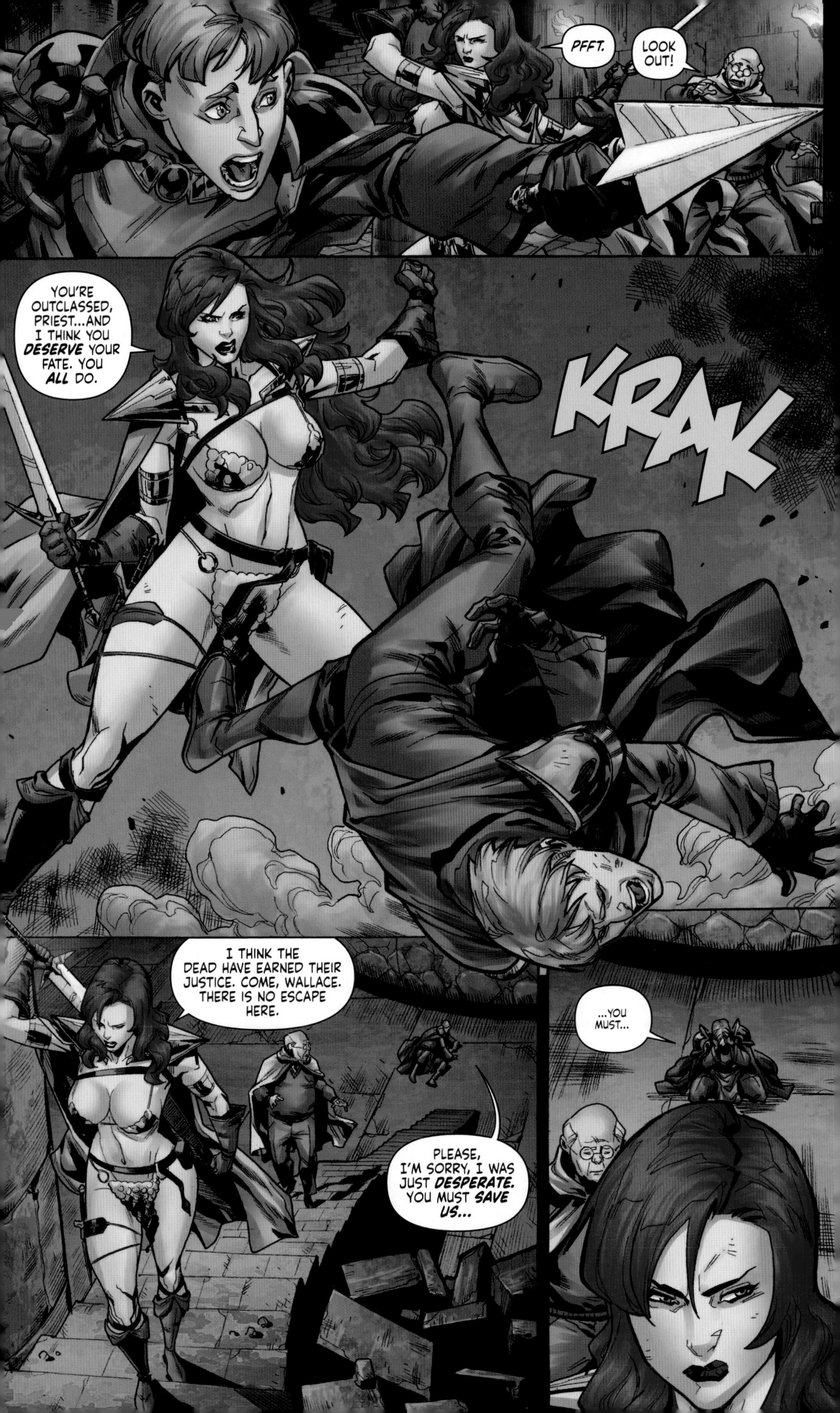
PFFT.
LOOK OUT!
YOU'RE OUTCLASSED, PRIEST...AND I THINK YOU ***DESERVE*** YOUR FATE. YOU ***ALL*** DO.
KRAK
I THINK THE DEAD HAVE EARNED THEIR JUSTICE. COME, WALLACE. THERE IS NO ESCAPE HERE.
PLEASE, I'M SORRY, I WAS JUST ***DESPERATE.*** YOU MUST ***SAVE US...***
...YOU MUST...

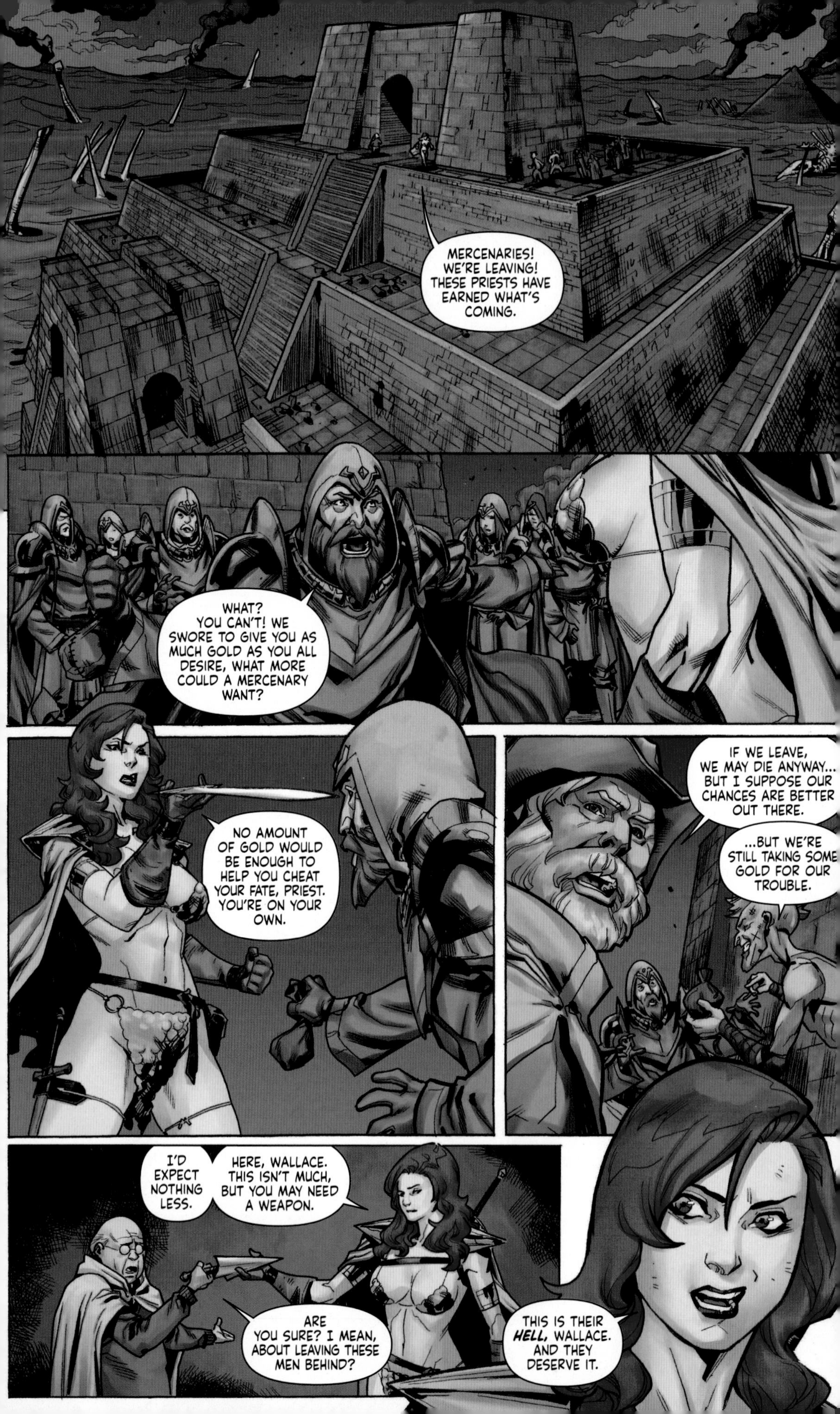
MERCENARIES! WE'RE LEAVING! THESE PRIESTS HAVE EARNED WHAT'S COMING.
WHAT? YOU CAN'T! WE SWORE TO GIVE YOU AS MUCH GOLD AS YOU ALL DESIRE, WHAT MORE COULD A MERCENARY WANT?
NO AMOUNT OF GOLD WOULD BE ENOUGH TO HELP YOU CHEAT YOUR FATE, PRIEST. YOU'RE ON YOUR OWN.
IF WE LEAVE, WE MAY DIE ANYWAY... BUT I SUPPOSE OUR CHANCES ARE BETTER OUT THERE.
...BUT WE'RE STILL TAKING SOME GOLD FOR OUR TROUBLE.
I'D EXPECT NOTHING LESS.
HERE, WALLACE. THIS ISN'T MUCH, BUT YOU MAY NEED A WEAPON.
ARE YOU SURE? I MEAN, ABOUT LEAVING THESE MEN BEHIND?
THIS IS THEIR ***HELL***, WALLACE. AND THEY DESERVE IT.

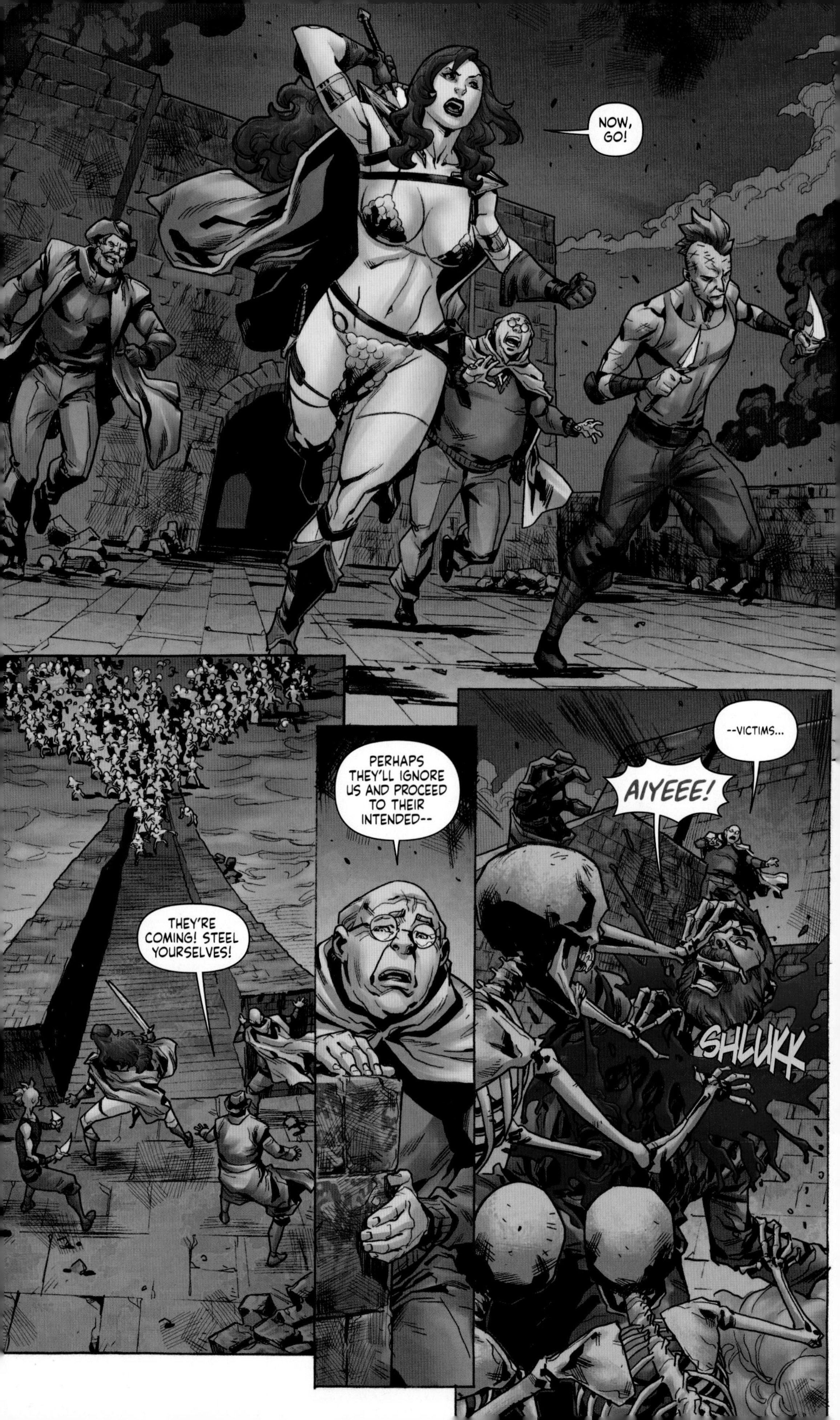
NOW, GO!
THEY'RE COMING! STEEL YOURSELVES!
PERHAPS THEY'LL IGNORE US AND PROCEED TO THEIR INTENDED--
--VICTIMS...
AIYEEE!
SHLUKK

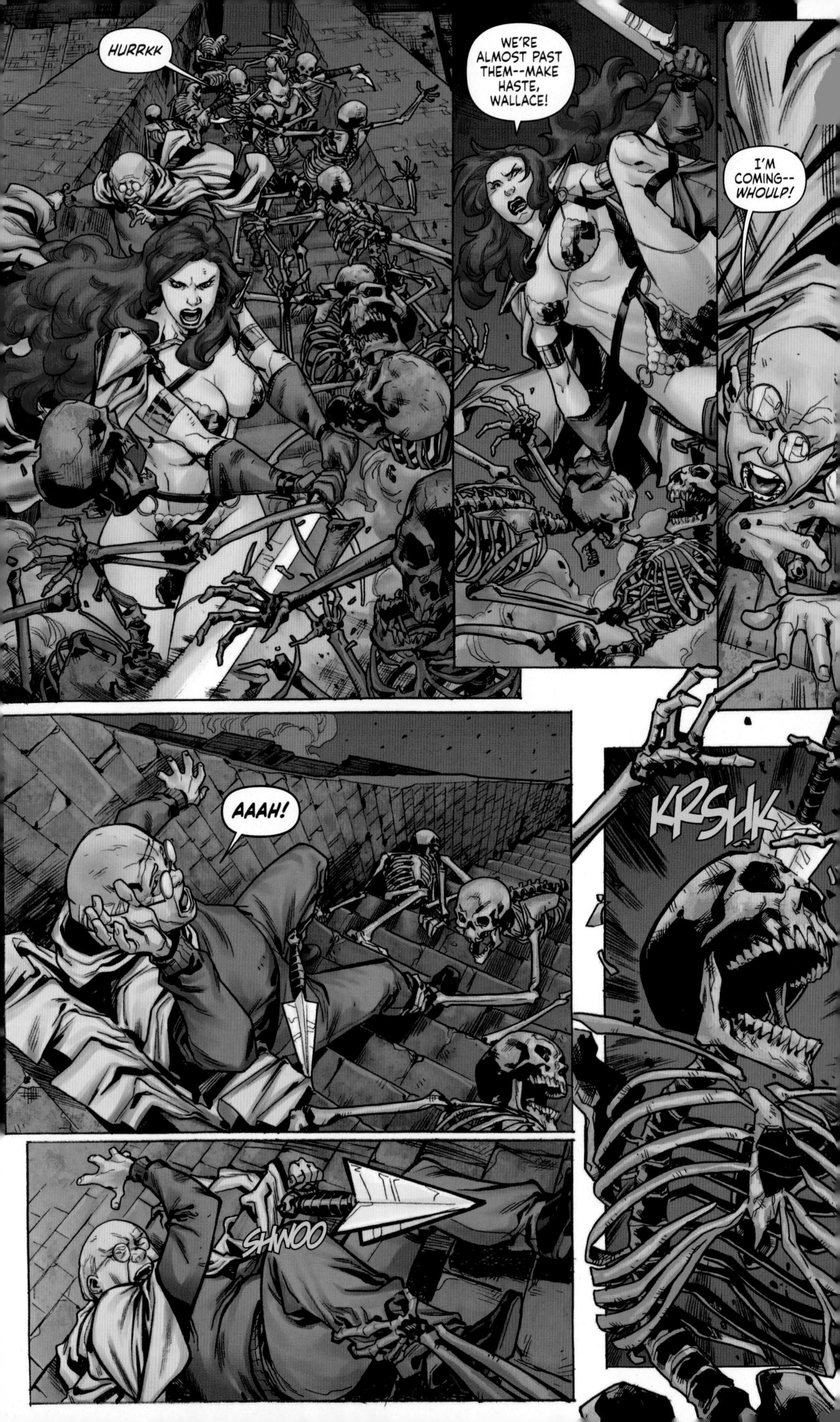
HURRKK
WE'RE ALMOST PAST THEM--MAKE HASTE, WALLACE!
I'M COMING-- WHOULP!
AAAH!
SHWOO
KRSHK

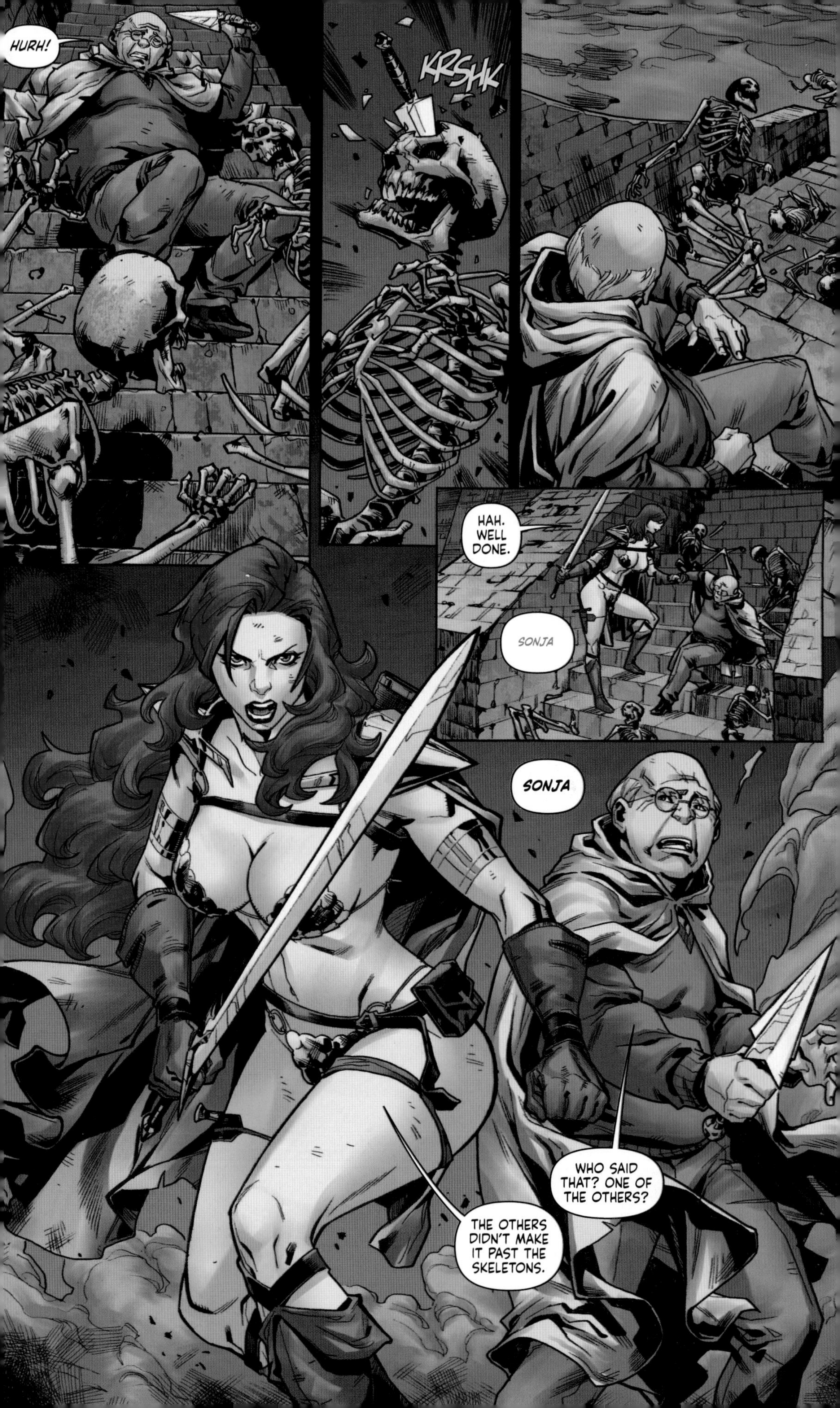
HURH!
KRSHK
HAH. WELL DONE.
SONJA
SONJA
WHO SAID THAT? ONE OF THE OTHERS?
THE OTHERS DIDN'T MAKE IT PAST THE SKELETONS.

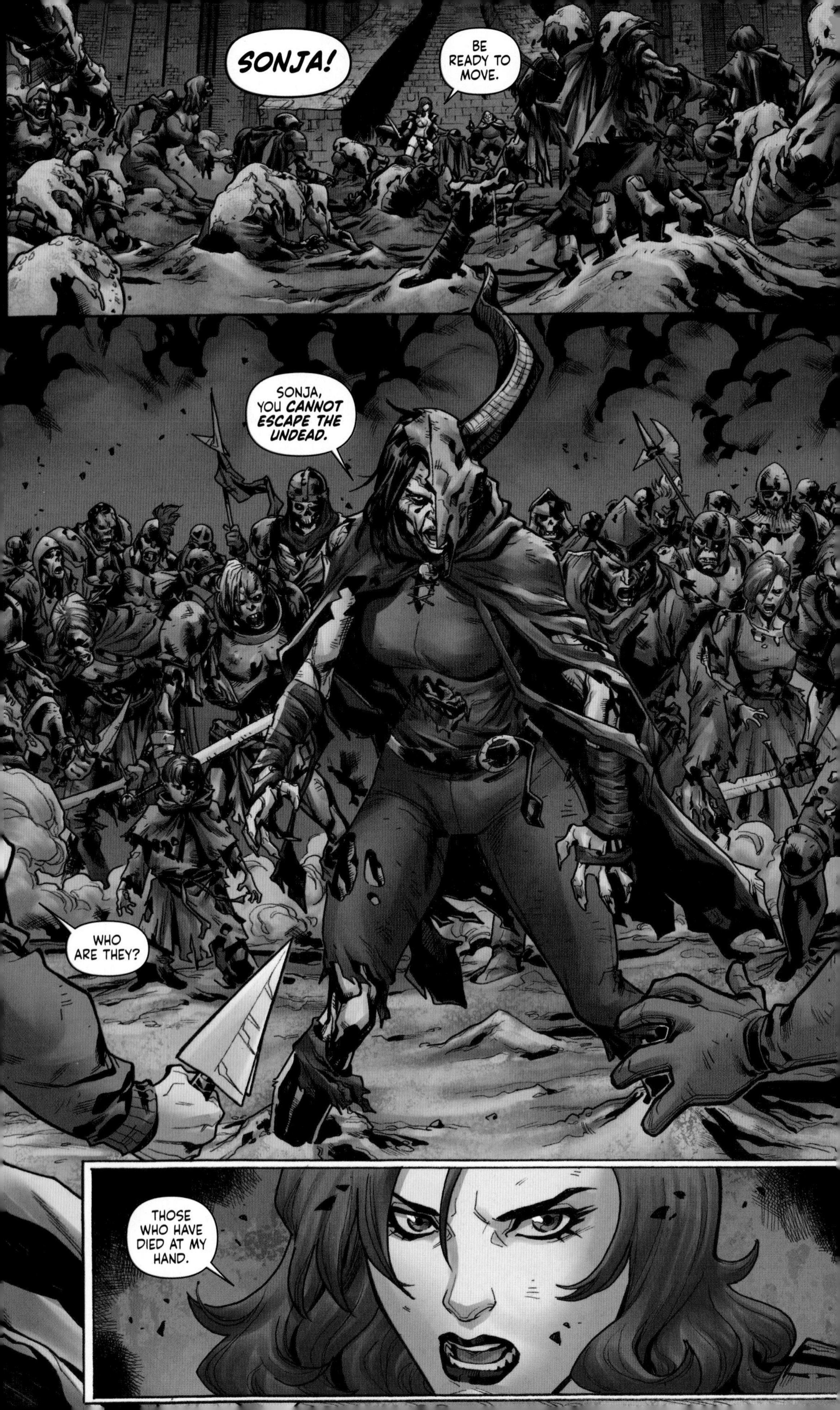
SONJA!
BE READY TO MOVE.
SONJA, YOU CANNOT ESCAPE THE UNDEAD.
WHO ARE THEY?
THOSE WHO HAVE DIED AT MY HAND.

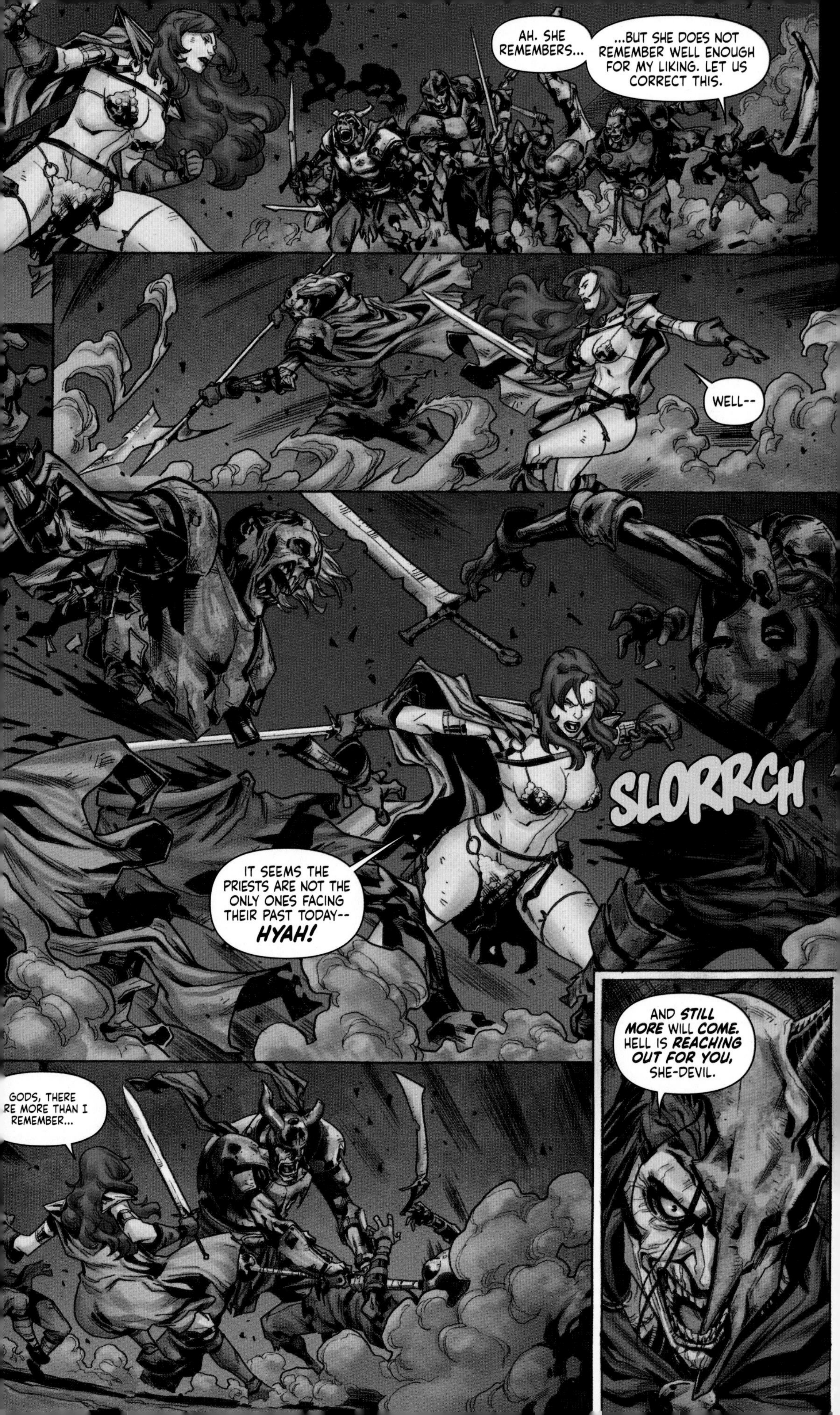
AH. SHE REMEMBERS...
...BUT SHE DOES NOT REMEMBER WELL ENOUGH FOR MY LIKING. LET US CORRECT THIS.
WELL--
SLORRCH
IT SEEMS THE PRIESTS ARE NOT THE ONLY ONES FACING THEIR PAST TODAY-- HYAH!
GODS, THERE RE MORE THAN I REMEMBER...
AND STILL MORE WILL COME. HELL IS REACHING OUT FOR YOU, SHE-DEVIL.

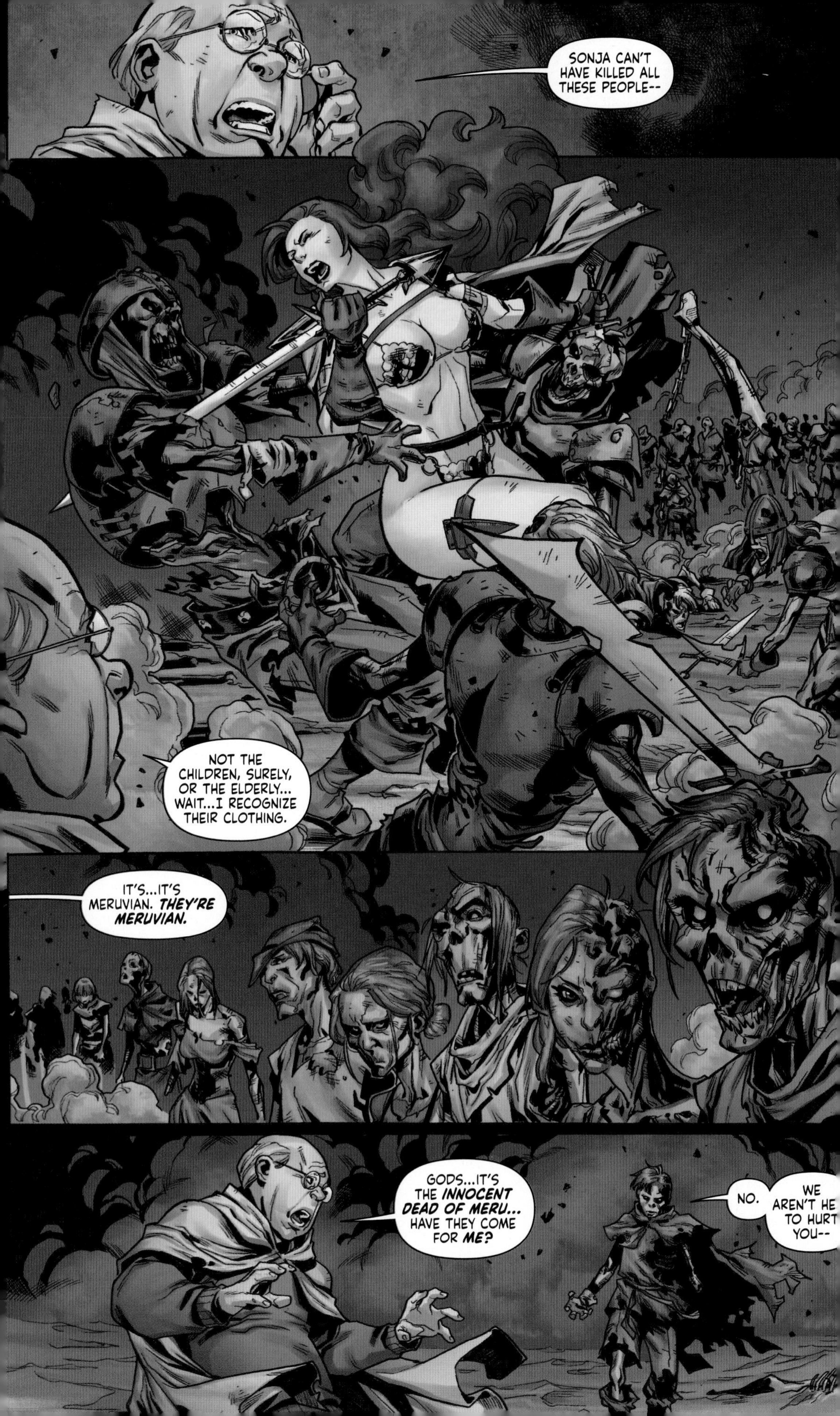
SONJA CAN'T HAVE KILLED ALL THESE PEOPLE--
NOT THE CHILDREN, SURELY, OR THE ELDERLY... WAIT...I RECOGNIZE THEIR CLOTHING.
IT'S...IT'S MERUVIAN. *THEY'RE MERUVIAN.*
GODS...IT'S THE *INNOCENT DEAD OF MERU...* HAVE THEY COME FOR *ME?*
NO.
WE AREN'T HE TO HURT YOU--

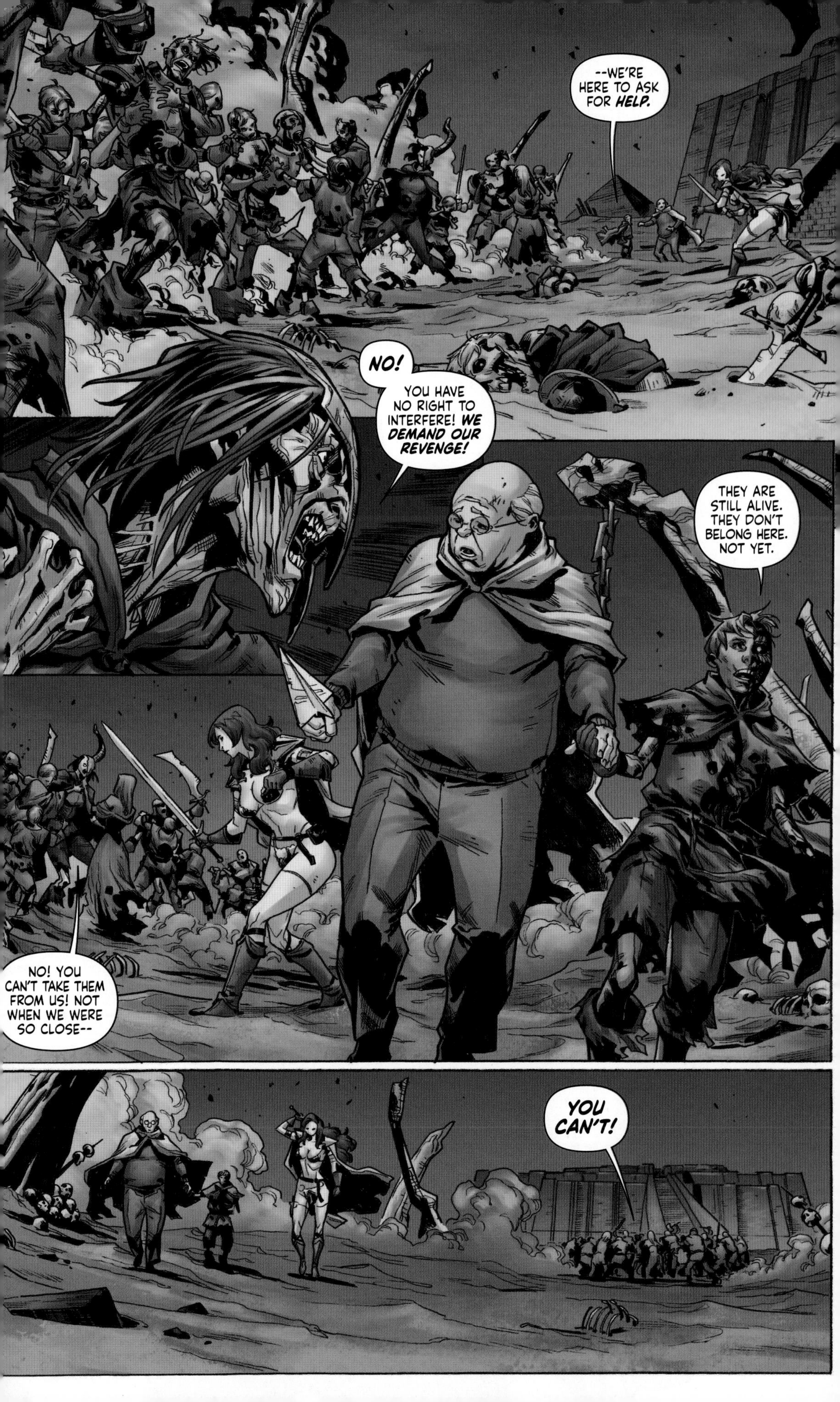
--WE'RE HERE TO ASK FOR **HELP.**
NO!
YOU HAVE NO RIGHT TO INTERFERE! **WE DEMAND OUR REVENGE!**
THEY ARE STILL ALIVE. THEY DON'T BELONG HERE. NOT YET.
NO! YOU CAN'T TAKE THEM FROM US! NOT WHEN WE WERE SO CLOSE--
YOU CAN'T!

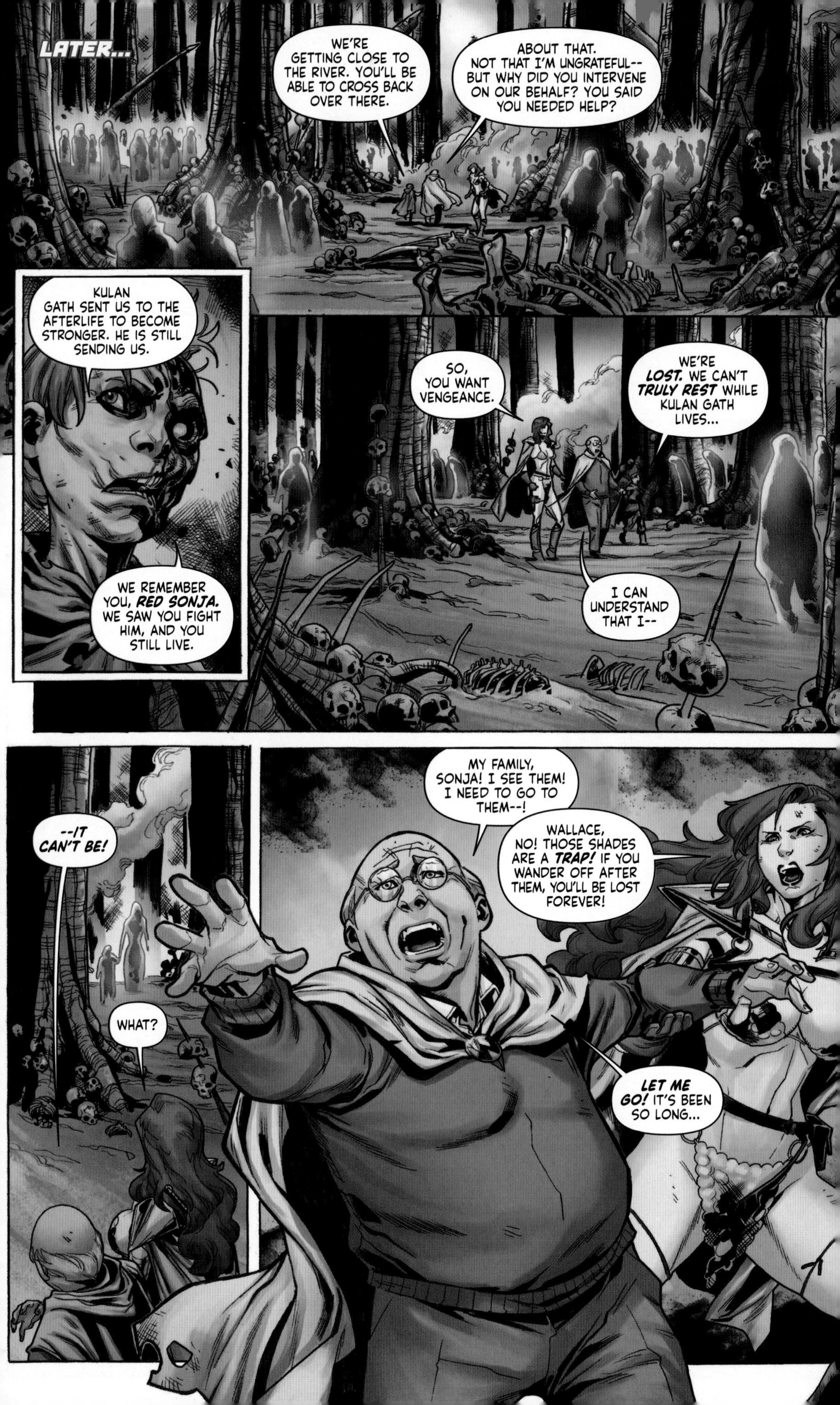
LATER...
WE'RE GETTING CLOSE TO THE RIVER. YOU'LL BE ABLE TO CROSS BACK OVER THERE.
ABOUT THAT. NOT THAT I'M UNGRATEFUL-- BUT WHY DID YOU INTERVENE ON OUR BEHALF? YOU SAID YOU NEEDED HELP?
KULAN GATH SENT US TO THE AFTERLIFE TO BECOME STRONGER. HE IS STILL SENDING US.
WE REMEMBER YOU, RED SONJA. WE SAW YOU FIGHT HIM, AND YOU STILL LIVE.
SO, YOU WANT VENGEANCE.
WE'RE LOST. WE CAN'T TRULY REST WHILE KULAN GATH LIVES...
I CAN UNDERSTAND THAT I--
--IT CAN'T BE!
WHAT?
MY FAMILY, SONJA! I SEE THEM! I NEED TO GO TO THEM--!
WALLACE, NO! THOSE SHADES ARE A TRAP! IF YOU WANDER OFF AFTER THEM, YOU'LL BE LOST FOREVER!
LET ME GO! IT'S BEEN SO LONG...

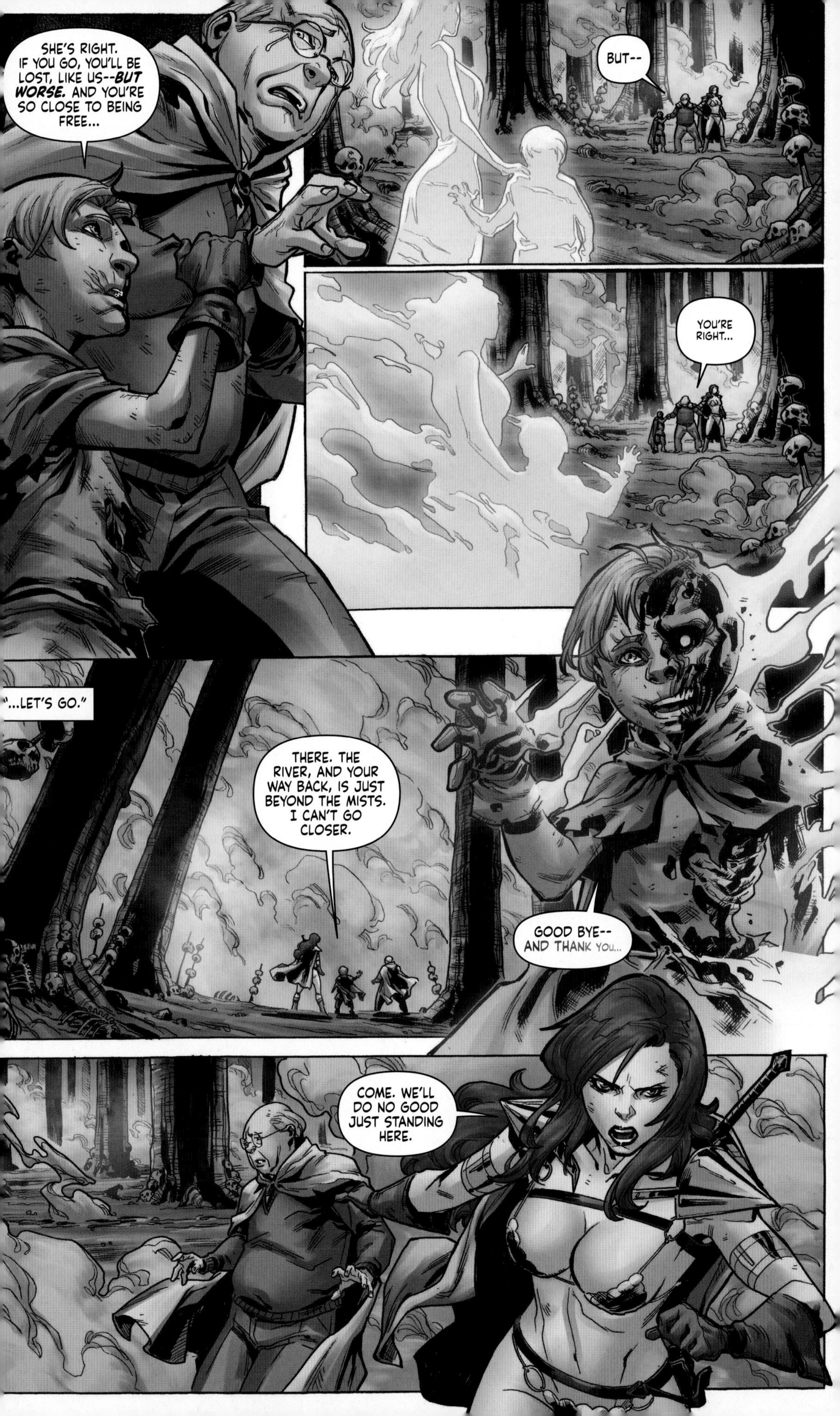
SHE'S RIGHT. IF YOU GO, YOU'LL BE LOST, LIKE US--***BUT WORSE.*** AND YOU'RE SO CLOSE TO BEING FREE...
BUT--
YOU'RE RIGHT...
"...LET'S GO."
THERE. THE RIVER, AND YOUR WAY BACK, IS JUST BEYOND THE MISTS. I CAN'T GO CLOSER.
GOOD BYE-- AND THANK YOU...
COME. WE'LL DO NO GOOD JUST STANDING HERE.

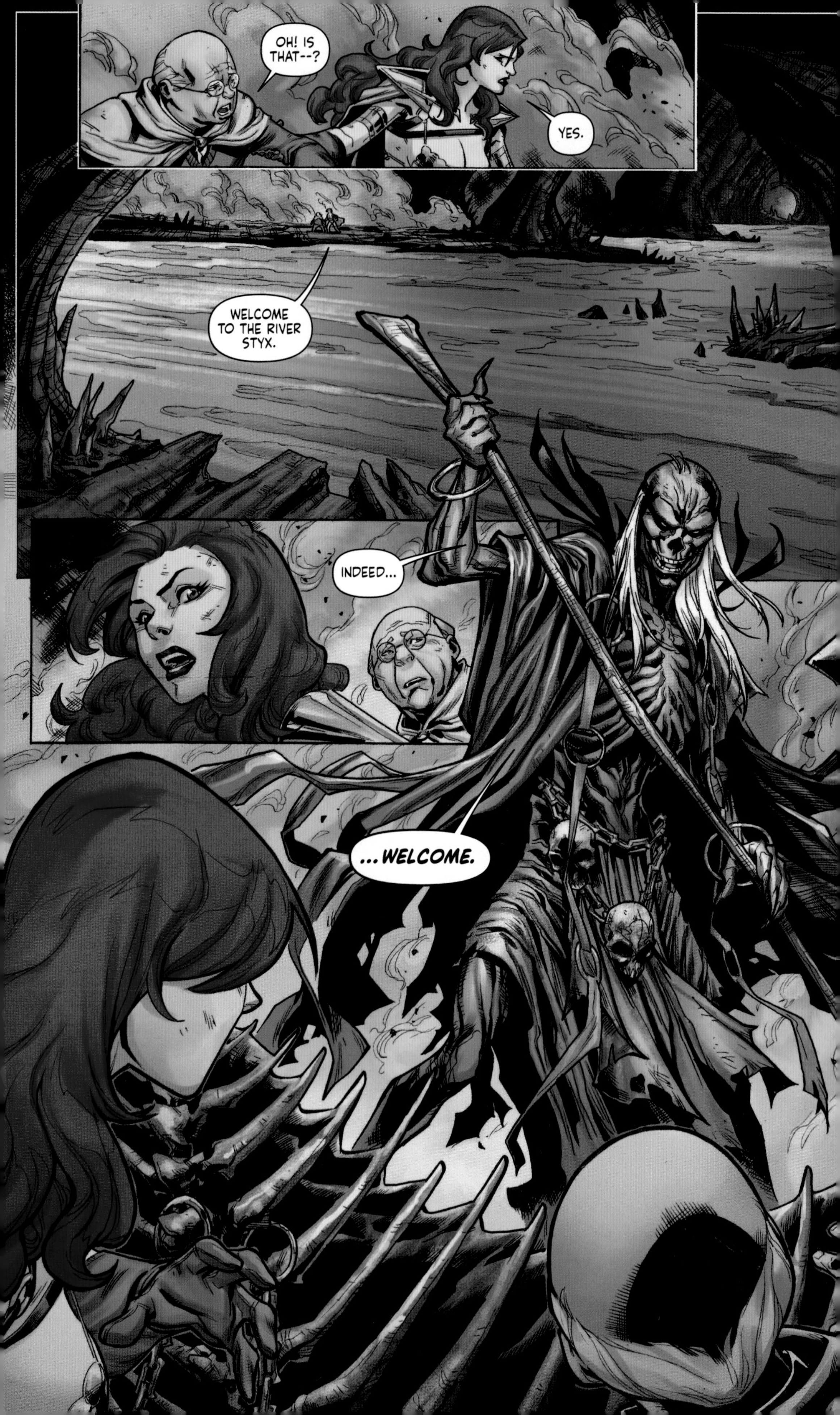
OH! IS THAT--?
YES.
WELCOME TO THE RIVER STYX.
INDEED...
...WELCOME.

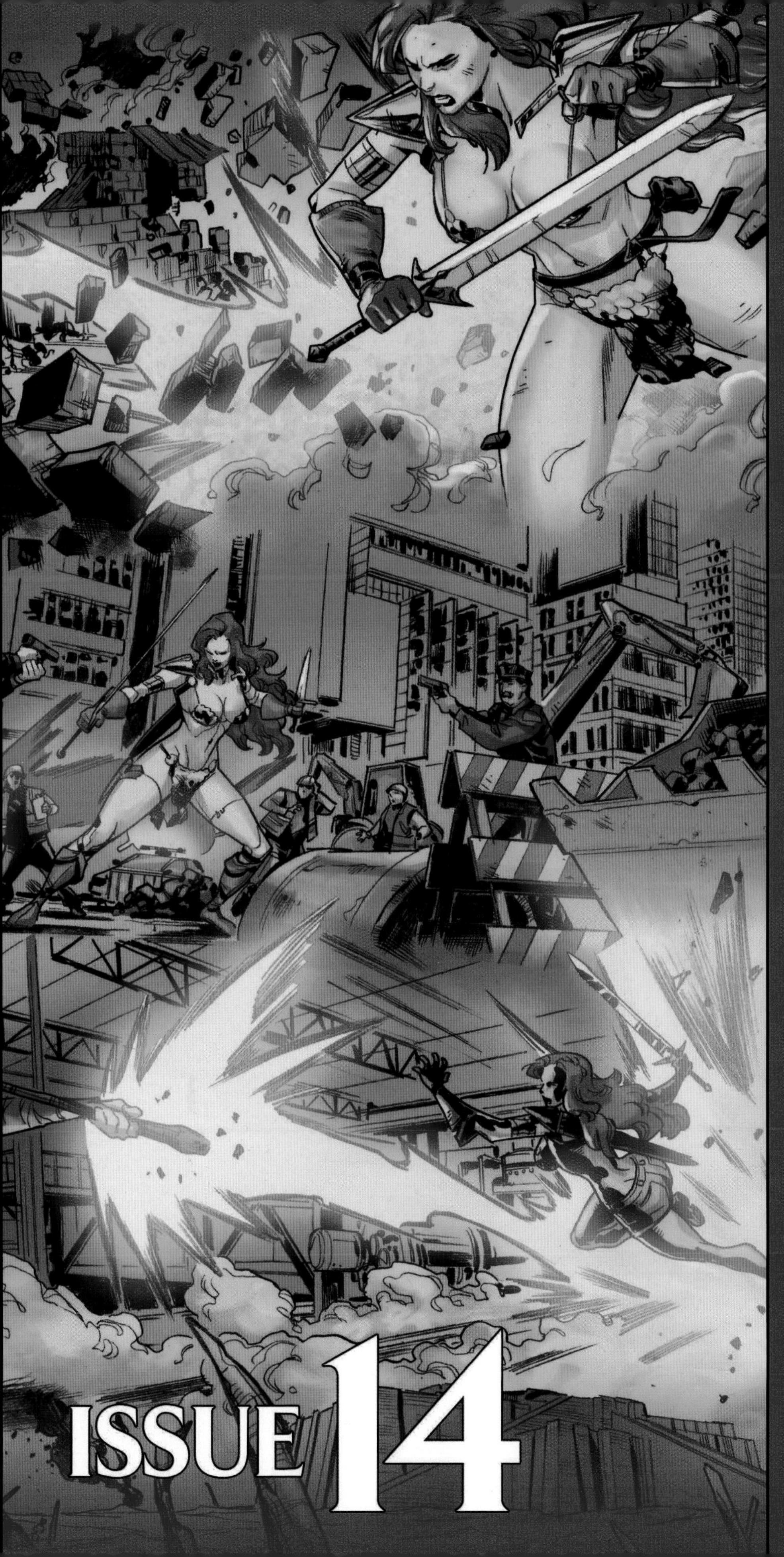
ISSUE 14

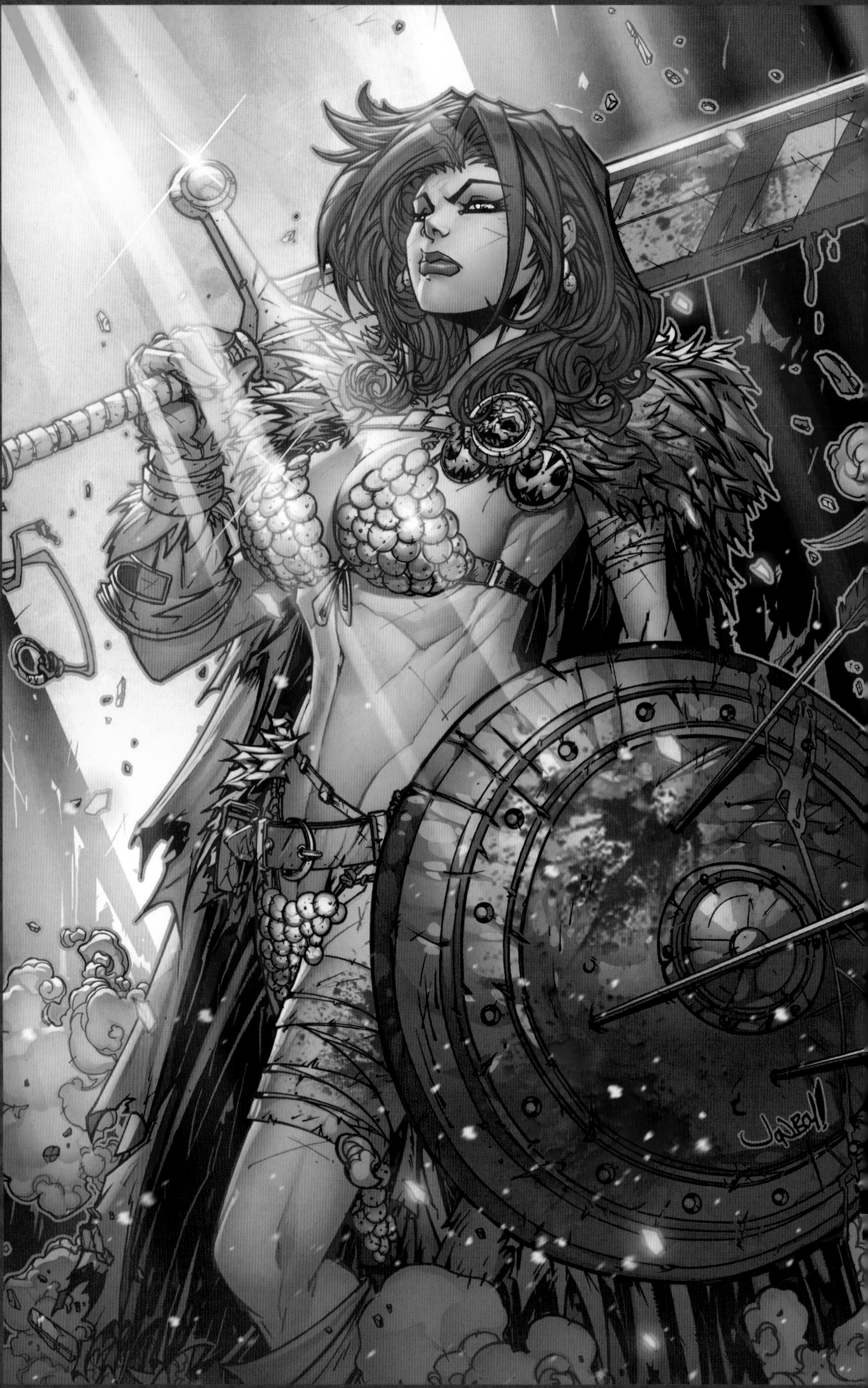

ISSUE #14: COVER ART BY JONBOY MEYERS

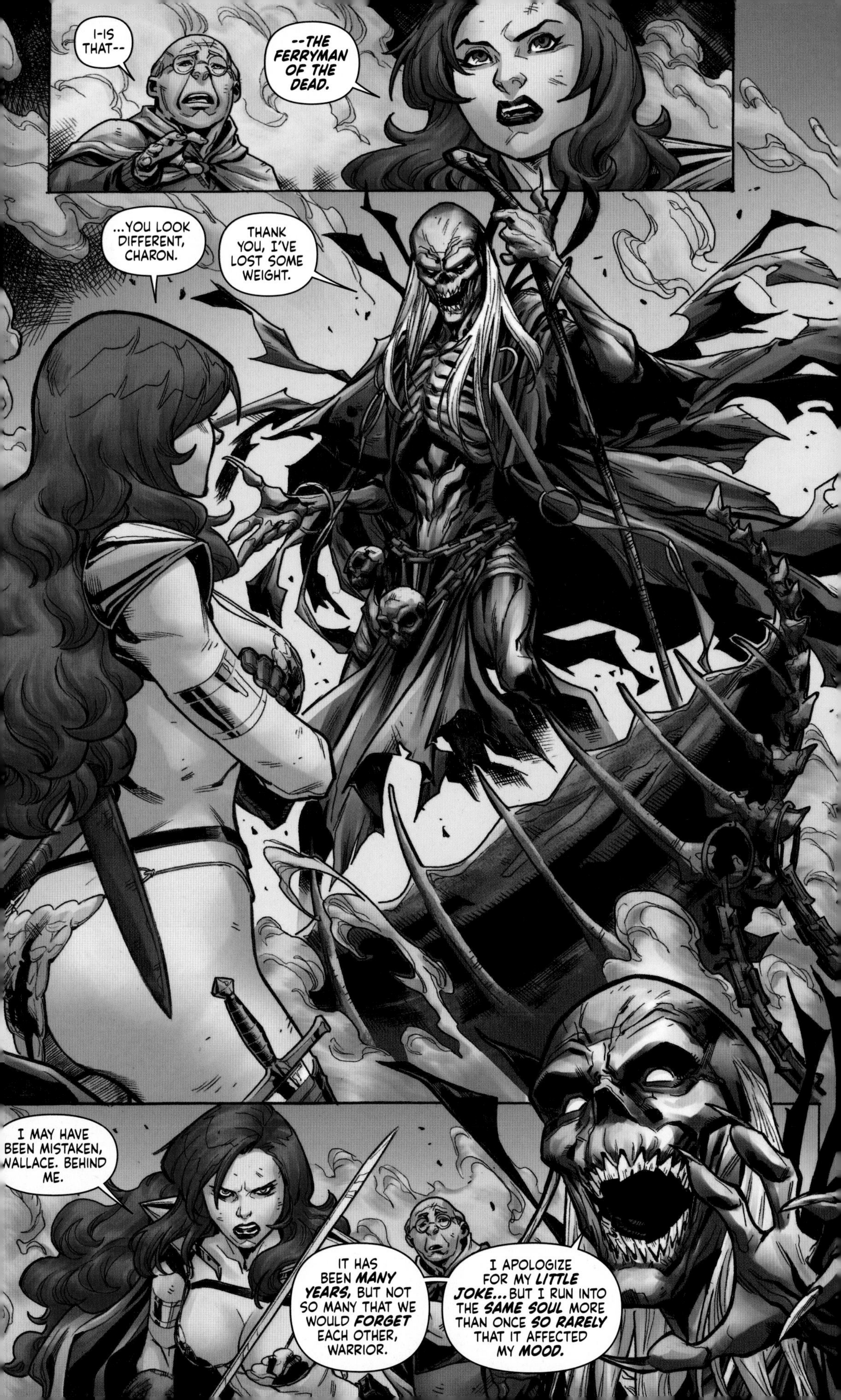

I-IS THAT--
--THE FERRYMAN OF THE DEAD.
...YOU LOOK DIFFERENT, CHARON.
THANK YOU, I'VE LOST SOME WEIGHT.
I MAY HAVE BEEN MISTAKEN, WALLACE. BEHIND ME.
I APOLOGIZE FOR MY LITTLE JOKE... BUT I RUN INTO THE SAME SOUL MORE THAN ONCE SO RARELY THAT IT AFFECTED MY MOOD.
IT HAS BEEN MANY YEARS, BUT NOT SO MANY THAT WE WOULD FORGET EACH OTHER, WARRIOR.

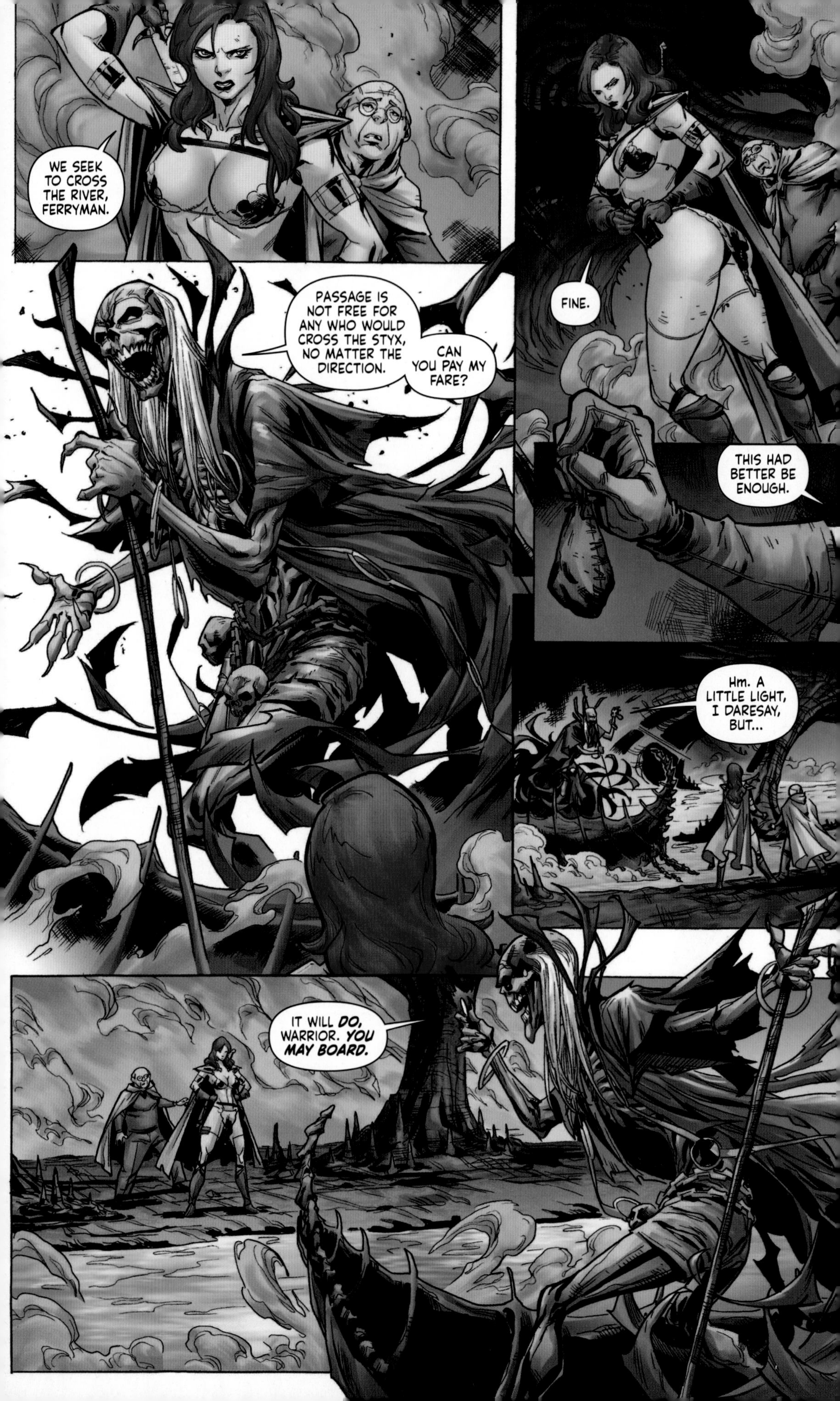
WE SEEK TO CROSS THE RIVER, FERRYMAN.
PASSAGE IS NOT FREE FOR ANY WHO WOULD CROSS THE STYX, NO MATTER THE DIRECTION.
CAN YOU PAY MY FARE?
FINE.
THIS HAD BETTER BE ENOUGH.
Hm. A LITTLE LIGHT, I DARESAY, BUT...
IT WILL DO, WARRIOR. YOU MAY BOARD.

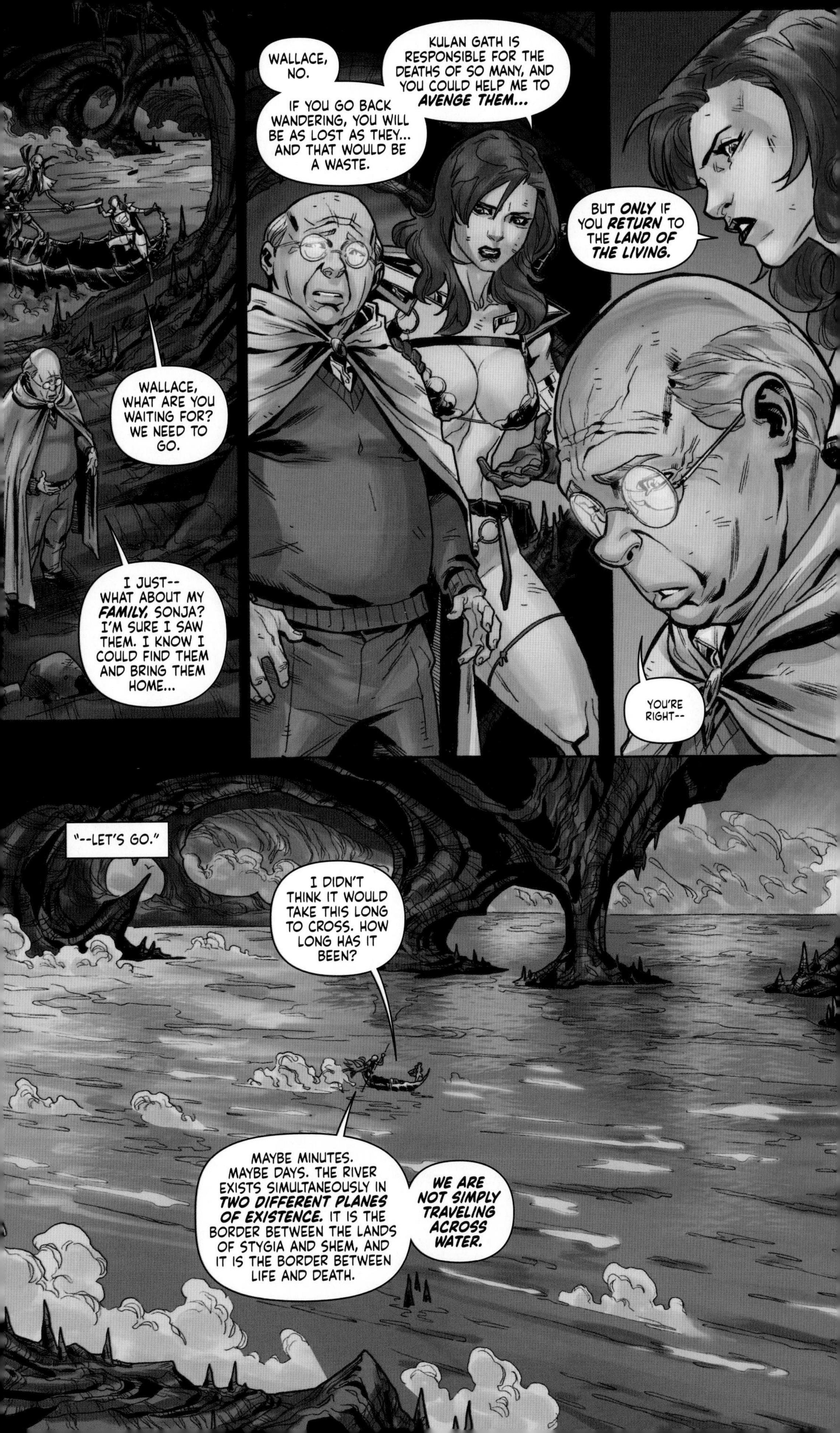
WALLACE, WHAT ARE YOU WAITING FOR? WE NEED TO GO.
I JUST-- WHAT ABOUT MY FAMILY, SONJA? I'M SURE I SAW THEM. I KNOW I COULD FIND THEM AND BRING THEM HOME...
WALLACE, NO.
IF YOU GO BACK WANDERING, YOU WILL BE AS LOST AS THEY... AND THAT WOULD BE A WASTE.
KULAN GATH IS RESPONSIBLE FOR THE DEATHS OF SO MANY, AND YOU COULD HELP ME TO AVENGE THEM...
BUT ONLY IF YOU RETURN TO THE LAND OF THE LIVING.
YOU'RE RIGHT--
"--LET'S GO."
I DIDN'T THINK IT WOULD TAKE THIS LONG TO CROSS. HOW LONG HAS IT BEEN?
MAYBE MINUTES. MAYBE DAYS. THE RIVER EXISTS SIMULTANEOUSLY IN TWO DIFFERENT PLANES OF EXISTENCE. IT IS THE BORDER BETWEEN THE LANDS OF STYGIA AND SHEM, AND IT IS THE BORDER BETWEEN LIFE AND DEATH.
WE ARE NOT SIMPLY TRAVELING ACROSS WATER.

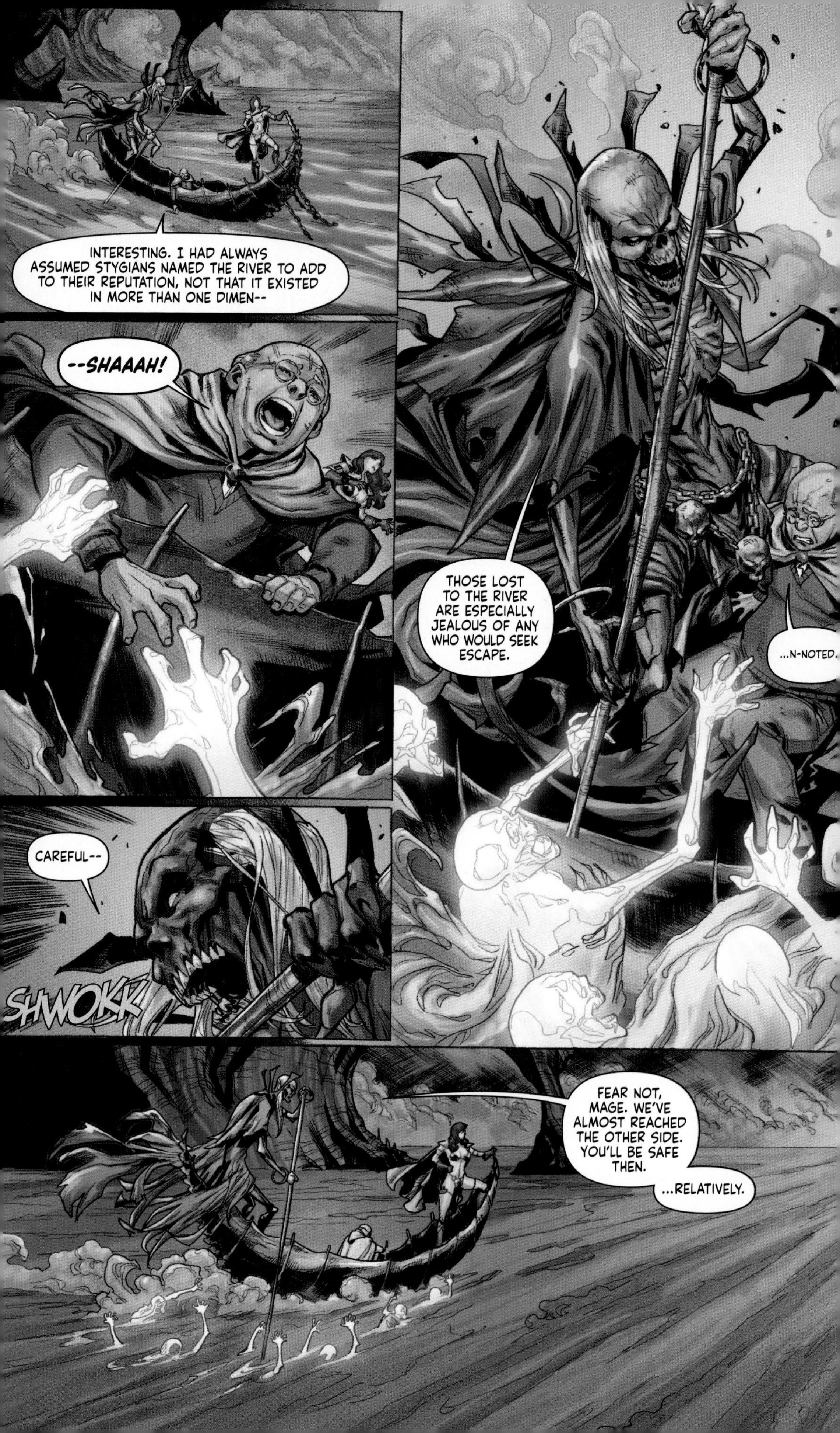

INTERESTING. I HAD ALWAYS ASSUMED STYGIANS NAMED THE RIVER TO ADD TO THEIR REPUTATION, NOT THAT IT EXISTED IN MORE THAN ONE DIMEN--
--SHAAAH!
CAREFUL--
SHWOKK
THOSE LOST TO THE RIVER ARE ESPECIALLY JEALOUS OF ANY WHO WOULD SEEK ESCAPE.
...N-NOTED.
FEAR NOT, MAGE. WE'VE ALMOST REACHED THE OTHER SIDE. YOU'LL BE SAFE THEN.
...RELATIVELY.

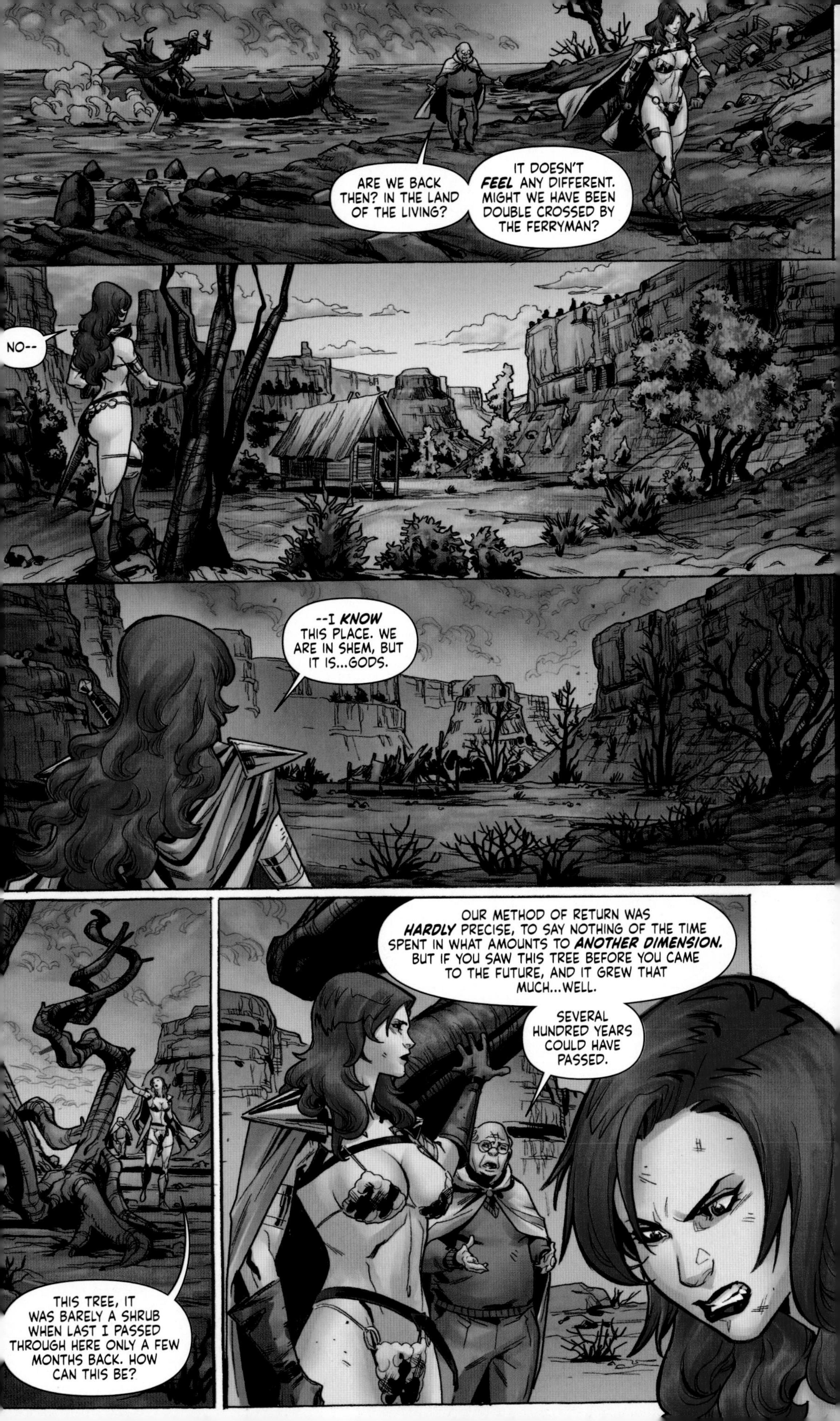
ARE WE BACK THEN? IN THE LAND OF THE LIVING?
IT DOESN'T **FEEL** ANY DIFFERENT. MIGHT WE HAVE BEEN DOUBLE CROSSED BY THE FERRYMAN?
NO--
--I **KNOW** THIS PLACE. WE ARE IN SHEM, BUT IT IS...GODS.
THIS TREE, IT WAS BARELY A SHRUB WHEN LAST I PASSED THROUGH HERE ONLY A FEW MONTHS BACK. HOW CAN THIS BE?
OUR METHOD OF RETURN WAS **HARDLY** PRECISE, TO SAY NOTHING OF THE TIME SPENT IN WHAT AMOUNTS TO **ANOTHER DIMENSION.** BUT IF YOU SAW THIS TREE BEFORE YOU CAME TO THE FUTURE, AND IT GREW THAT MUCH...WELL.
SEVERAL HUNDRED YEARS COULD HAVE PASSED.

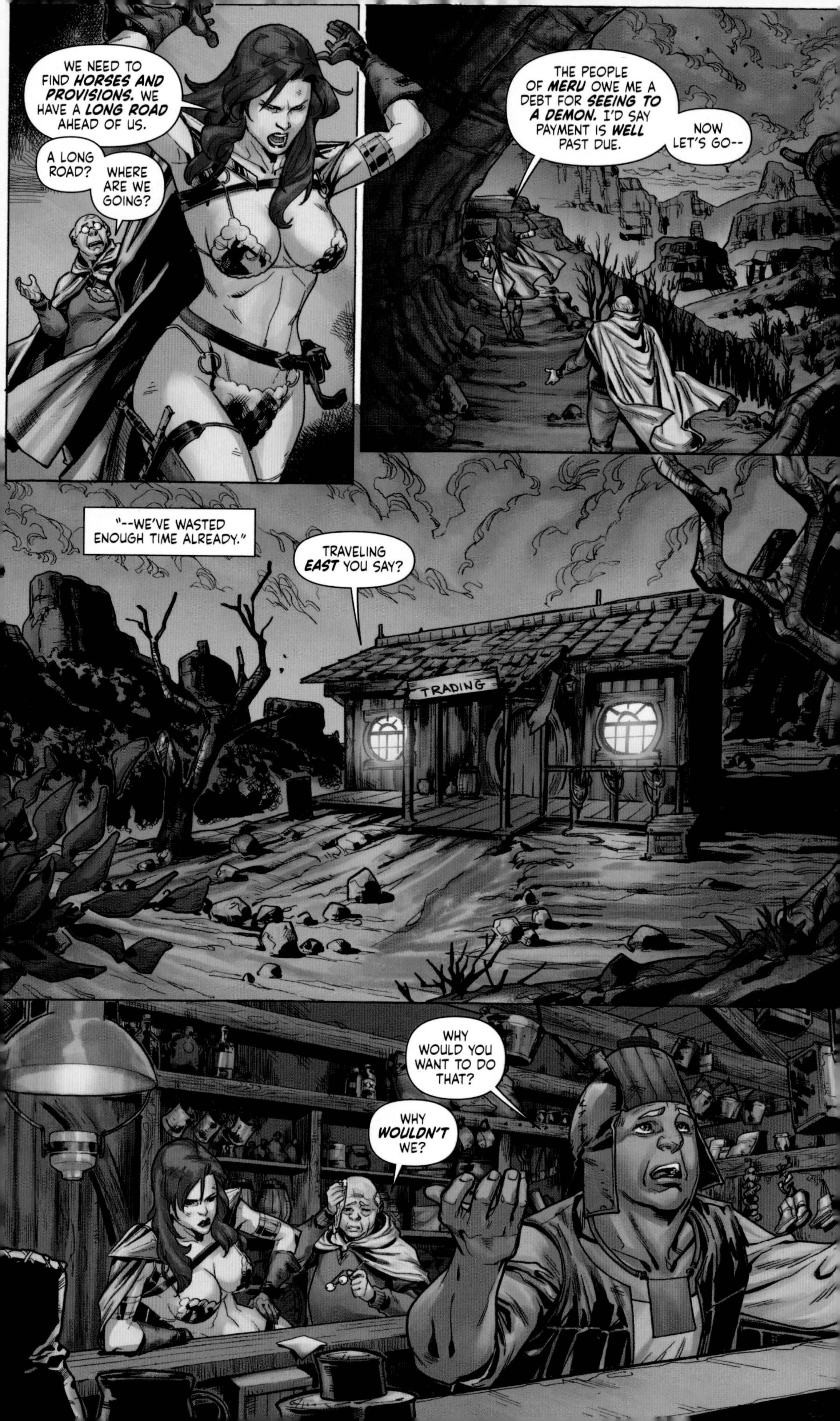
WE NEED TO FIND HORSES AND PROVISIONS. WE HAVE A LONG ROAD AHEAD OF US.
A LONG ROAD?
WHERE ARE WE GOING?
THE PEOPLE OF MERU OWE ME A DEBT FOR SEEING TO A DEMON. I'D SAY PAYMENT IS WELL PAST DUE.
NOW LET'S GO--
"--WE'VE WASTED ENOUGH TIME ALREADY."
TRAVELING EAST YOU SAY?
TRADING
WHY WOULD YOU WANT TO DO THAT?
WHY WOULDN'T WE?

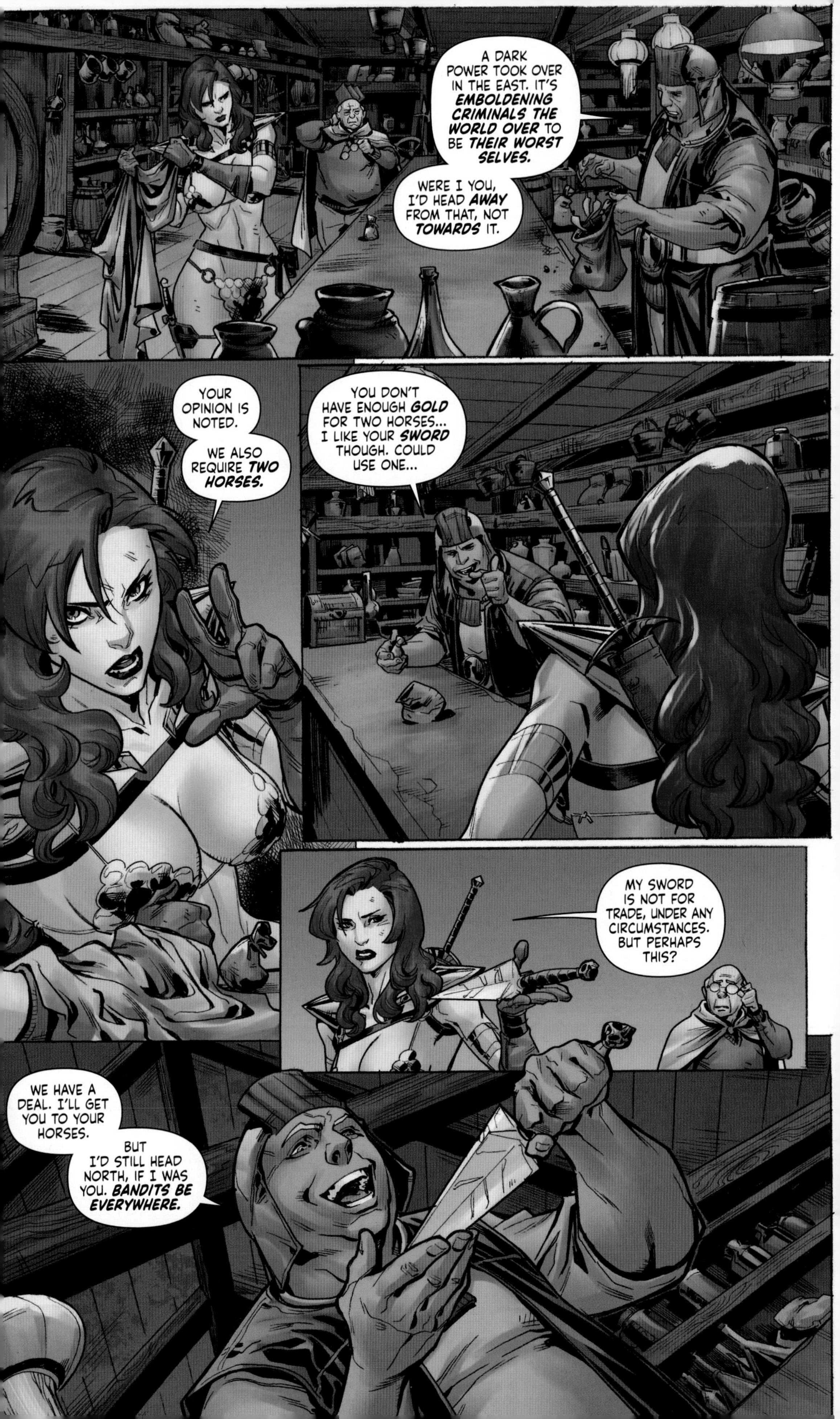
A DARK POWER TOOK OVER IN THE EAST. IT'S **EMBOLDENING CRIMINALS THE WORLD OVER** TO BE **THEIR WORST SELVES.**
WERE I YOU, I'D HEAD **AWAY** FROM THAT, NOT **TOWARDS** IT.
YOUR OPINION IS NOTED.
WE ALSO REQUIRE **TWO HORSES.**
YOU DON'T HAVE ENOUGH **GOLD** FOR TWO HORSES... I LIKE YOUR **SWORD** THOUGH. COULD USE ONE...
MY SWORD IS NOT FOR TRADE, UNDER ANY CIRCUMSTANCES. BUT PERHAPS THIS?
WE HAVE A DEAL. I'LL GET YOU TO YOUR HORSES.
BUT I'D STILL HEAD NORTH, IF I WAS YOU. **BANDITS BE EVERYWHERE.**

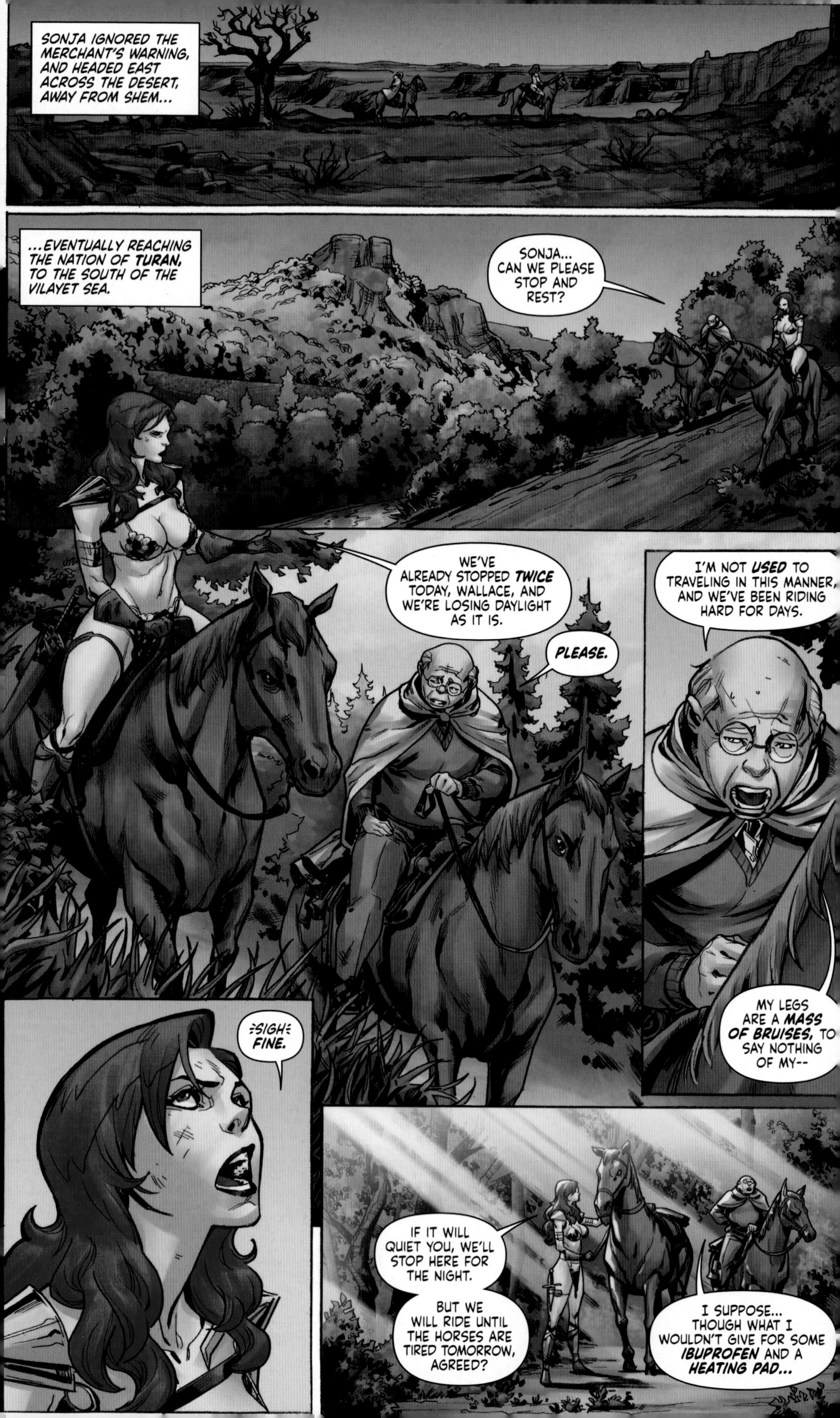
SONJA IGNORED THE MERCHANT'S WARNING, AND HEADED EAST ACROSS THE DESERT, AWAY FROM SHEM...
...EVENTUALLY REACHING THE NATION OF TURAN, TO THE SOUTH OF THE VILAYET SEA.
SONJA... CAN WE PLEASE STOP AND REST?
WE'VE ALREADY STOPPED TWICE TODAY, WALLACE, AND WE'RE LOSING DAYLIGHT AS IT IS.
PLEASE.
I'M NOT USED TO TRAVELING IN THIS MANNER, AND WE'VE BEEN RIDING HARD FOR DAYS.
MY LEGS ARE A MASS OF BRUISES, TO SAY NOTHING OF MY--
SIGH FINE.
IF IT WILL QUIET YOU, WE'LL STOP HERE FOR THE NIGHT.
BUT WE WILL RIDE UNTIL THE HORSES ARE TIRED TOMORROW, AGREED?
I SUPPOSE... THOUGH WHAT I WOULDN'T GIVE FOR SOME IBUPROFEN AND A HEATING PAD...

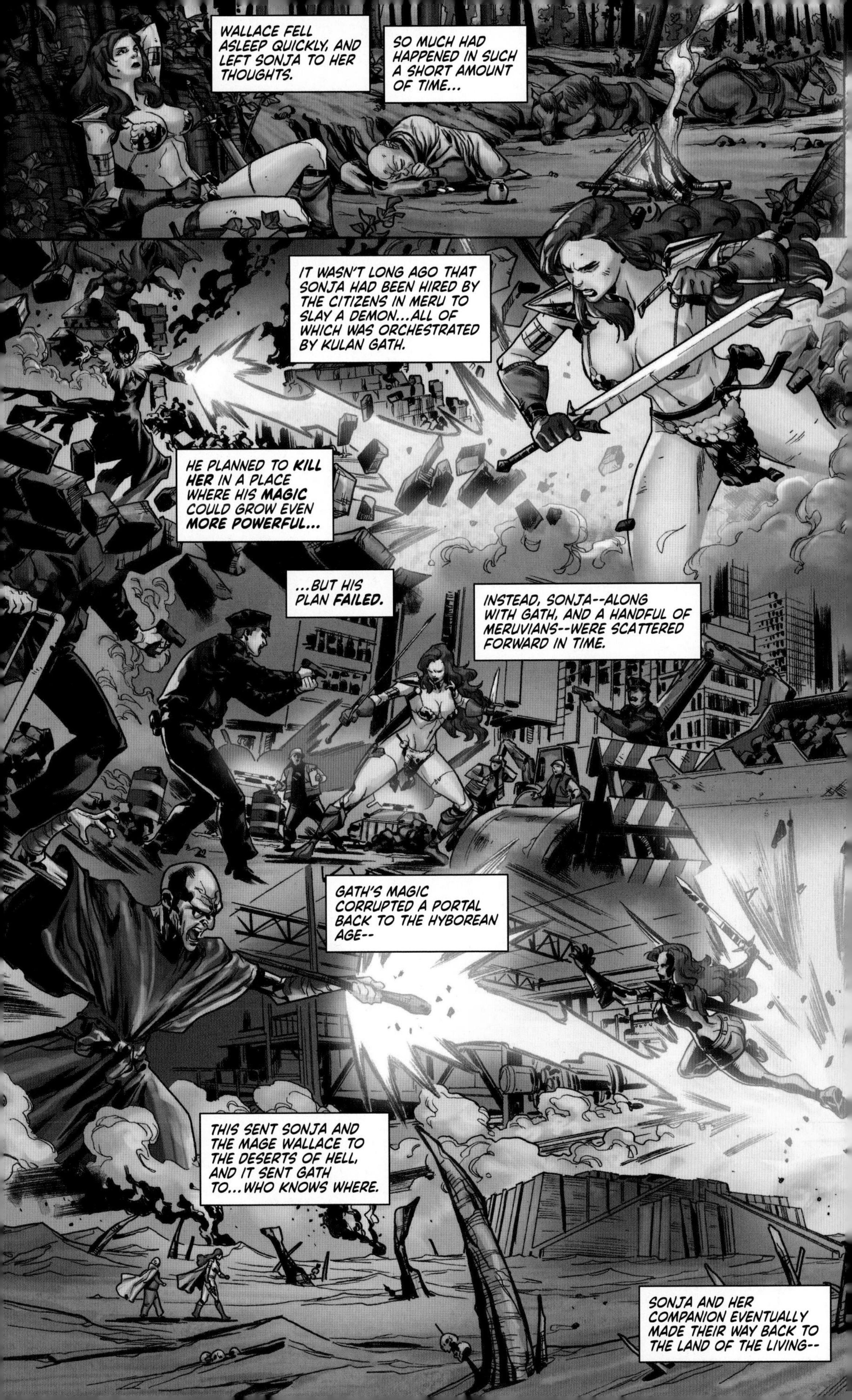
WALLACE FELL ASLEEP QUICKLY, AND LEFT SONJA TO HER THOUGHTS.
SO MUCH HAD HAPPENED IN SUCH A SHORT AMOUNT OF TIME...
IT WASN'T LONG AGO THAT SONJA HAD BEEN HIRED BY THE CITIZENS IN MERU TO SLAY A DEMON...ALL OF WHICH WAS ORCHESTRATED BY KULAN GATH.
HE PLANNED TO **KILL HER** IN A PLACE WHERE HIS **MAGIC** COULD GROW EVEN **MORE POWERFUL...**
...BUT HIS PLAN **FAILED.**
INSTEAD, SONJA--ALONG WITH GATH, AND A HANDFUL OF MERUVIANS--WERE SCATTERED FORWARD IN TIME.
GATH'S MAGIC CORRUPTED A PORTAL BACK TO THE HYBOREAN AGE--
THIS SENT SONJA AND THE MAGE WALLACE TO THE DESERTS OF HELL, AND IT SENT GATH TO...WHO KNOWS WHERE.
SONJA AND HER COMPANION EVENTUALLY MADE THEIR WAY BACK TO THE LAND OF THE LIVING--

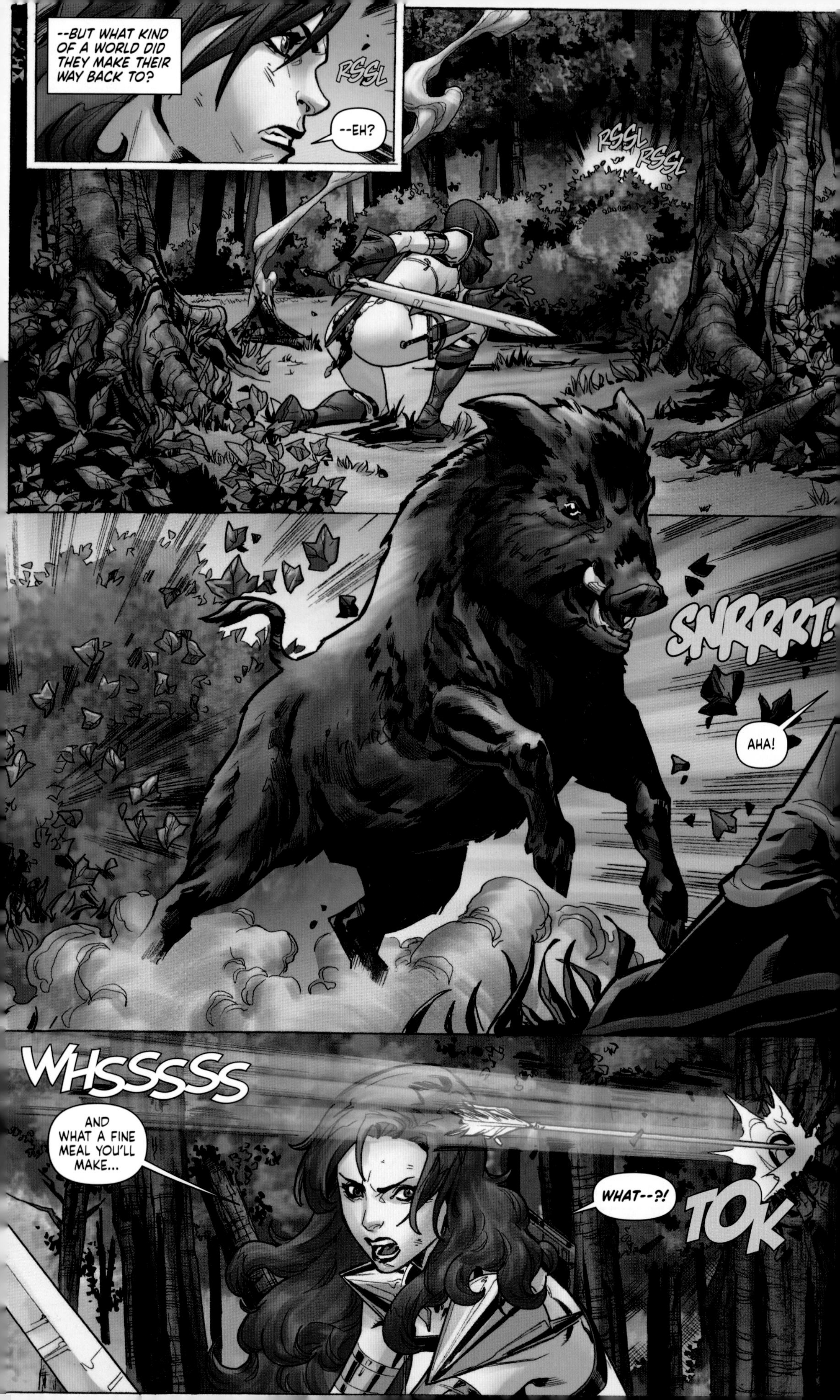
--BUT WHAT KIND OF A WORLD DID THEY MAKE THEIR WAY BACK TO?
RSSL
--EH?
RSSL RSSL
SNRRRT!
AHA!
WHSSSSS
AND WHAT A FINE MEAL YOU'LL MAKE...
WHAT--?!
TOK

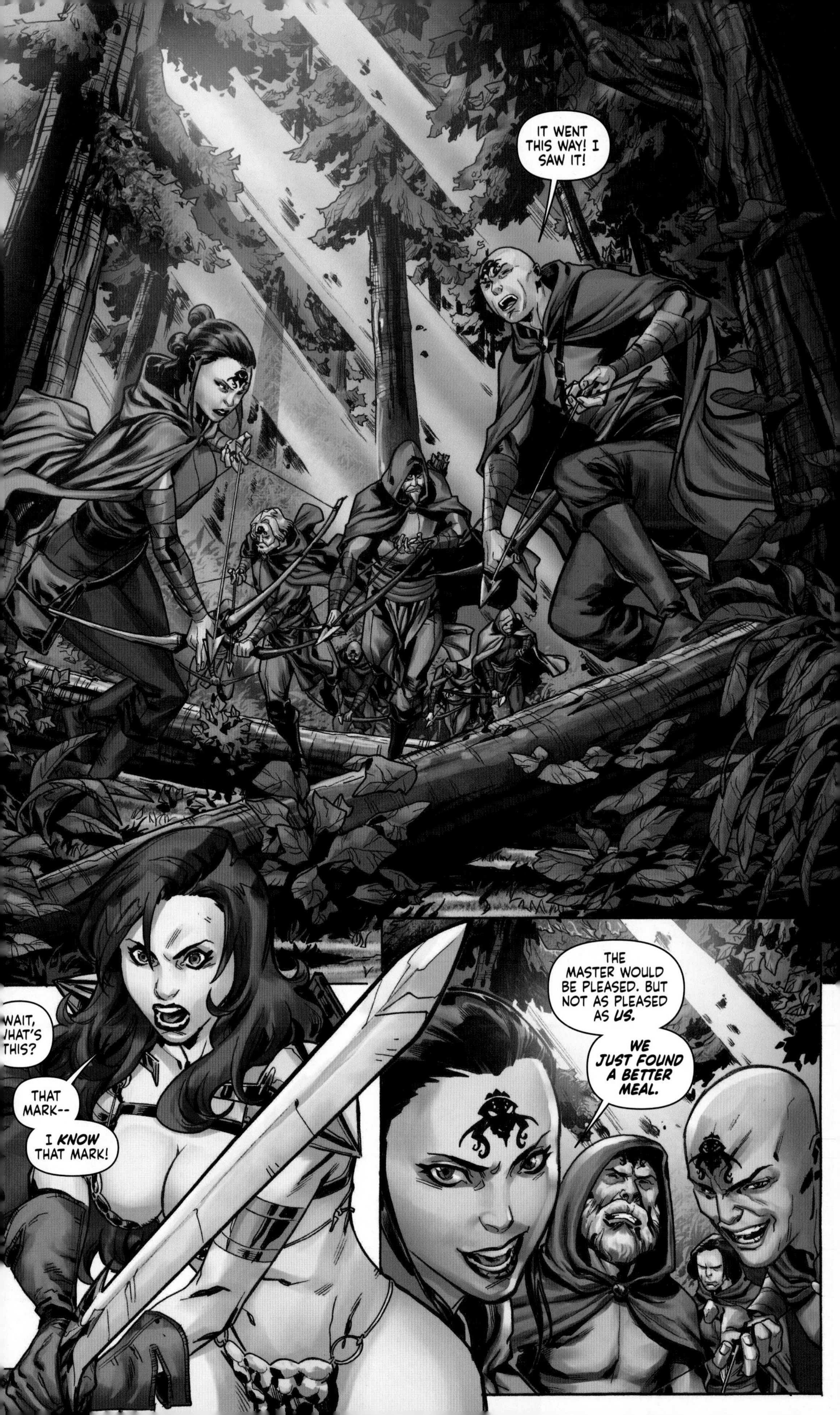
IT WENT THIS WAY! I SAW IT!
WAIT, WHAT'S THIS?
THAT MARK--
I KNOW THAT MARK!
THE MASTER WOULD BE PLEASED. BUT NOT AS PLEASED AS US.
WE JUST FOUND A BETTER MEAL.

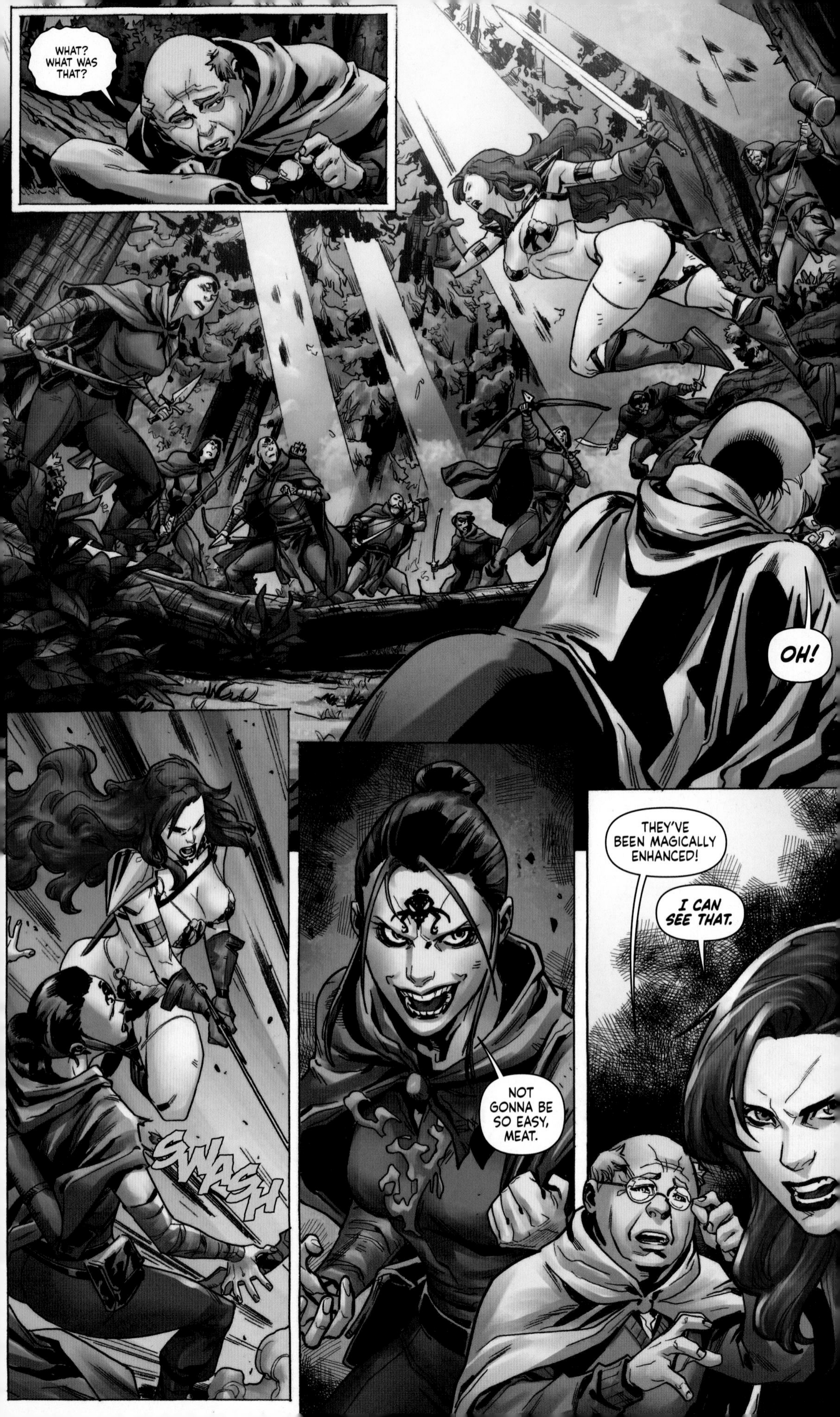
WHAT? WHAT WAS THAT?
OH!
SWASH
NOT GONNA BE SO EASY, MEAT.
THEY'VE BEEN MAGICALLY ENHANCED!
I CAN SEE THAT.

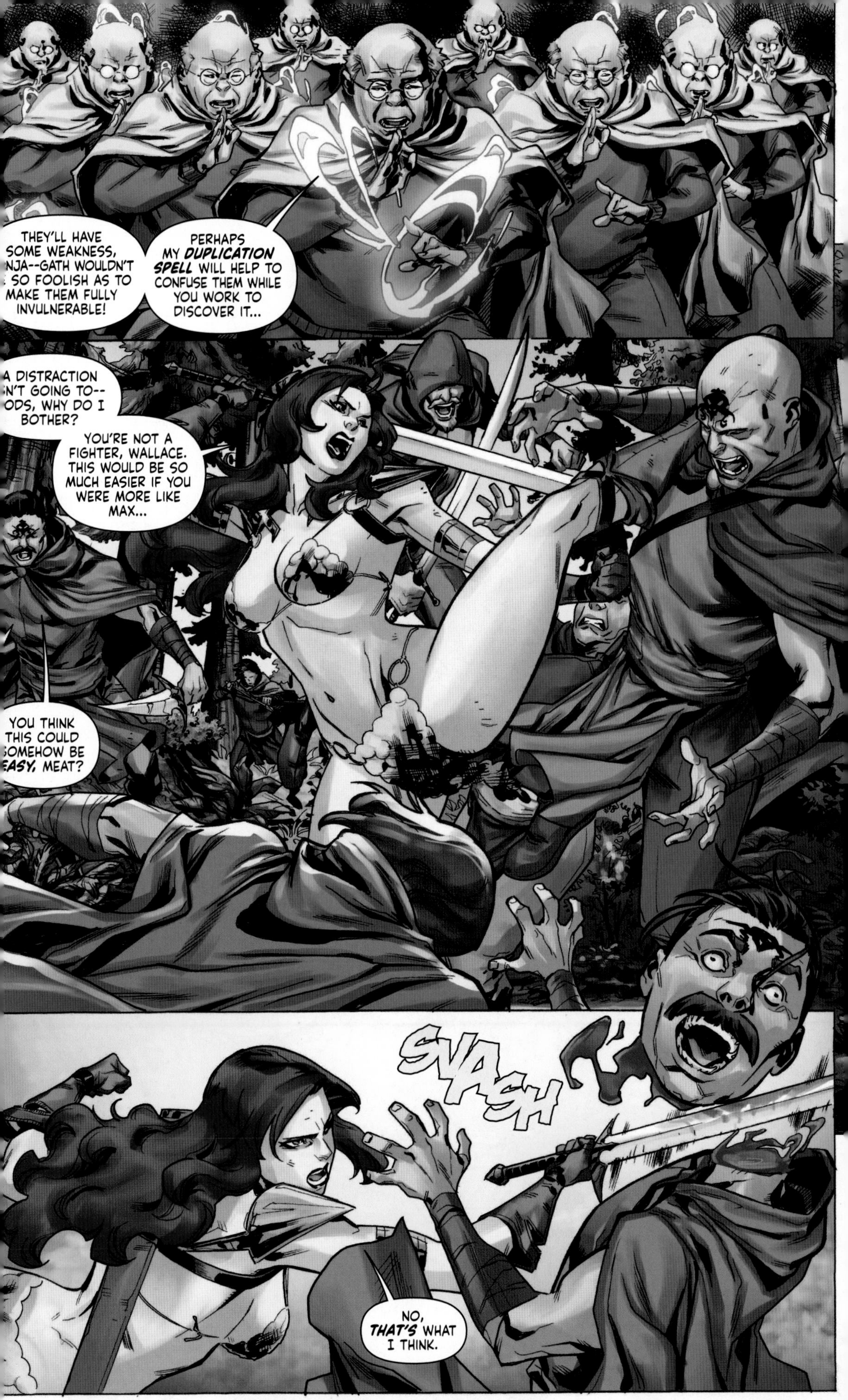
THEY'LL HAVE SOME WEAKNESS, NJA--GATH WOULDN'T SO FOOLISH AS TO MAKE THEM FULLY INVULNERABLE!
PERHAPS MY DUPLICATION SPELL WILL HELP TO CONFUSE THEM WHILE YOU WORK TO DISCOVER IT...
A DISTRACTION N'T GOING TO-- ODS, WHY DO I BOTHER?
YOU'RE NOT A FIGHTER, WALLACE. THIS WOULD BE SO MUCH EASIER IF YOU WERE MORE LIKE MAX...
YOU THINK THIS COULD SOMEHOW BE EASY, MEAT?
SWASH
NO, THAT'S WHAT I THINK.

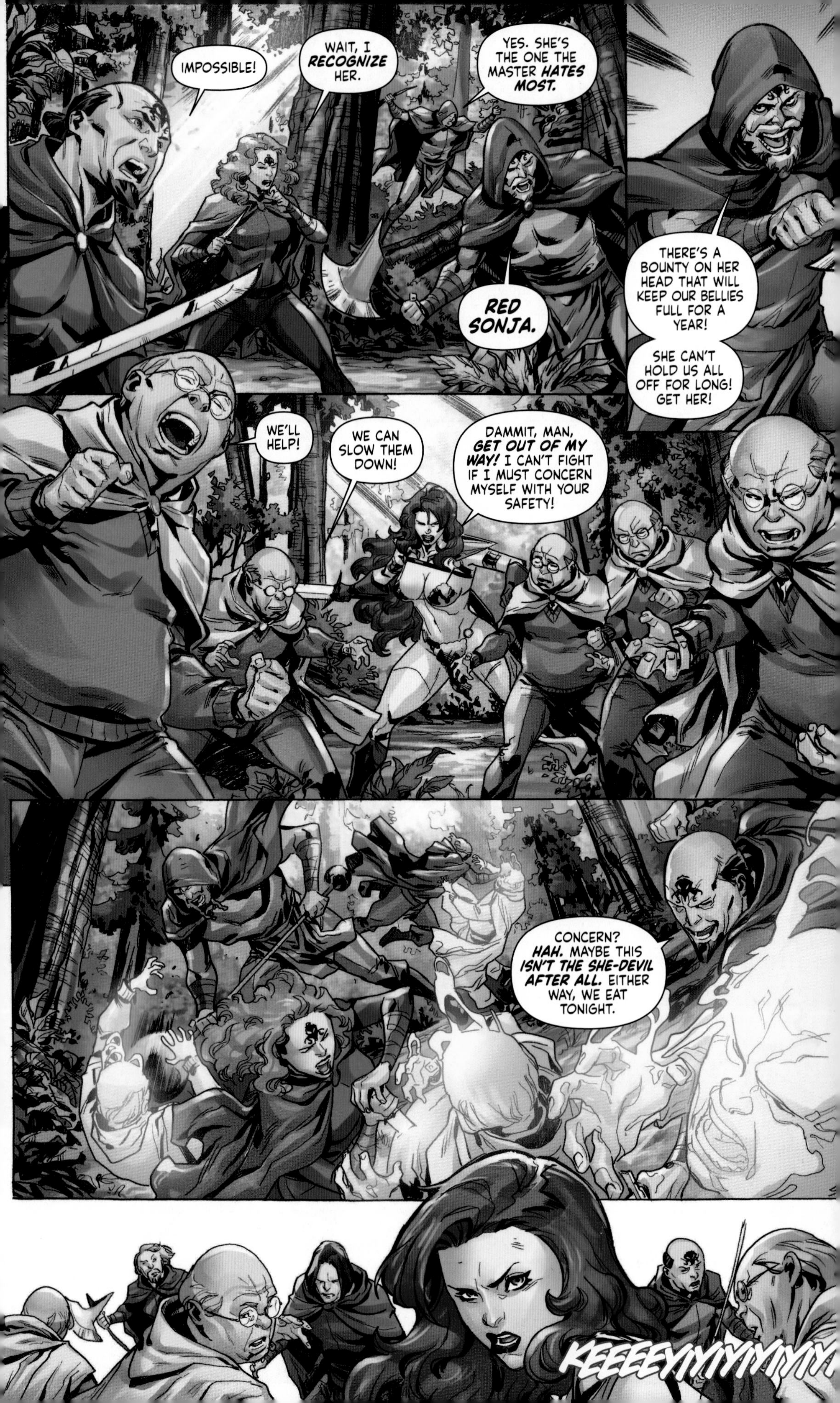
IMPOSSIBLE!
WAIT, I RECOGNIZE HER.
YES. SHE'S THE ONE THE MASTER HATES MOST.
RED SONJA.
THERE'S A BOUNTY ON HER HEAD THAT WILL KEEP OUR BELLIES FULL FOR A YEAR!
SHE CAN'T HOLD US ALL OFF FOR LONG! GET HER!
WE'LL HELP!
WE CAN SLOW THEM DOWN!
DAMMIT, MAN, GET OUT OF MY WAY! I CAN'T FIGHT IF I MUST CONCERN MYSELF WITH YOUR SAFETY!
CONCERN? HAH. MAYBE THIS ISN'T THE SHE-DEVIL AFTER ALL. EITHER WAY, WE EAT TONIGHT.
KEEEEEYIYIYIYIYIYI

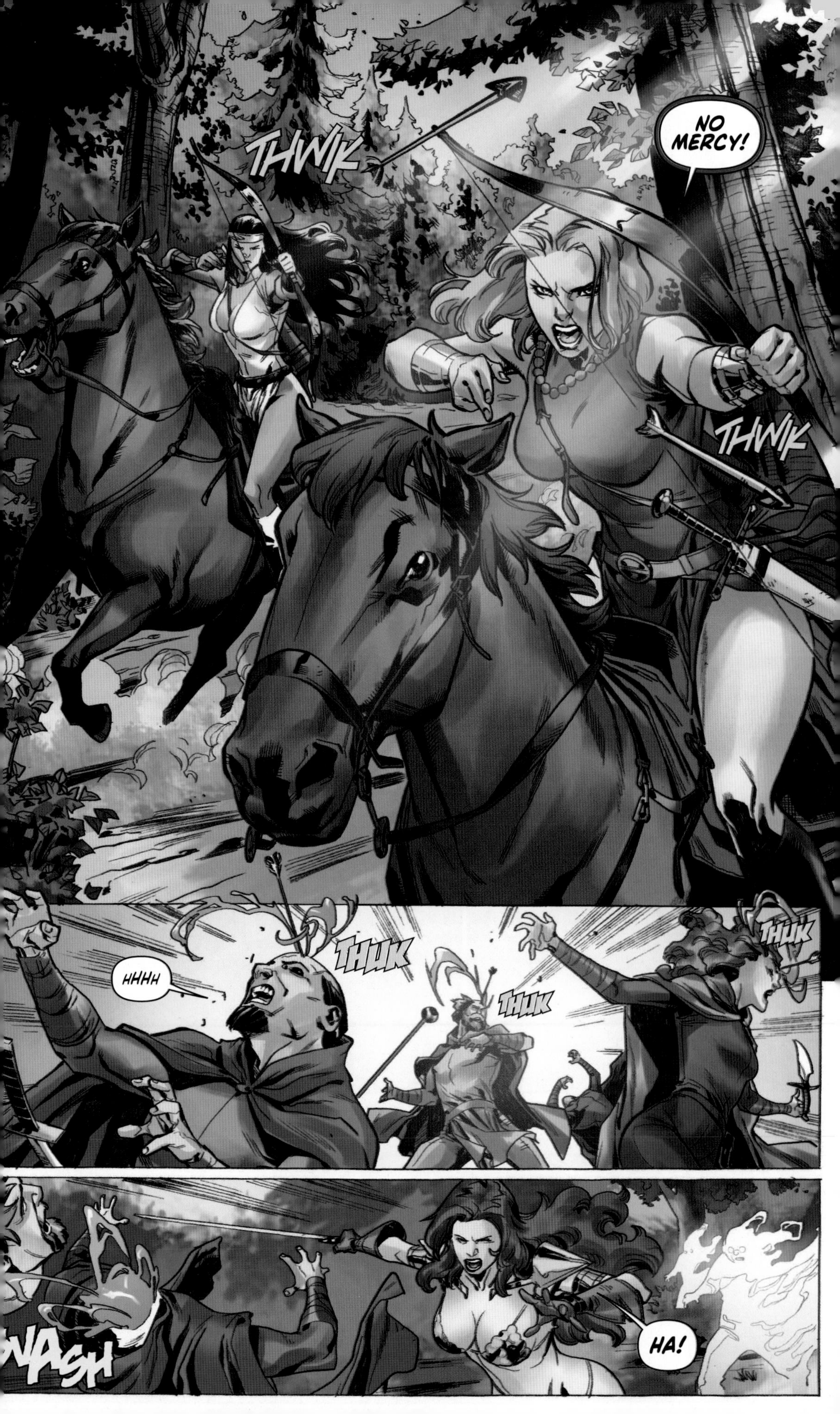
THWIK
NO MERCY!
THWIK
HHHH
THUK
THUK
THUK
HA!

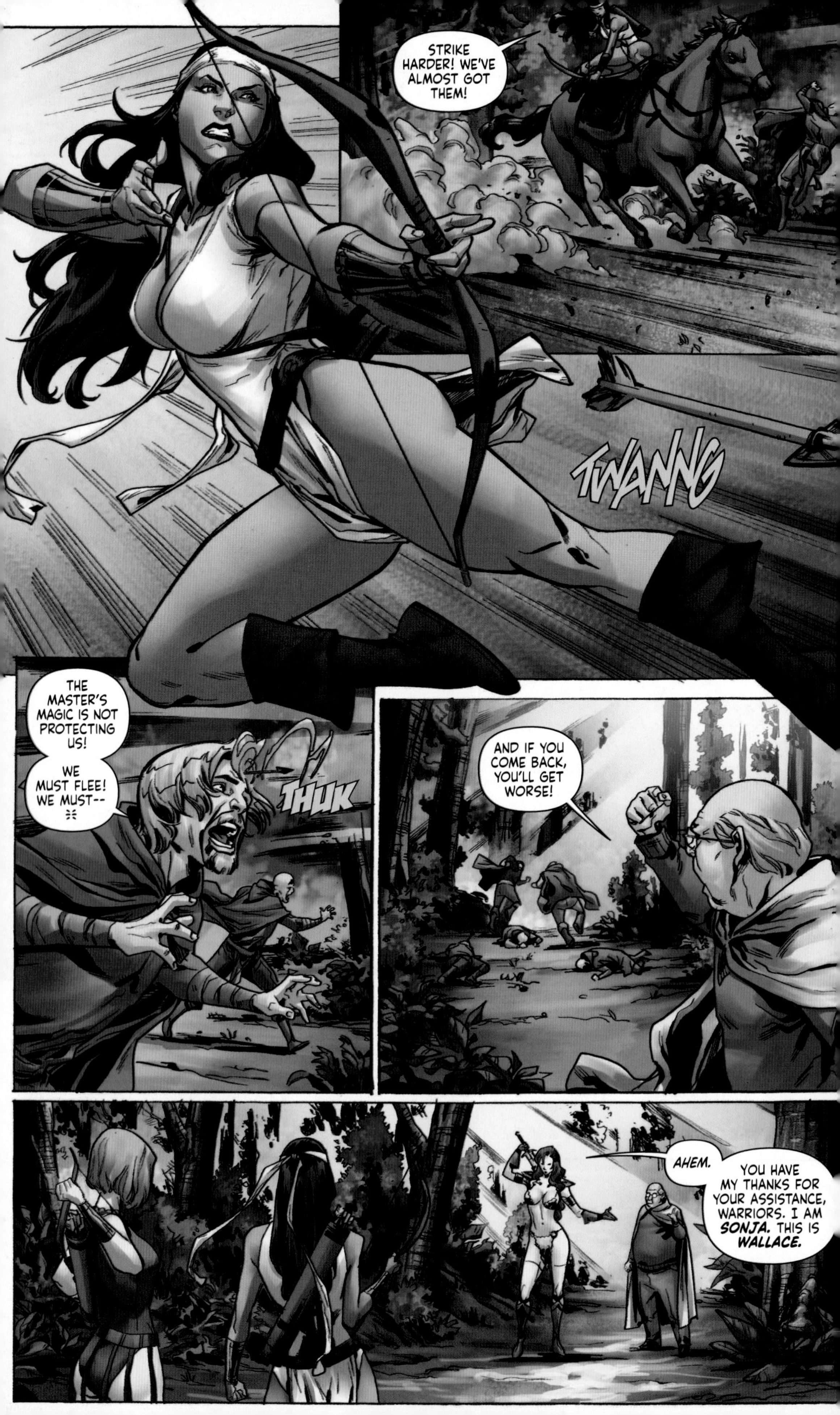
STRIKE HARDER! WE'VE ALMOST GOT THEM!
TWANNG
THE MASTER'S MAGIC IS NOT PROTECTING US!
WE MUST FLEE! WE MUST--
THUK
AND IF YOU COME BACK, YOU'LL GET WORSE!
AHEM.
YOU HAVE MY THANKS FOR YOUR ASSISTANCE, WARRIORS. I AM SONJA. THIS IS WALLACE.

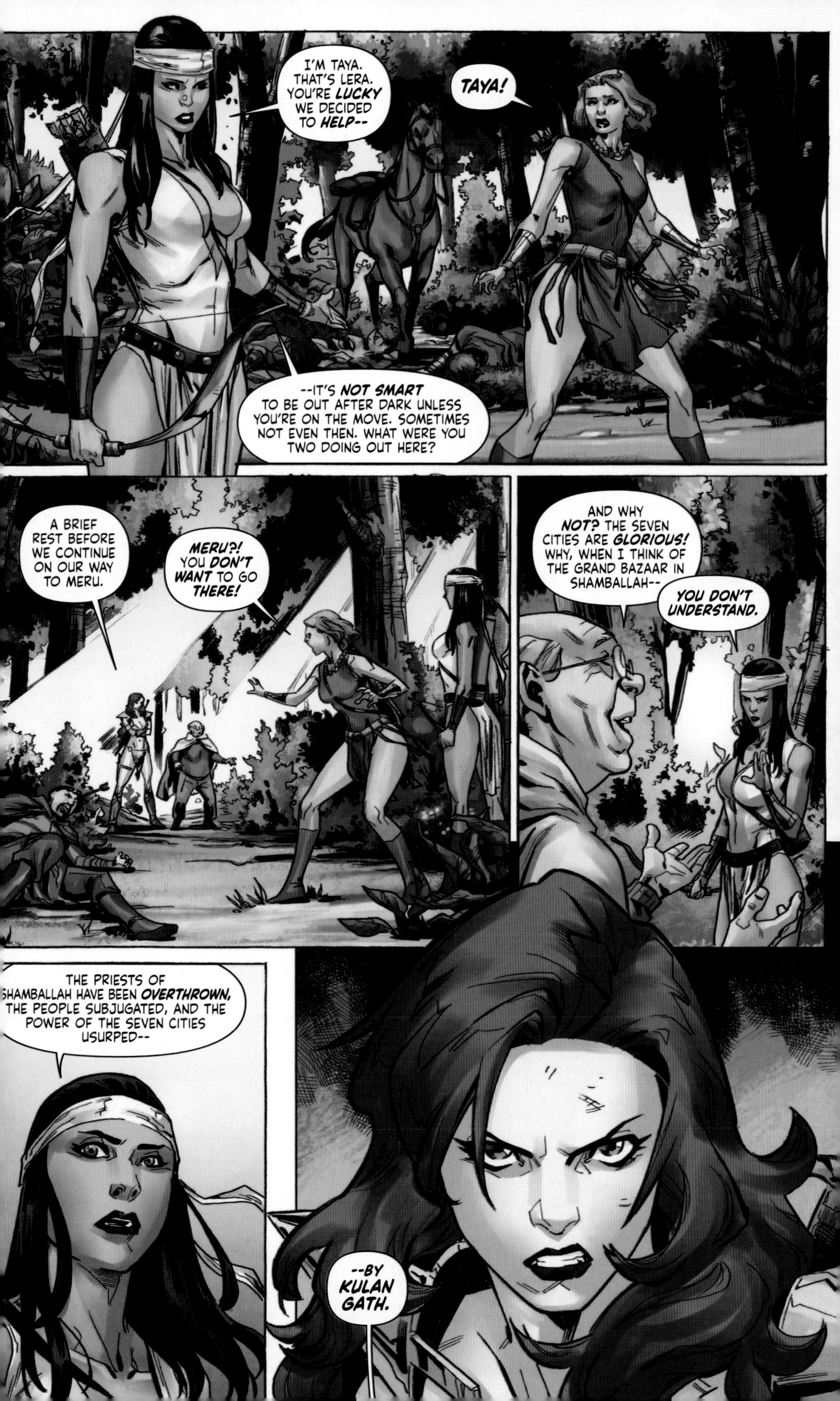
I'M TAYA. THAT'S LERA. YOU'RE LUCKY WE DECIDED TO HELP--
TAYA!
--IT'S NOT SMART TO BE OUT AFTER DARK UNLESS YOU'RE ON THE MOVE. SOMETIMES NOT EVEN THEN. WHAT WERE YOU TWO DOING OUT HERE?
A BRIEF REST BEFORE WE CONTINUE ON OUR WAY TO MERU.
MERU?! YOU DON'T WANT TO GO THERE!
AND WHY NOT? THE SEVEN CITIES ARE GLORIOUS! WHY, WHEN I THINK OF THE GRAND BAZAAR IN SHAMBALLAH--
YOU DON'T UNDERSTAND.
THE PRIESTS OF SHAMBALLAH HAVE BEEN OVERTHROWN, THE PEOPLE SUBJUGATED, AND THE POWER OF THE SEVEN CITIES USURPED--
--BY KULAN GATH.

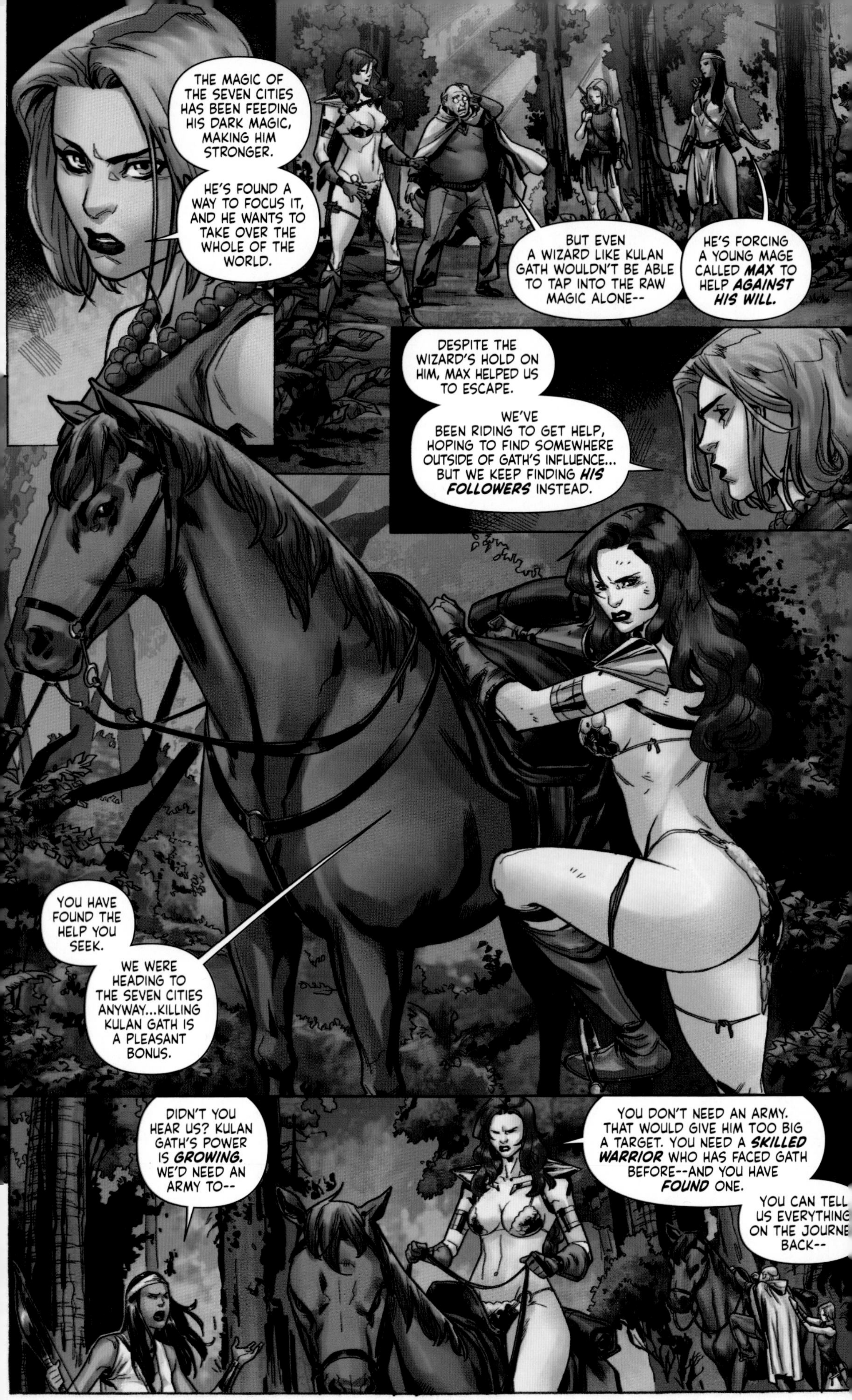

THE MAGIC OF THE SEVEN CITIES HAS BEEN FEEDING HIS DARK MAGIC, MAKING HIM STRONGER.
HE'S FOUND A WAY TO FOCUS IT, AND HE WANTS TO TAKE OVER THE WHOLE OF THE WORLD.
BUT EVEN A WIZARD LIKE KULAN GATH WOULDN'T BE ABLE TO TAP INTO THE RAW MAGIC ALONE--
HE'S FORCING A YOUNG MAGE CALLED **MAX** TO HELP **AGAINST HIS WILL.**
DESPITE THE WIZARD'S HOLD ON HIM, MAX HELPED US TO ESCAPE.
WE'VE BEEN RIDING TO GET HELP, HOPING TO FIND SOMEWHERE OUTSIDE OF GATH'S INFLUENCE... BUT WE KEEP FINDING **HIS FOLLOWERS** INSTEAD.
YOU HAVE FOUND THE HELP YOU SEEK.
WE WERE HEADING TO THE SEVEN CITIES ANYWAY...KILLING KULAN GATH IS A PLEASANT BONUS.
DIDN'T YOU HEAR US? KULAN GATH'S POWER IS **GROWING.** WE'D NEED AN ARMY TO--
YOU DON'T NEED AN ARMY. THAT WOULD GIVE HIM TOO BIG A TARGET. YOU NEED A **SKILLED WARRIOR** WHO HAS FACED GATH BEFORE--AND YOU HAVE **FOUND** ONE.
YOU CAN TELL US EVERYTHING ON THE JOURNE BACK--

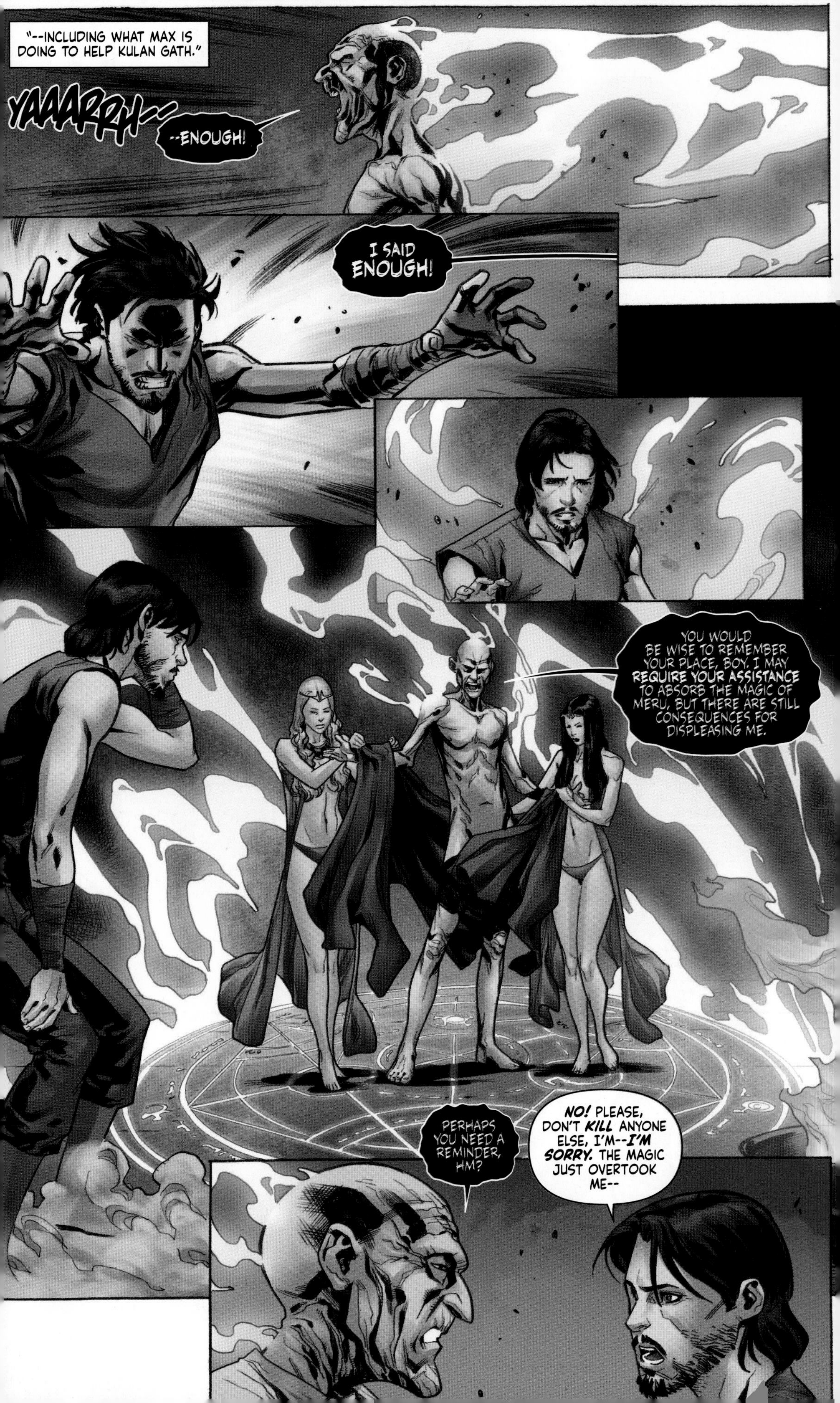
"--INCLUDING WHAT MAX IS DOING TO HELP KULAN GATH."
YAAARRH--
--ENOUGH!
I SAID ENOUGH!
YOU WOULD BE WISE TO REMEMBER YOUR PLACE, BOY. I MAY REQUIRE YOUR ASSISTANCE TO ABSORB THE MAGIC OF MERU, BUT THERE ARE STILL CONSEQUENCES FOR DISPLEASING ME.
PERHAPS YOU NEED A REMINDER, HM?
NO! PLEASE, DON'T KILL ANYONE ELSE, I'M--I'M SORRY. THE MAGIC JUST OVERTOOK ME--

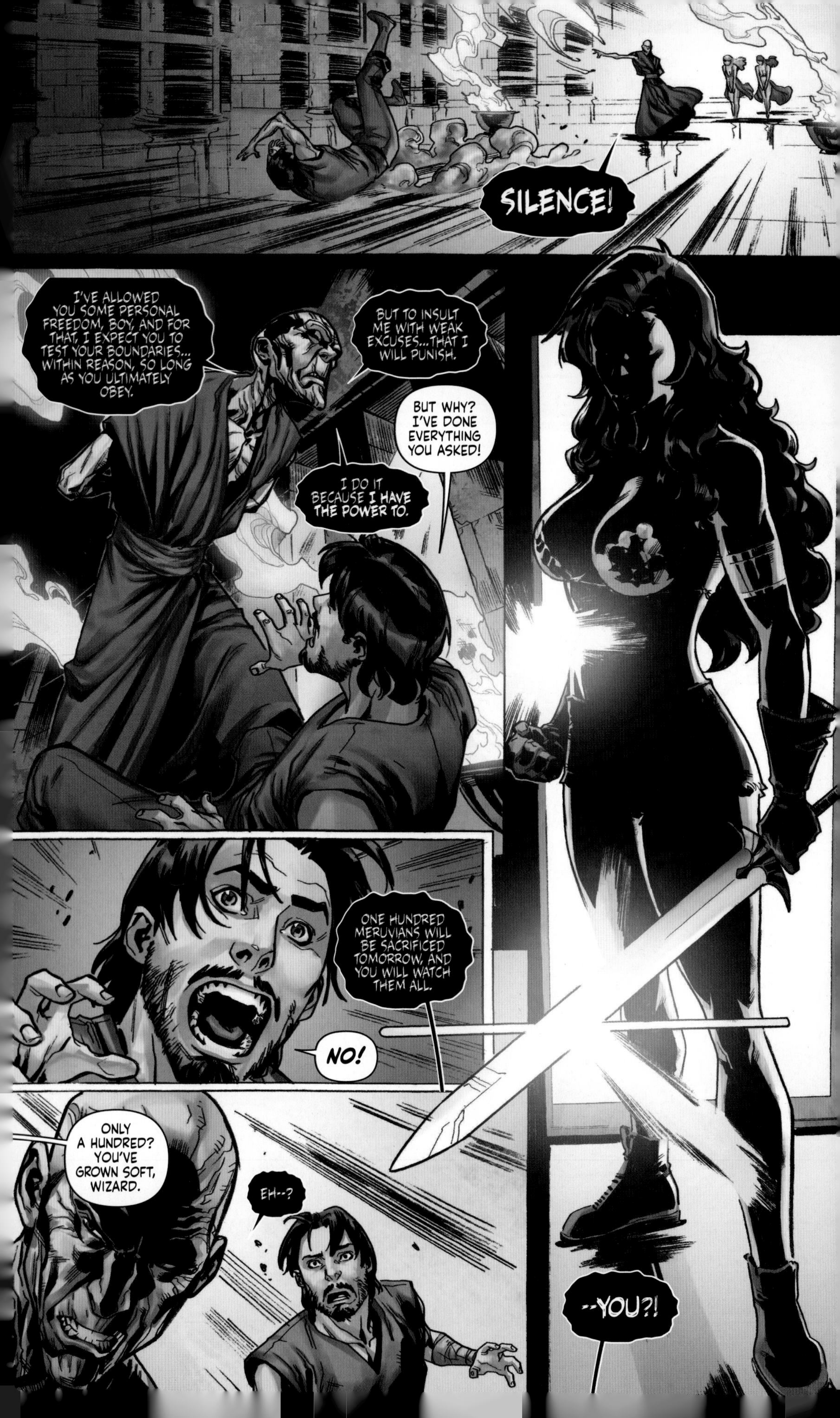
SILENCE!
I'VE ALLOWED YOU SOME PERSONAL FREEDOM, BOY, AND FOR THAT, I EXPECT YOU TO TEST YOUR BOUNDARIES... WITHIN REASON, SO LONG AS YOU ULTIMATELY OBEY.
BUT TO INSULT ME WITH WEAK EXCUSES...THAT I WILL PUNISH.
BUT WHY? I'VE DONE EVERYTHING YOU ASKED!
I DO IT BECAUSE I HAVE THE POWER TO.
ONE HUNDRED MERUVIANS WILL BE SACRIFICED TOMORROW, AND YOU WILL WATCH THEM ALL.
NO!
ONLY A HUNDRED? YOU'VE GROWN SOFT, WIZARD.
EH--?
--YOU?!

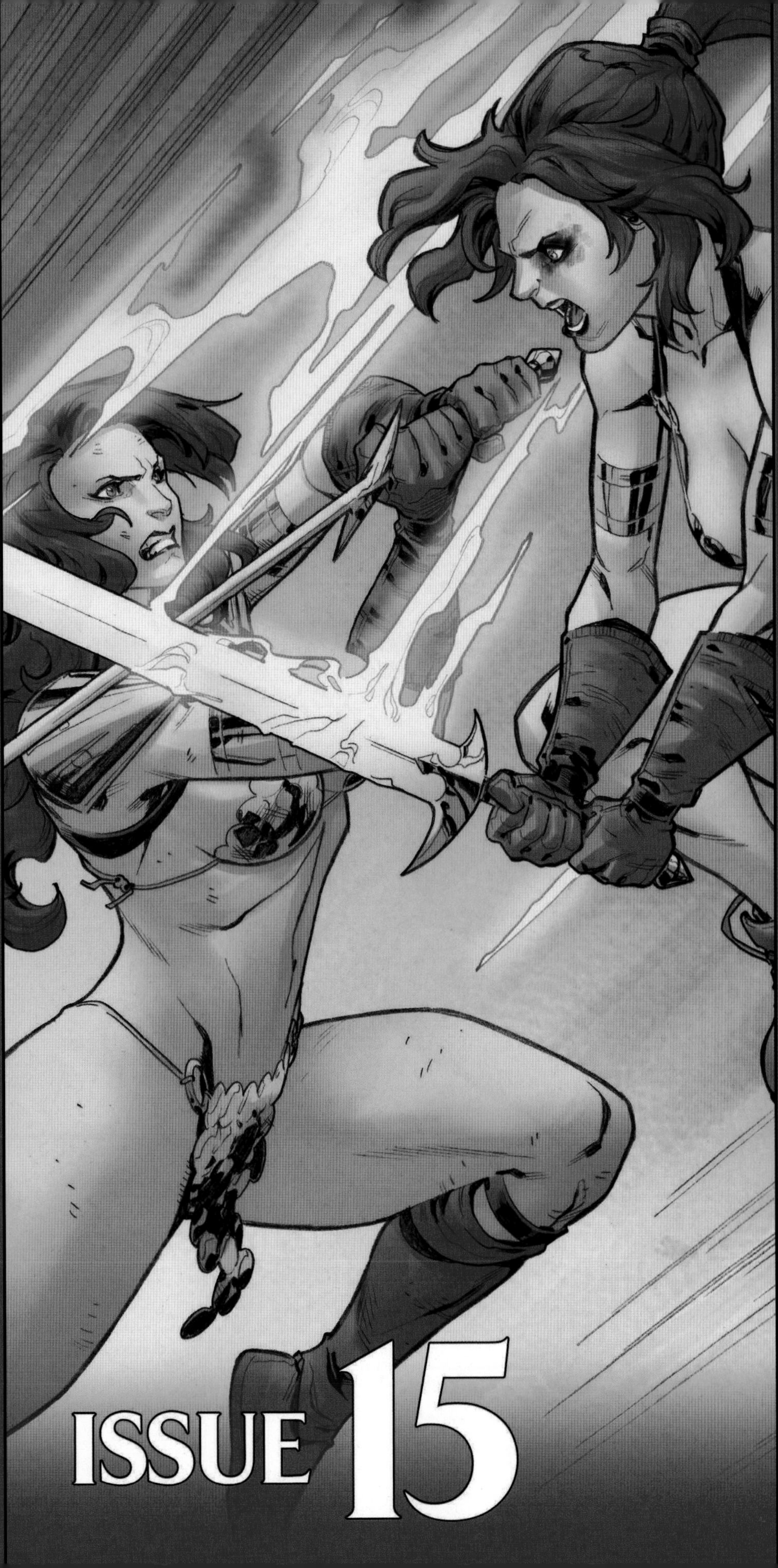
ISSUE 15

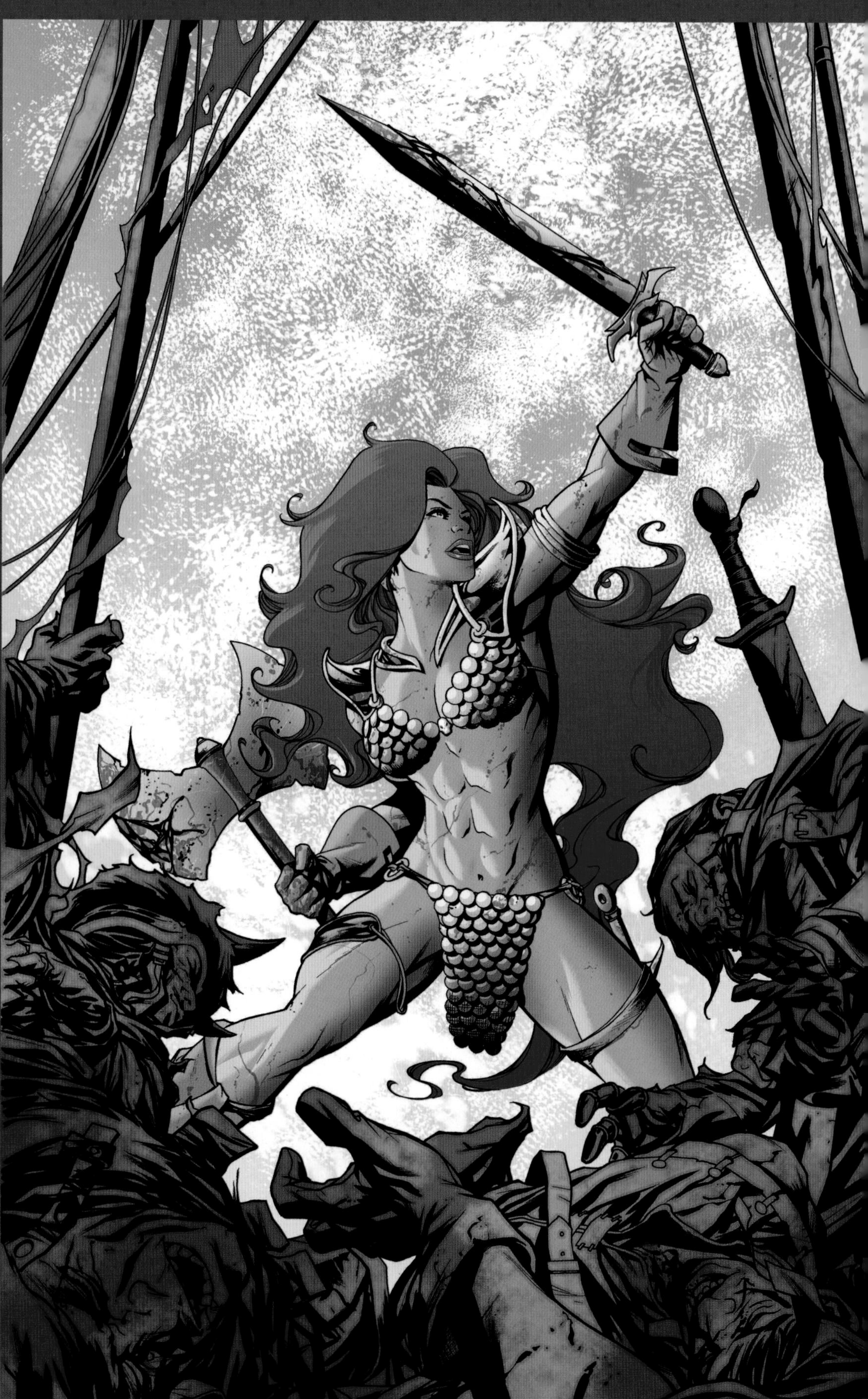

ISSUE #15: COVER ART BY **MIKE McKONE**

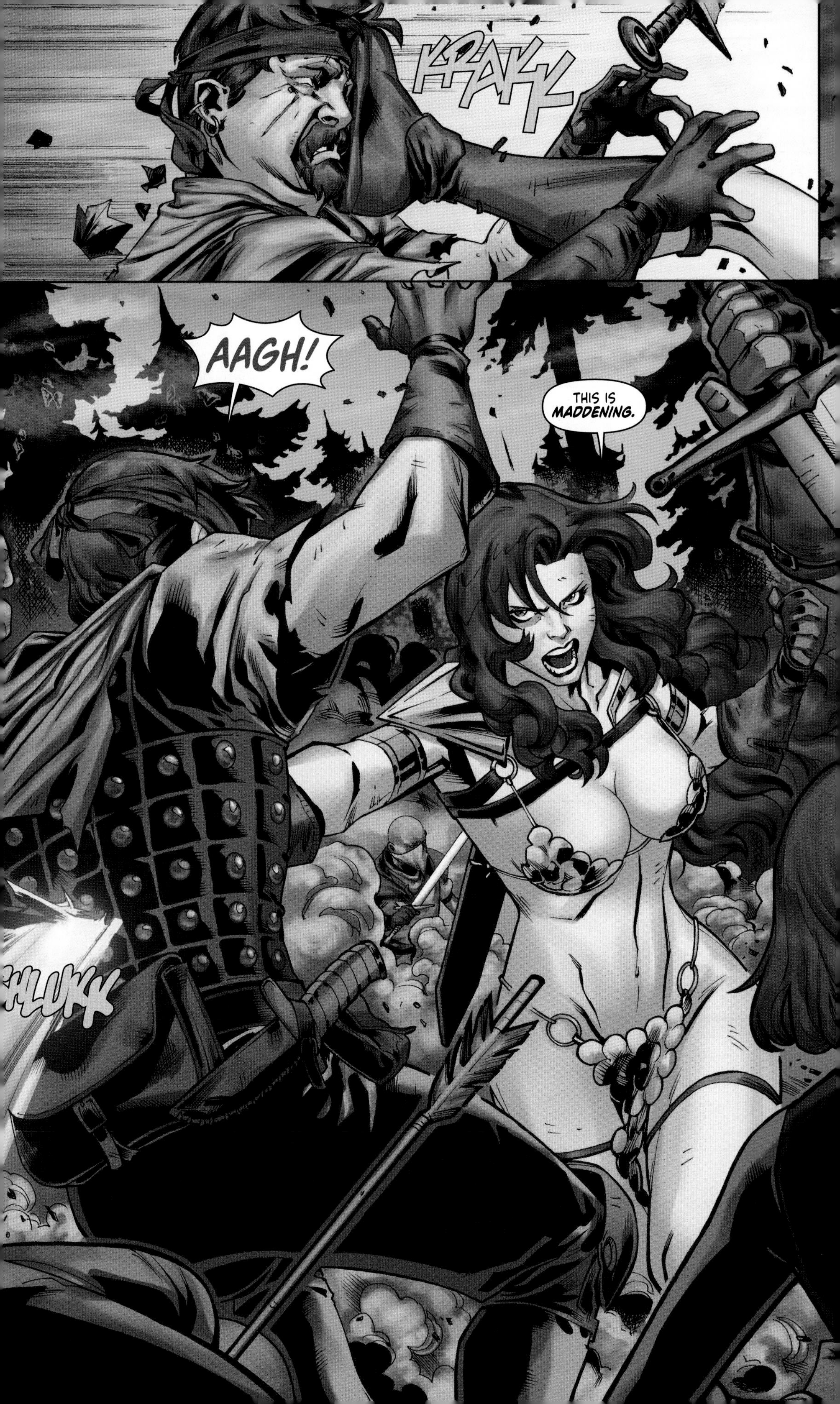

KRAKK
AAGH!
THIS IS MADDENING.
HLUKK

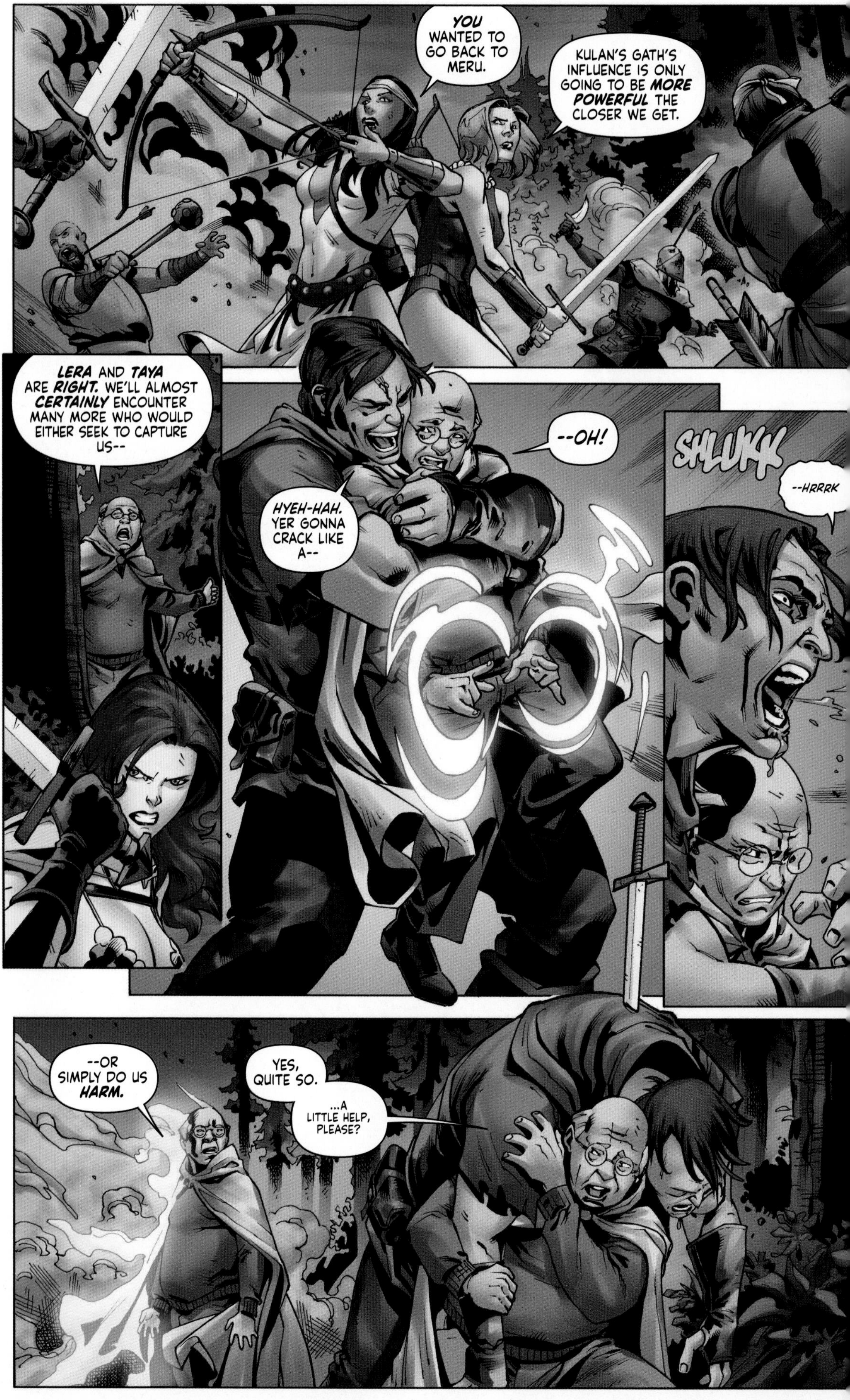

YOU WANTED TO GO BACK TO MERU.
KULAN'S GATH'S INFLUENCE IS ONLY GOING TO BE MORE POWERFUL THE CLOSER WE GET.
LERA AND TAYA ARE RIGHT. WE'LL ALMOST CERTAINLY ENCOUNTER MANY MORE WHO WOULD EITHER SEEK TO CAPTURE US--
HYEH-HAH. YER GONNA CRACK LIKE A--
--OH!
SHLUKK
--HRRRK
--OR SIMPLY DO US HARM.
YES, QUITE SO.
...A LITTLE HELP, PLEASE?

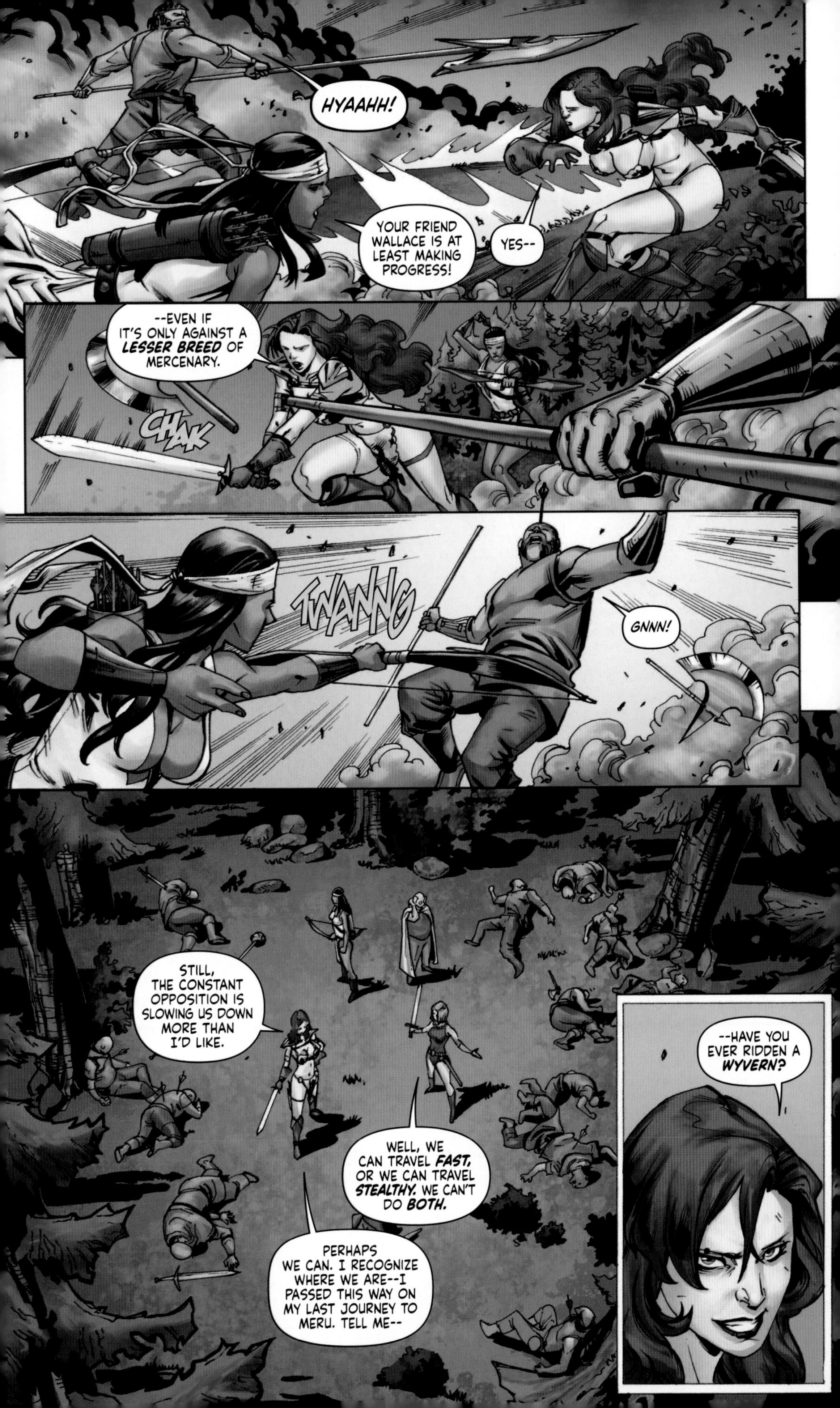

HYAAHH!
YOUR FRIEND WALLACE IS AT LEAST MAKING PROGRESS!
YES--
--EVEN IF IT'S ONLY AGAINST A ***LESSER BREED*** OF MERCENARY.
CHAK
TWANNG
GNNN!
STILL, THE CONSTANT OPPOSITION IS SLOWING US DOWN MORE THAN I'D LIKE.
WELL, WE CAN TRAVEL ***FAST,*** OR WE CAN TRAVEL ***STEALTHY.*** WE CAN'T DO ***BOTH.***
PERHAPS WE CAN. I RECOGNIZE WHERE WE ARE--I PASSED THIS WAY ON MY LAST JOURNEY TO MERU. TELL ME--
--HAVE YOU EVER RIDDEN A ***WYVERN?***

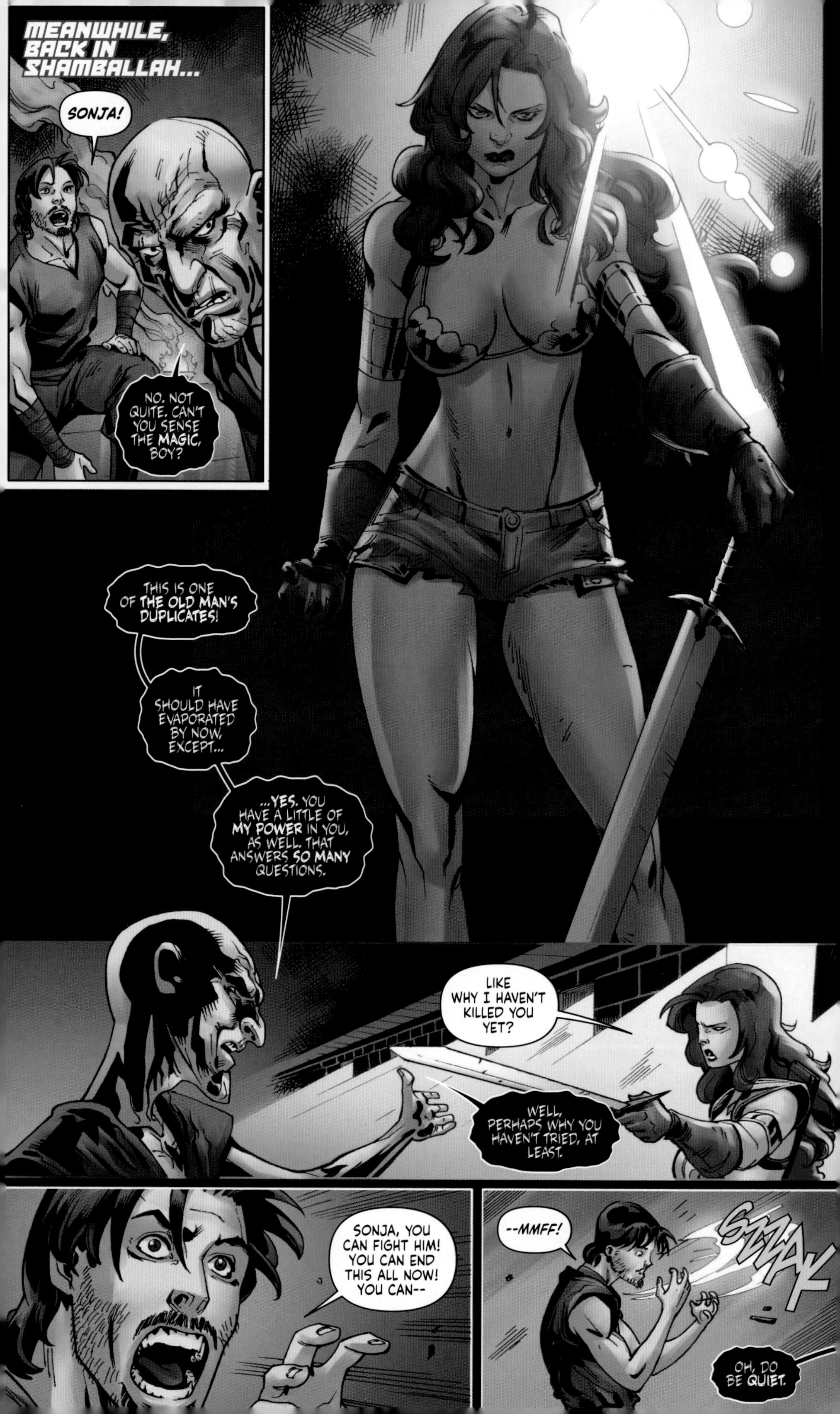
MEANWHILE, BACK IN SHAMBALLAH...
SONJA!
NO. NOT QUITE. CAN'T YOU SENSE THE MAGIC, BOY?
THIS IS ONE OF THE OLD MAN'S DUPLICATES!
IT SHOULD HAVE EVAPORATED BY NOW, EXCEPT...
...YES. YOU HAVE A LITTLE OF MY POWER IN YOU, AS WELL. THAT ANSWERS SO MANY QUESTIONS.
LIKE WHY I HAVEN'T KILLED YOU YET?
WELL, PERHAPS WHY YOU HAVEN'T TRIED, AT LEAST.
SONJA, YOU CAN FIGHT HIM! YOU CAN END THIS ALL NOW! YOU CAN--
--MMFF!
SMAK
OH, DO BE QUIET.

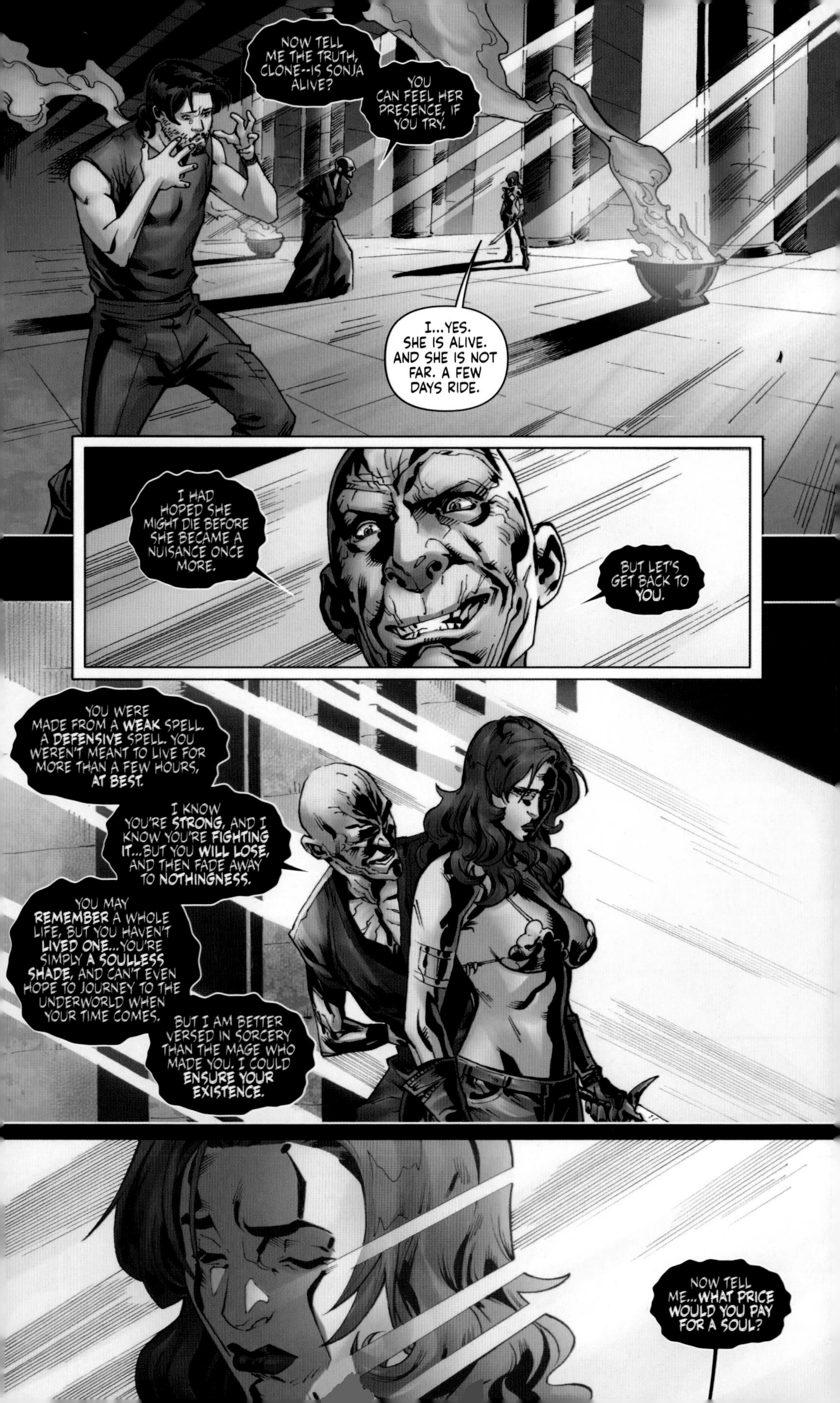
NOW TELL ME THE TRUTH, CLONE--IS SONJA ALIVE?
YOU CAN FEEL HER PRESENCE, IF YOU TRY.
I...YES. SHE IS ALIVE. AND SHE IS NOT FAR. A FEW DAYS RIDE.
I HAD HOPED SHE MIGHT DIE BEFORE SHE BECAME A NUISANCE ONCE MORE.
BUT LET'S GET BACK TO YOU.
YOU WERE MADE FROM A WEAK SPELL. A DEFENSIVE SPELL. YOU WEREN'T MEANT TO LIVE FOR MORE THAN A FEW HOURS, AT BEST.
I KNOW YOU'RE STRONG, AND I KNOW YOU'RE FIGHTING IT...BUT YOU WILL LOSE, AND THEN FADE AWAY TO NOTHINGNESS.
YOU MAY REMEMBER A WHOLE LIFE, BUT YOU HAVEN'T LIVED ONE...YOU'RE SIMPLY A SOULLESS SHADE, AND CAN'T EVEN HOPE TO JOURNEY TO THE UNDERWORLD WHEN YOUR TIME COMES.
BUT I AM BETTER VERSED IN SORCERY THAN THE MAGE WHO MADE YOU. I COULD ENSURE YOUR EXISTENCE.
NOW TELL ME...WHAT PRICE WOULD YOU PAY FOR A SOUL?

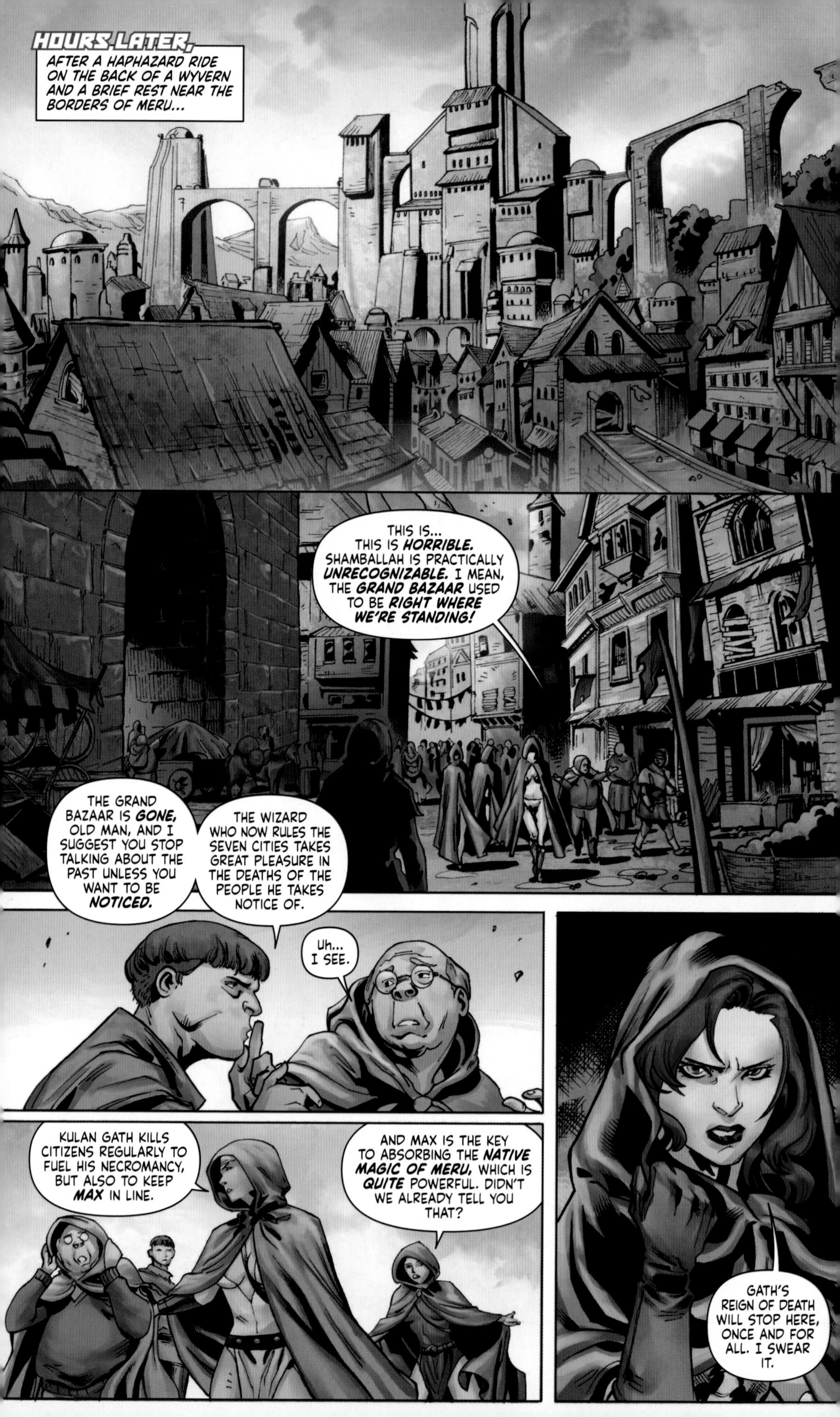
HOURS LATER,
AFTER A HAPHAZARD RIDE ON THE BACK OF A WYVERN AND A BRIEF REST NEAR THE BORDERS OF MERU...
THIS IS... THIS IS HORRIBLE. SHAMBALLAH IS PRACTICALLY UNRECOGNIZABLE. I MEAN, THE GRAND BAZAAR USED TO BE RIGHT WHERE WE'RE STANDING!
THE GRAND BAZAAR IS GONE, OLD MAN, AND I SUGGEST YOU STOP TALKING ABOUT THE PAST UNLESS YOU WANT TO BE NOTICED.
THE WIZARD WHO NOW RULES THE SEVEN CITIES TAKES GREAT PLEASURE IN THE DEATHS OF THE PEOPLE HE TAKES NOTICE OF.
Uh... I SEE.
KULAN GATH KILLS CITIZENS REGULARLY TO FUEL HIS NECROMANCY, BUT ALSO TO KEEP MAX IN LINE.
AND MAX IS THE KEY TO ABSORBING THE NATIVE MAGIC OF MERU, WHICH IS QUITE POWERFUL. DIDN'T WE ALREADY TELL YOU THAT?
GATH'S REIGN OF DEATH WILL STOP HERE, ONCE AND FOR ALL. I SWEAR IT.

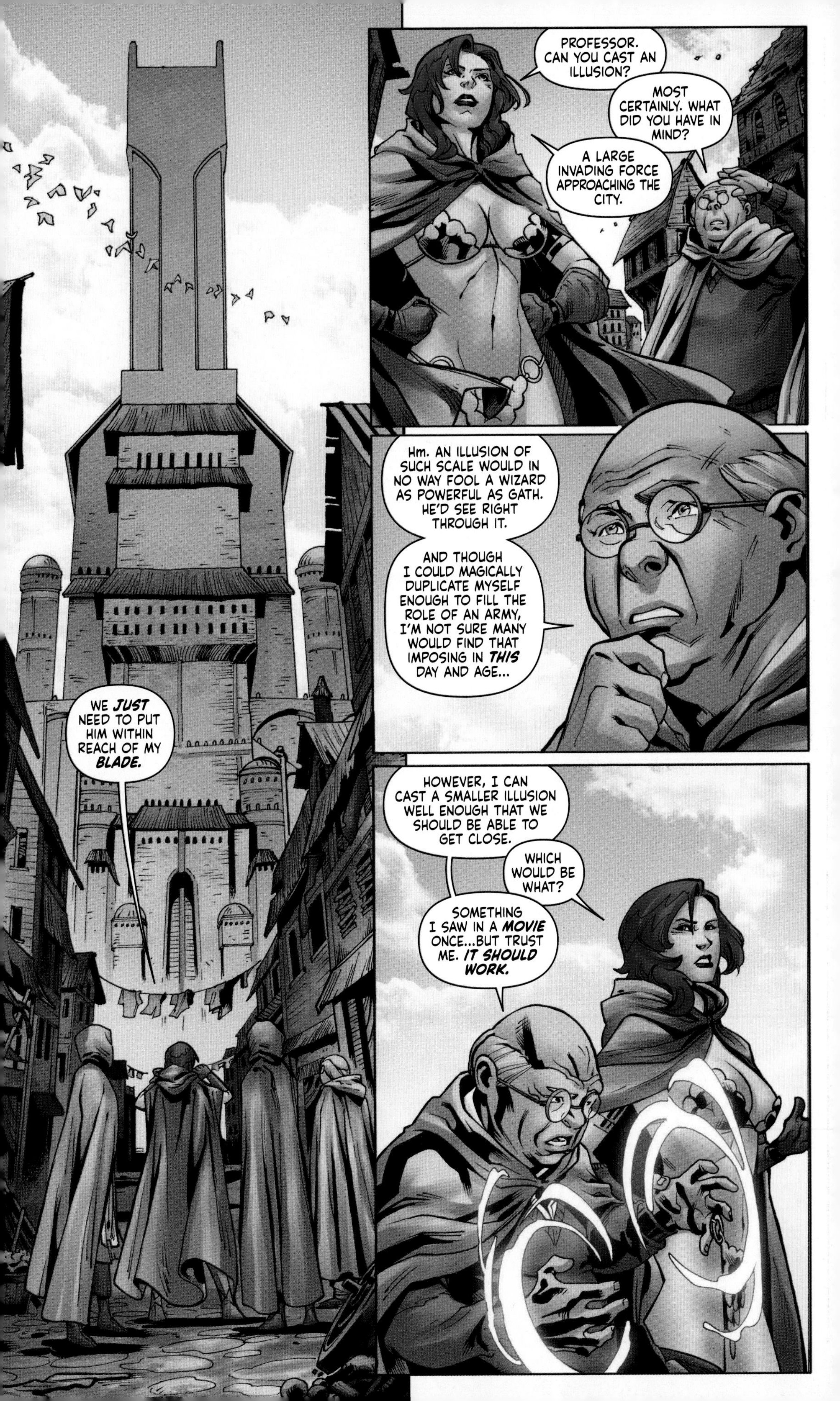

PROFESSOR. CAN YOU CAST AN ILLUSION?
MOST CERTAINLY. WHAT DID YOU HAVE IN MIND?
A LARGE INVADING FORCE APPROACHING THE CITY.
Hm. AN ILLUSION OF SUCH SCALE WOULD IN NO WAY FOOL A WIZARD AS POWERFUL AS GATH. HE'D SEE RIGHT THROUGH IT.
AND THOUGH I COULD MAGICALLY DUPLICATE MYSELF ENOUGH TO FILL THE ROLE OF AN ARMY, I'M NOT SURE MANY WOULD FIND THAT IMPOSING IN *THIS* DAY AND AGE...
WE *JUST* NEED TO PUT HIM WITHIN REACH OF MY *BLADE.*
HOWEVER, I CAN CAST A SMALLER ILLUSION WELL ENOUGH THAT WE SHOULD BE ABLE TO GET CLOSE.
WHICH WOULD BE WHAT?
SOMETHING I SAW IN A *MOVIE* ONCE...BUT TRUST ME. *IT SHOULD WORK.*

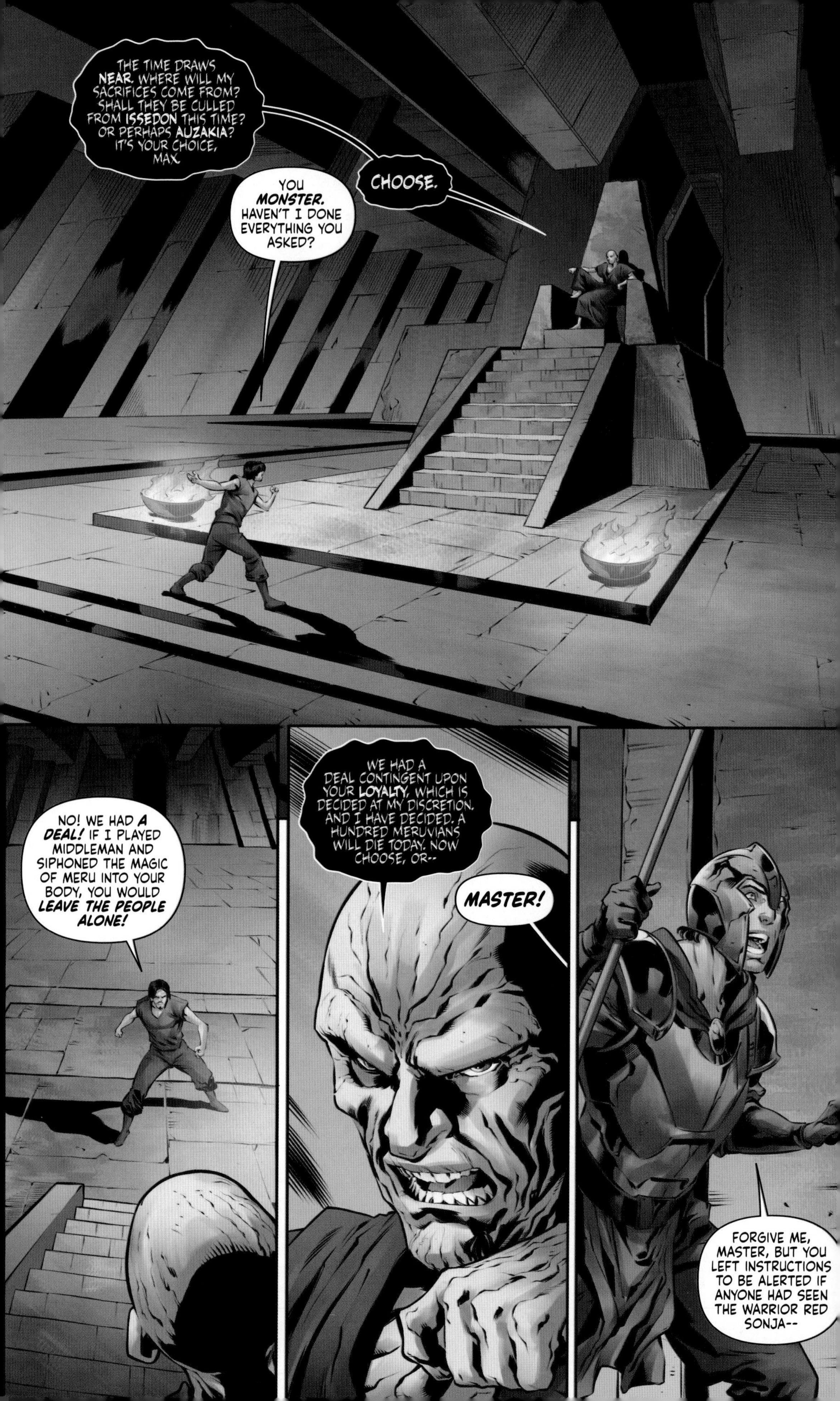
THE TIME DRAWS NEAR. WHERE WILL MY SACRIFICES COME FROM? SHALL THEY BE CULLED FROM ISSEDON THIS TIME? OR PERHAPS AUZAKIA? IT'S YOUR CHOICE, MAX.
CHOOSE.
YOU MONSTER. HAVEN'T I DONE EVERYTHING YOU ASKED?
NO! WE HAD A DEAL! IF I PLAYED MIDDLEMAN AND SIPHONED THE MAGIC OF MERU INTO YOUR BODY, YOU WOULD LEAVE THE PEOPLE ALONE!
WE HAD A DEAL CONTINGENT UPON YOUR LOYALTY, WHICH IS DECIDED AT MY DISCRETION. AND I HAVE DECIDED. A HUNDRED MERUVIANS WILL DIE TODAY. NOW CHOOSE, OR--
MASTER!
FORGIVE ME, MASTER, BUT YOU LEFT INSTRUCTIONS TO BE ALERTED IF ANYONE HAD SEEN THE WARRIOR RED SONJA--

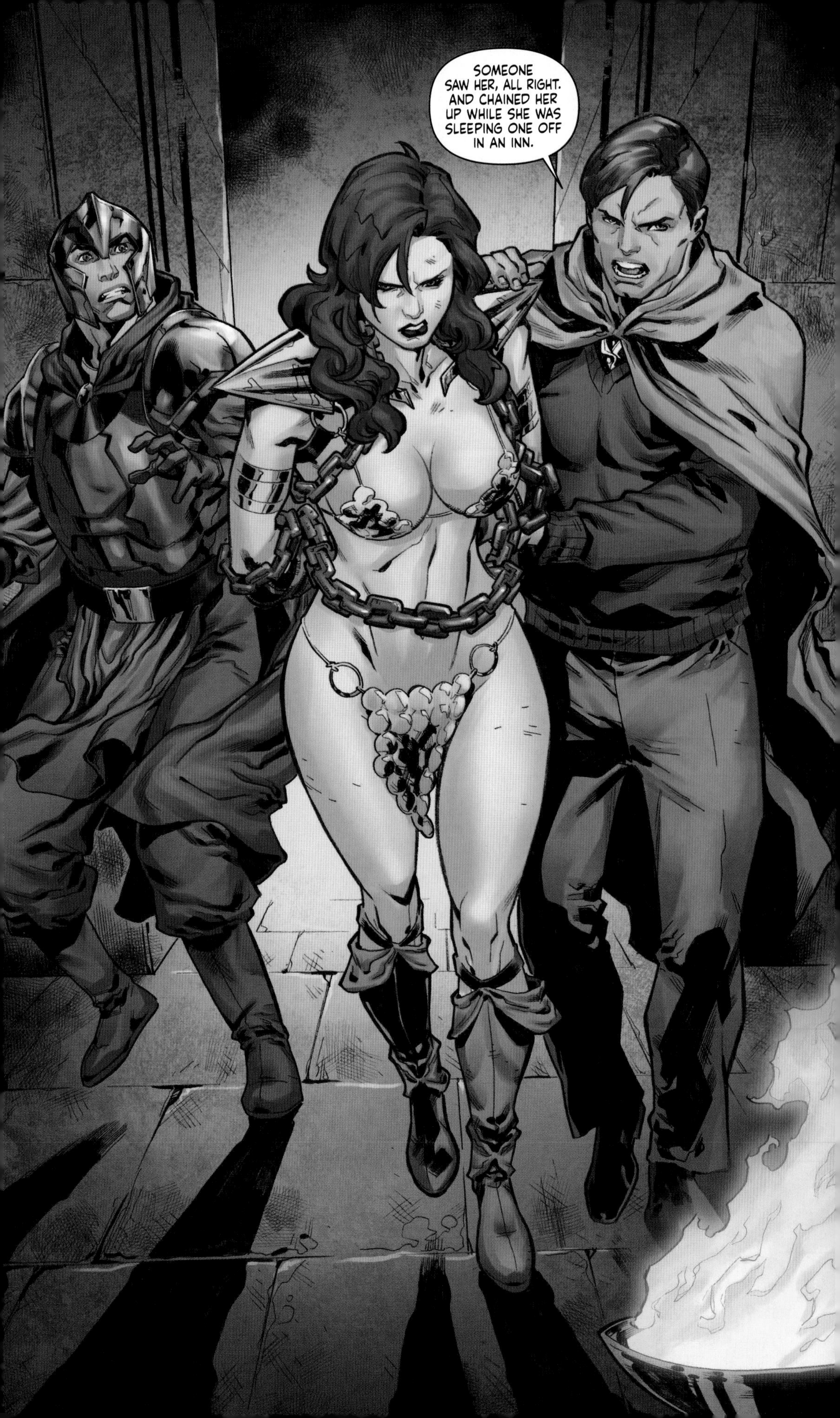
SOMEONE SAW HER, ALL RIGHT. AND CHAINED HER UP WHILE SHE WAS SLEEPING ONE OFF IN AN INN.

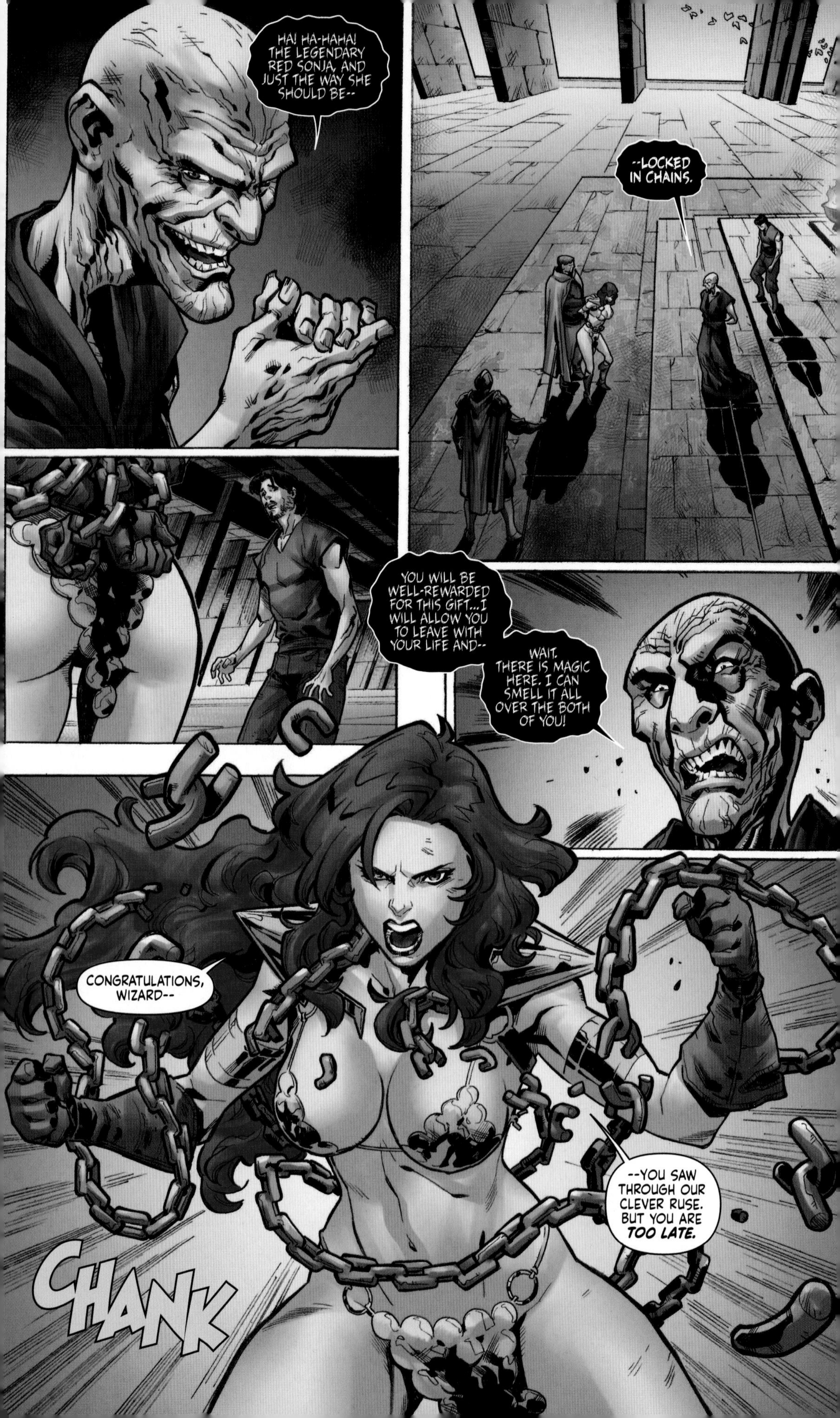
HA! HA-HAHA! THE LEGENDARY RED SONJA, AND JUST THE WAY SHE SHOULD BE--
--LOCKED IN CHAINS.
YOU WILL BE WELL-REWARDED FOR THIS GIFT...I WILL ALLOW YOU TO LEAVE WITH YOUR LIFE AND--
WAIT. THERE IS MAGIC HERE. I CAN SMELL IT ALL OVER THE BOTH OF YOU!
CONGRATULATIONS, WIZARD--
--YOU SAW THROUGH OUR CLEVER RUSE. BUT YOU ARE TOO LATE.
CHANK

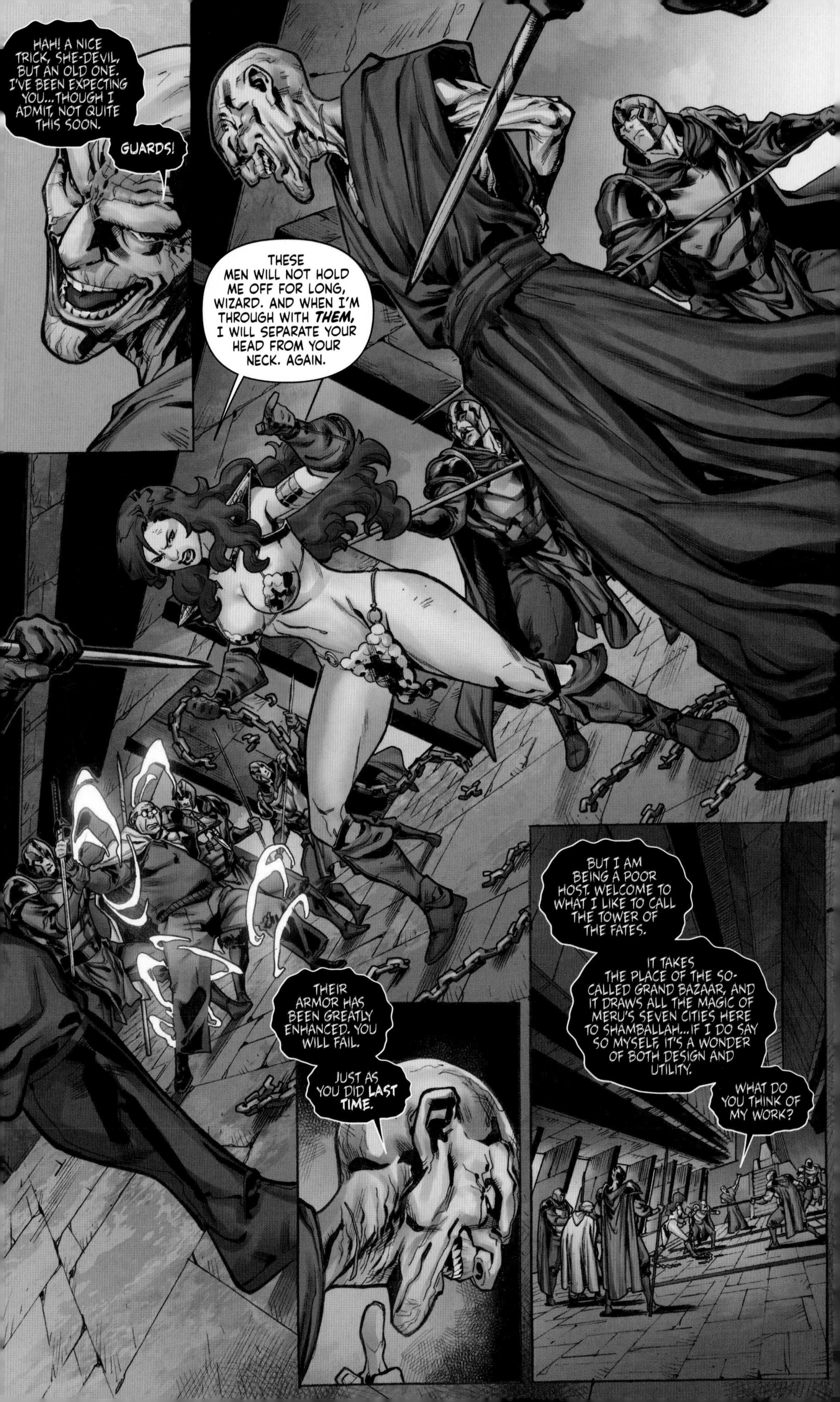
HAH! A NICE TRICK, SHE-DEVIL, BUT AN OLD ONE. I'VE BEEN EXPECTING YOU...THOUGH I ADMIT, NOT QUITE THIS SOON.
GUARDS!
THESE MEN WILL NOT HOLD ME OFF FOR LONG, WIZARD. AND WHEN I'M THROUGH WITH *THEM,* I WILL SEPARATE YOUR HEAD FROM YOUR NECK. AGAIN.
THEIR ARMOR HAS BEEN GREATLY ENHANCED. YOU WILL FAIL.
JUST AS YOU DID **LAST TIME.**
BUT I AM BEING A POOR HOST. WELCOME TO WHAT I LIKE TO CALL THE TOWER OF THE FATES.
IT TAKES THE PLACE OF THE SO-CALLED GRAND BAZAAR, AND IT DRAWS ALL THE MAGIC OF MERU'S SEVEN CITIES HERE TO SHAMBALLAH...IF I DO SAY SO MYSELF, IT'S A WONDER OF BOTH DESIGN AND UTILITY.
WHAT DO YOU THINK OF MY WORK?

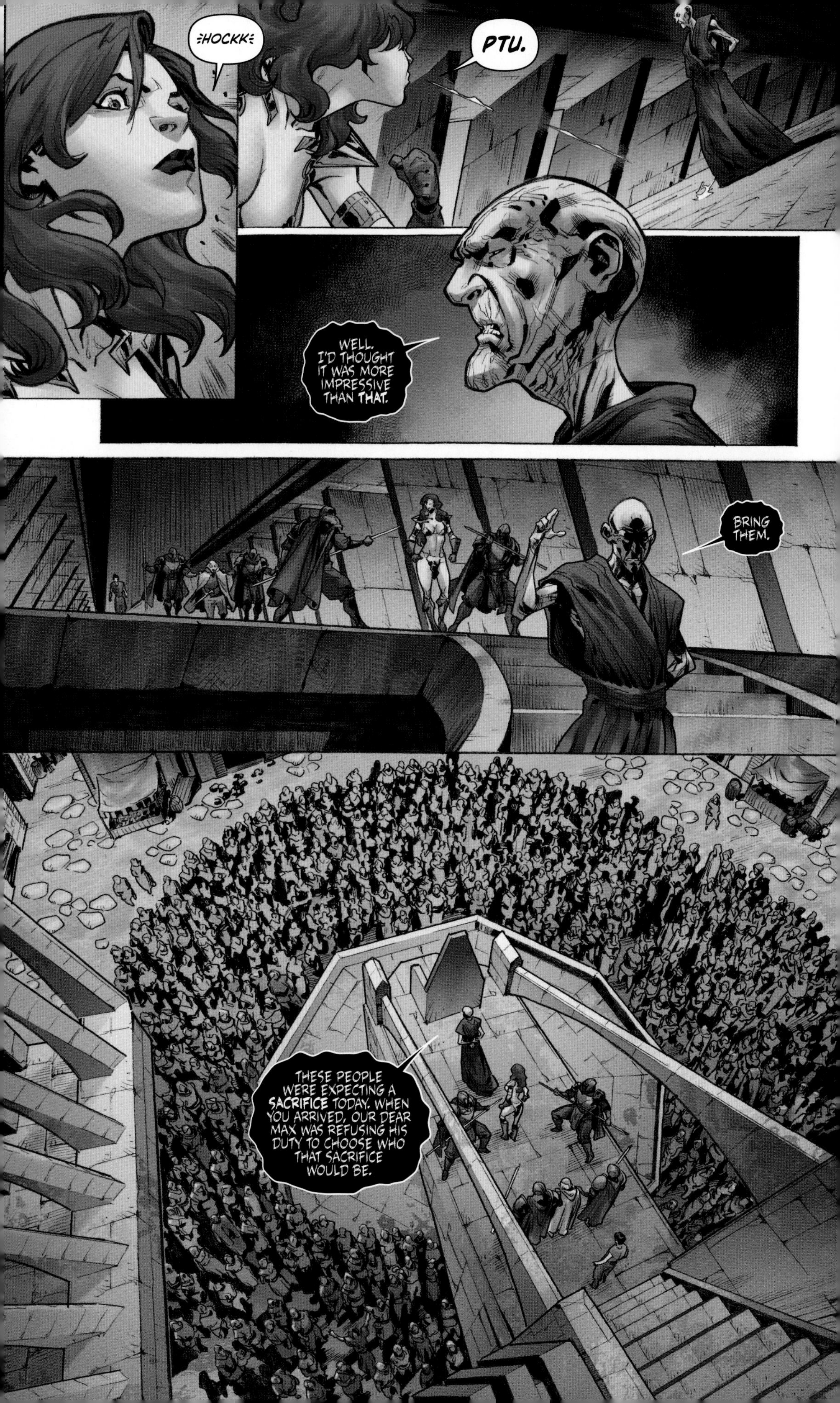
HOCKK
PTU.
WELL. I'D THOUGHT IT WAS MORE IMPRESSIVE THAN THAT.
BRING THEM.
THESE PEOPLE WERE EXPECTING A SACRIFICE TODAY. WHEN YOU ARRIVED, OUR DEAR MAX WAS REFUSING HIS DUTY TO CHOOSE WHO THAT SACRIFICE WOULD BE.

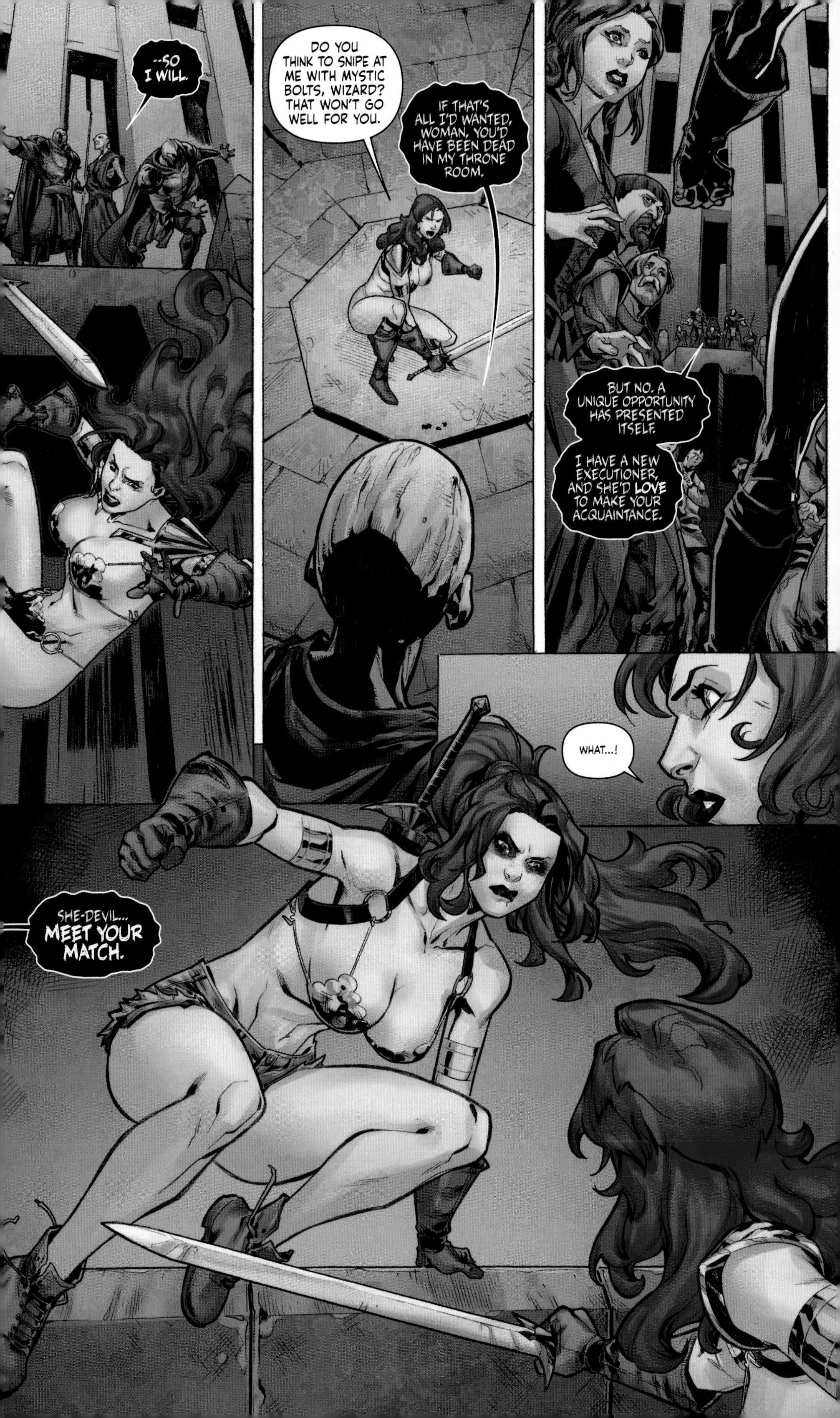
--SO I WILL.
DO YOU THINK TO SNIPE AT ME WITH MYSTIC BOLTS, WIZARD? THAT WON'T GO WELL FOR YOU.
IF THAT'S ALL I'D WANTED, WOMAN, YOU'D HAVE BEEN DEAD IN MY THRONE ROOM.
BUT NO. A UNIQUE OPPORTUNITY HAS PRESENTED ITSELF.
I HAVE A NEW EXECUTIONER, AND SHE'D **LOVE** TO MAKE YOUR ACQUAINTANCE.
WHAT...!
SHE-DEVIL... **MEET YOUR MATCH.**

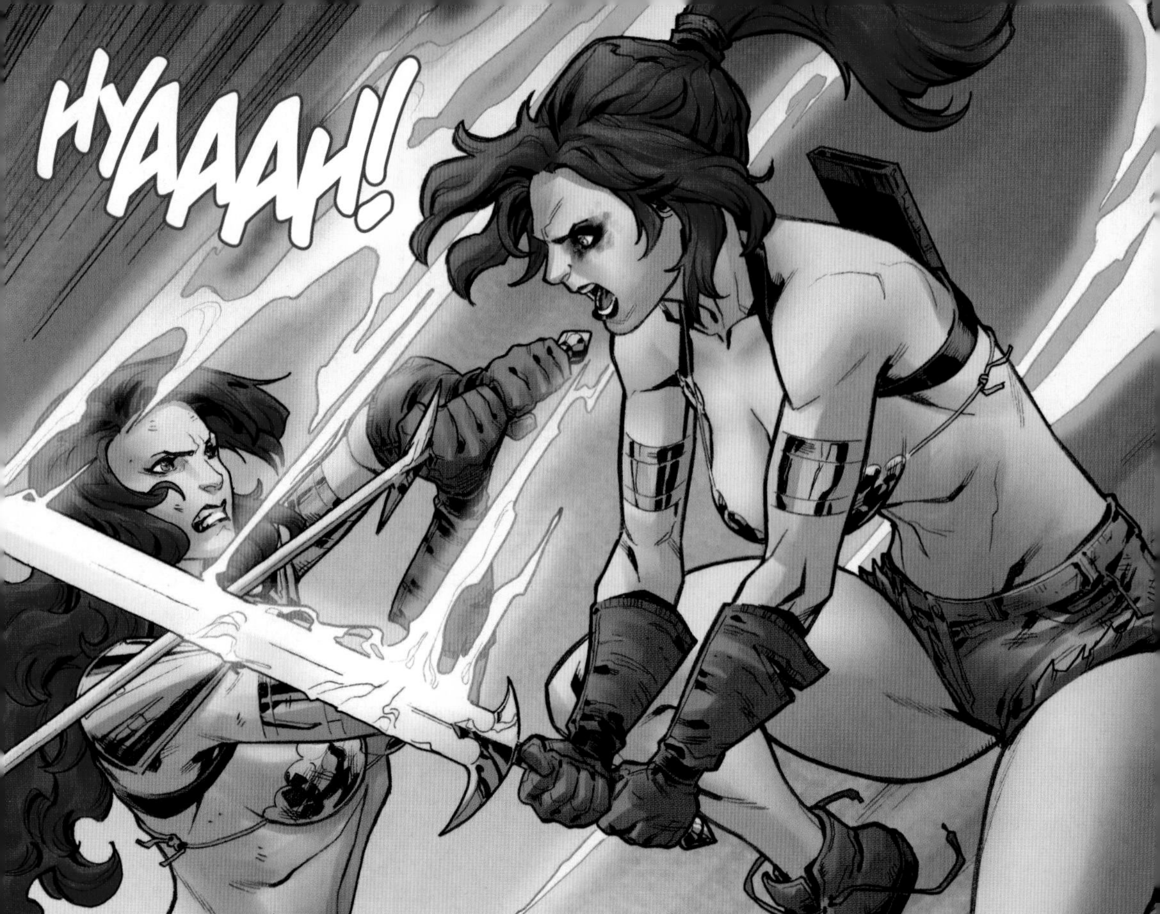
HYAAAH!!

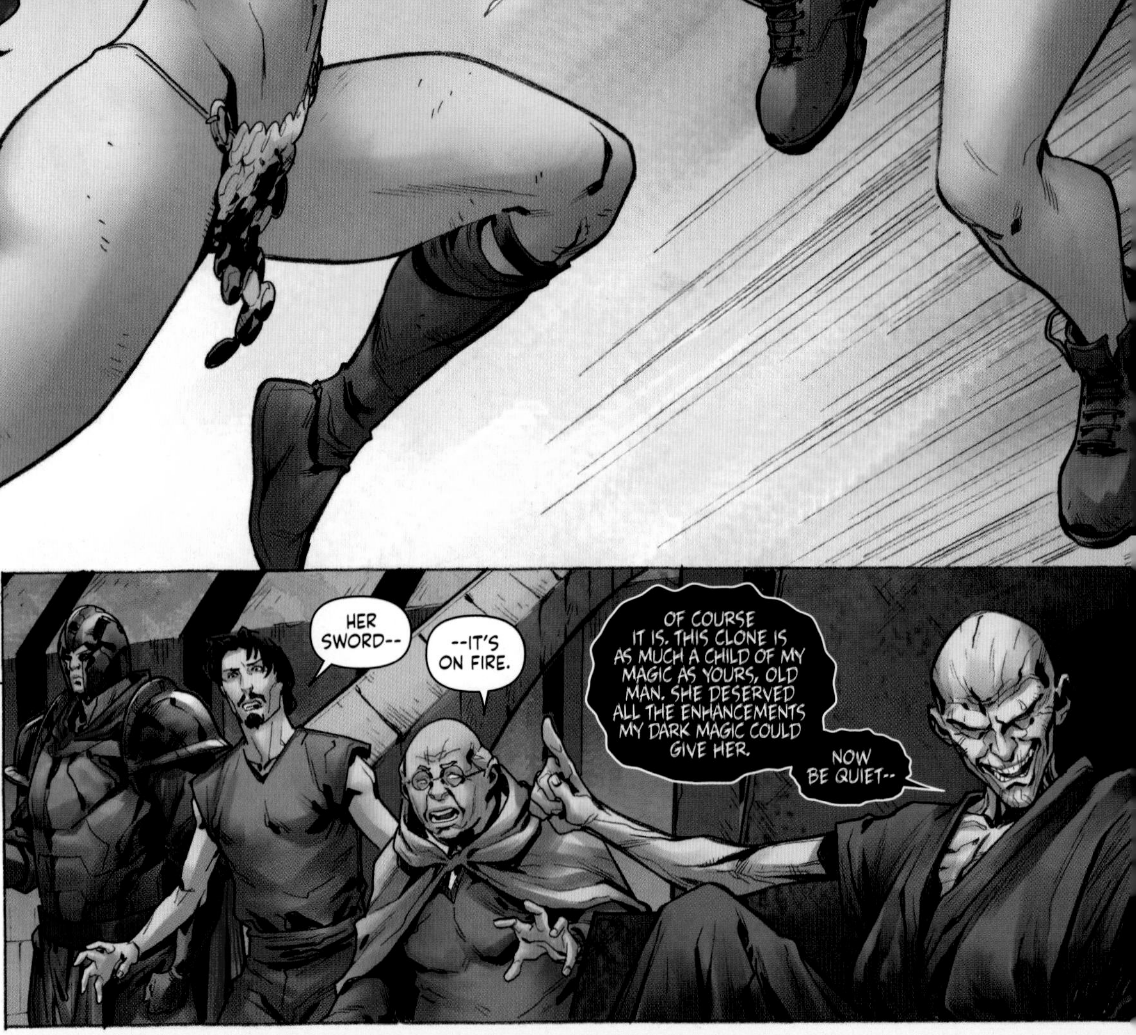
HER SWORD--
--IT'S ON FIRE.
OF COURSE IT IS. THIS CLONE IS AS MUCH A CHILD OF MY MAGIC AS YOURS, OLD MAN. SHE DESERVED ALL THE ENHANCEMENTS MY DARK MAGIC COULD GIVE HER.
NOW BE QUIET--

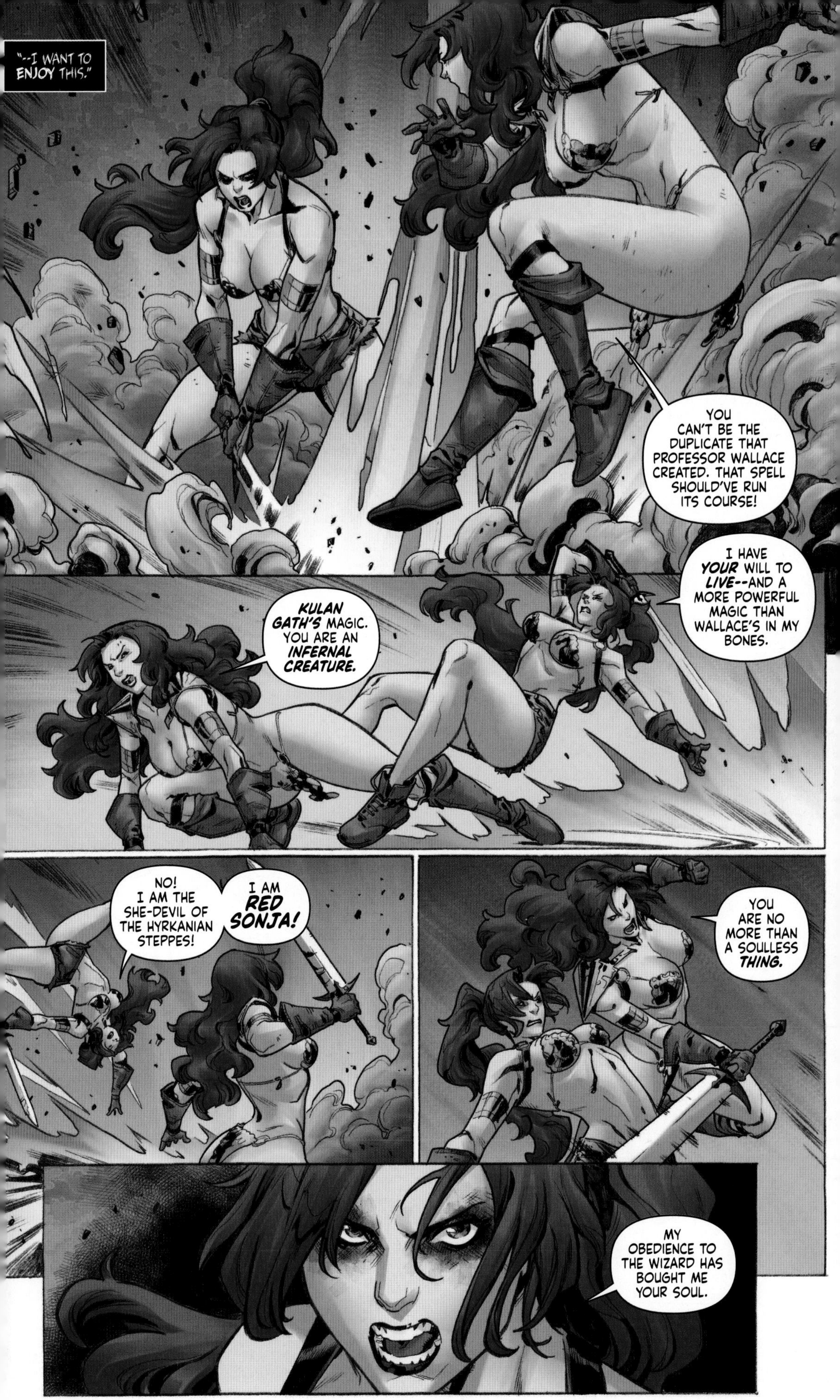
"--I WANT TO ENJOY THIS."
YOU CAN'T BE THE DUPLICATE THAT PROFESSOR WALLACE CREATED. THAT SPELL SHOULD'VE RUN ITS COURSE!
KULAN GATH'S MAGIC. YOU ARE AN INFERNAL CREATURE.
I HAVE YOUR WILL TO LIVE--AND A MORE POWERFUL MAGIC THAN WALLACE'S IN MY BONES.
NO! I AM THE SHE-DEVIL OF THE HYRKANIAN STEPPES!
I AM RED SONJA!
YOU ARE NO MORE THAN A SOULLESS THING.
MY OBEDIENCE TO THE WIZARD HAS BOUGHT ME YOUR SOUL.

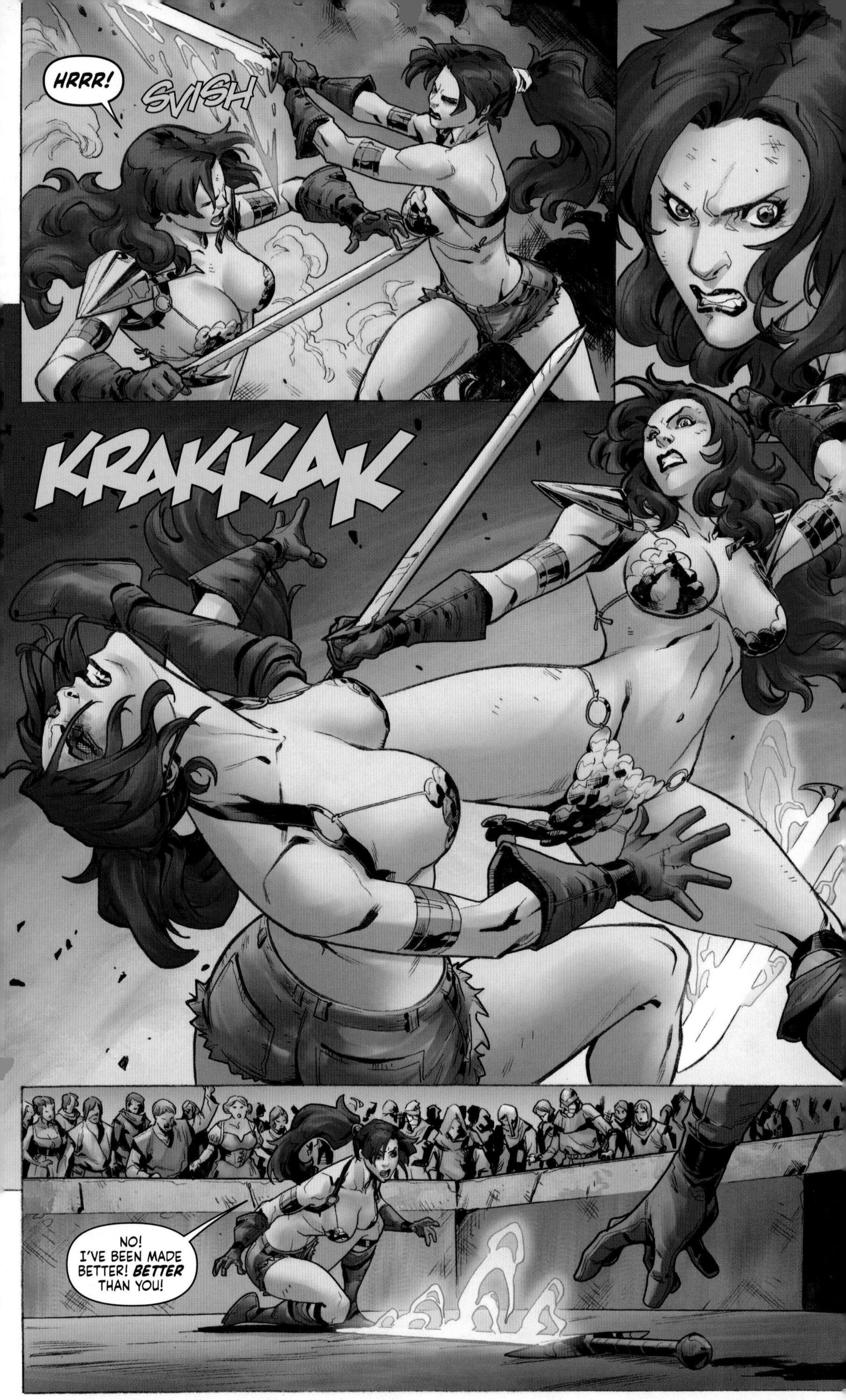
HRRR!
SVISH
KRAKKAK
NO! I'VE BEEN MADE BETTER! **BETTER** THAN YOU!

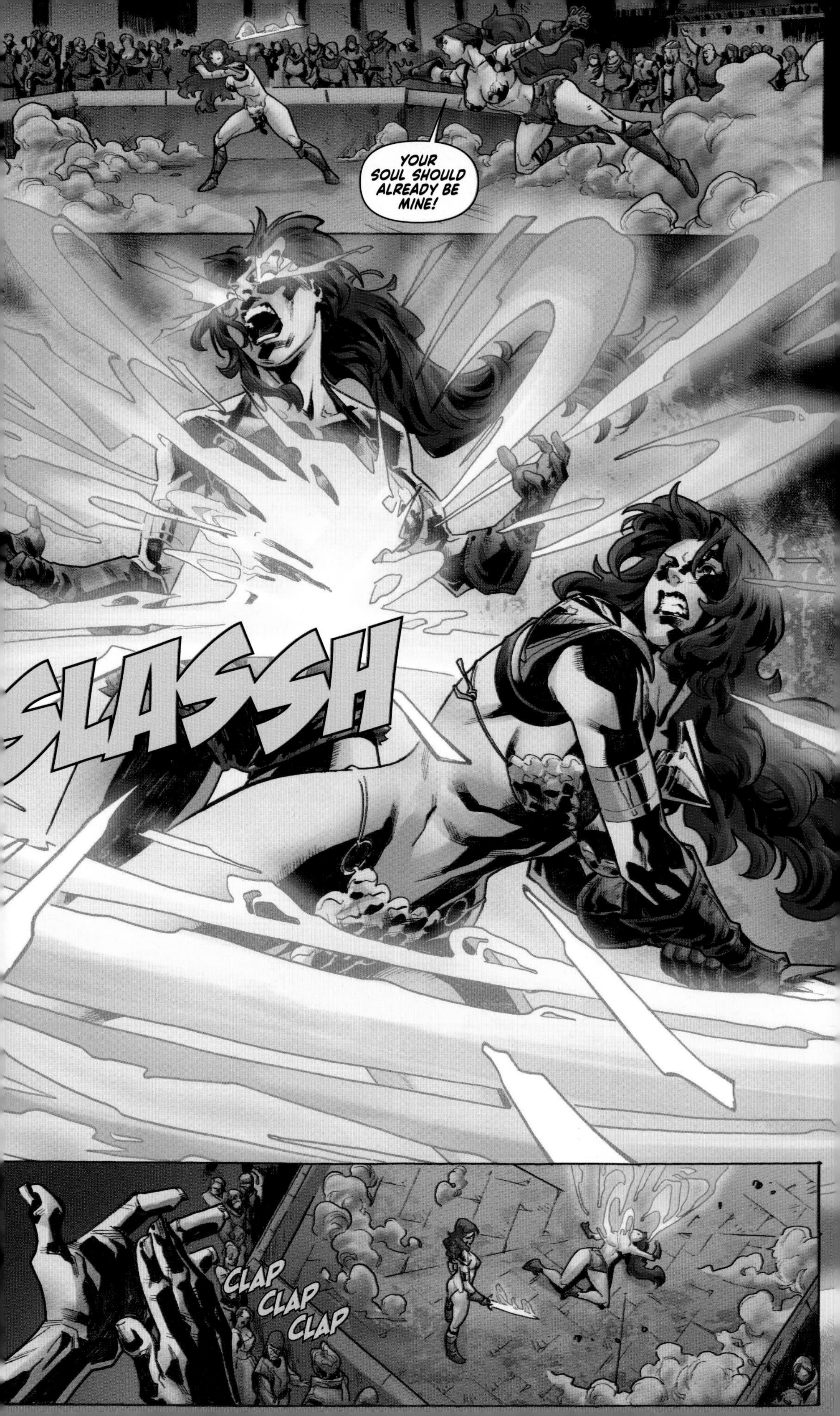
YOUR SOUL SHOULD ALREADY BE MINE!
SLASSH
CLAP
CLAP
CLAP

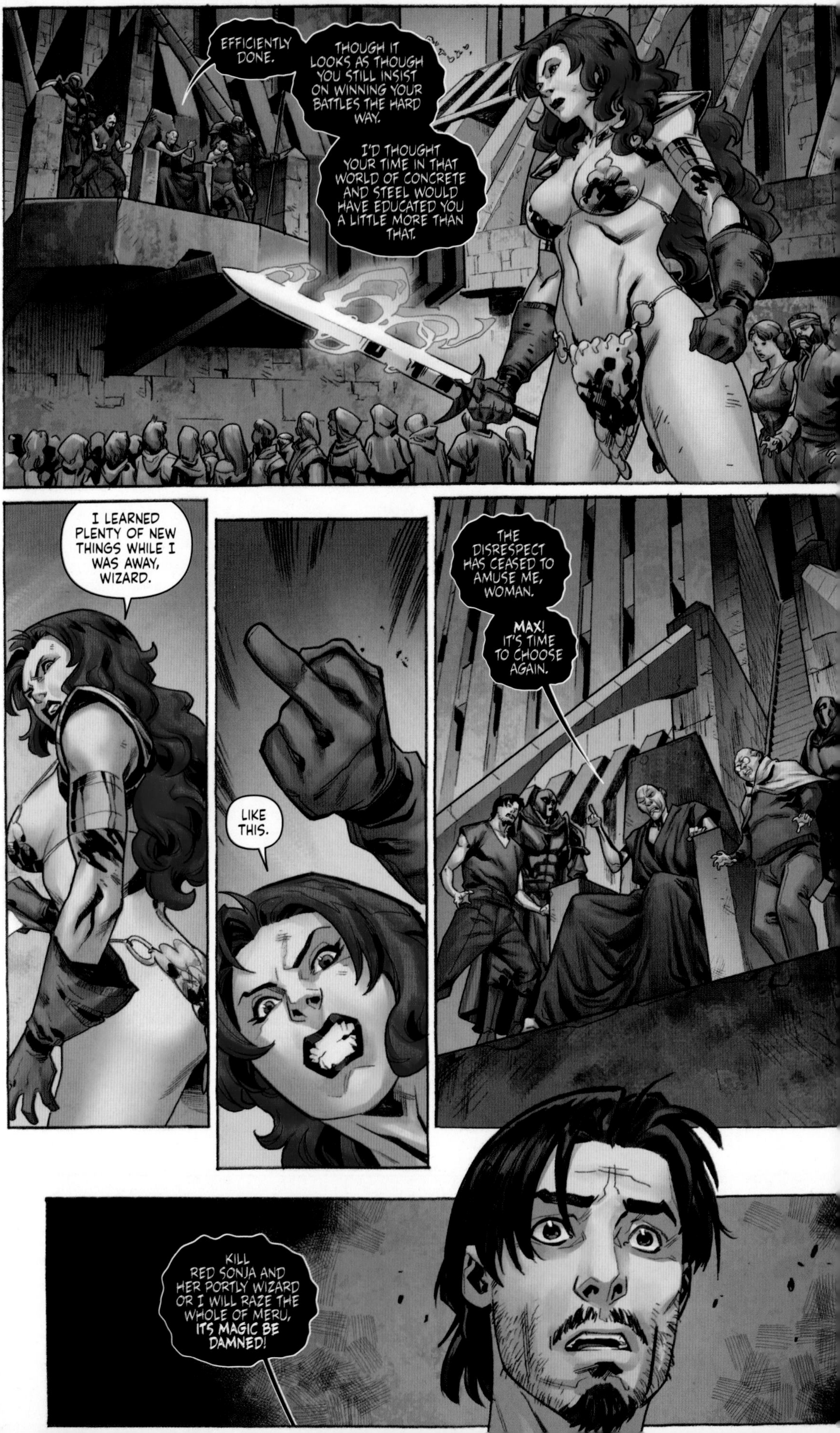
EFFICIENTLY DONE.
THOUGH IT LOOKS AS THOUGH YOU STILL INSIST ON WINNING YOUR BATTLES THE HARD WAY.
I'D THOUGHT YOUR TIME IN THAT WORLD OF CONCRETE AND STEEL WOULD HAVE EDUCATED YOU A LITTLE MORE THAN THAT.
I LEARNED PLENTY OF NEW THINGS WHILE I WAS AWAY, WIZARD.
LIKE THIS.
THE DISRESPECT HAS CEASED TO AMUSE ME, WOMAN.
MAX! IT'S TIME TO CHOOSE AGAIN.
KILL RED SONJA AND HER PORTLY WIZARD OR I WILL RAZE THE WHOLE OF MERU, ITS MAGIC BE DAMNED!

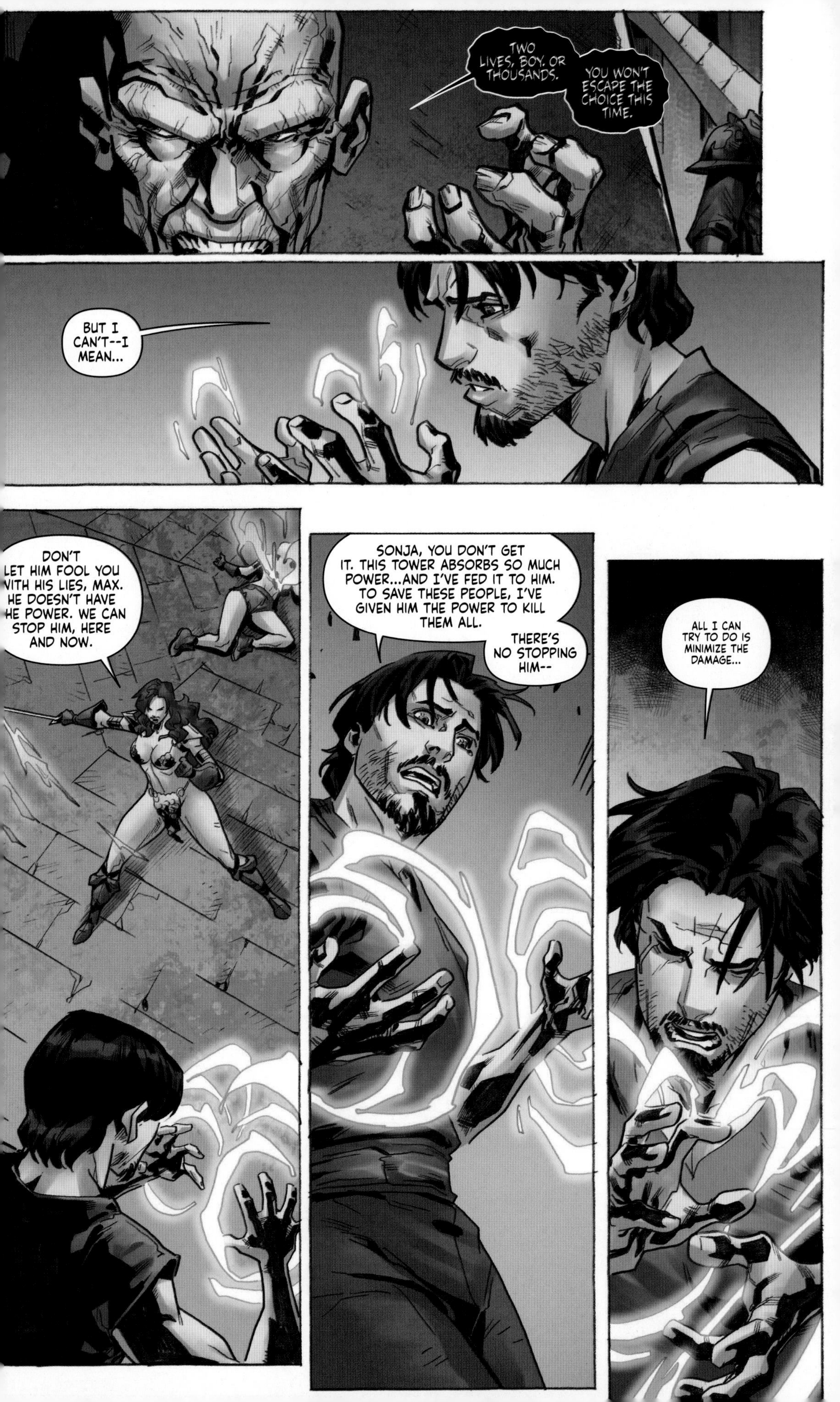

TWO LIVES, BOY. OR THOUSANDS.
YOU WON'T ESCAPE THE CHOICE THIS TIME.
BUT I CAN'T--I MEAN...
DON'T LET HIM FOOL YOU VITH HIS LIES, MAX. HE DOESN'T HAVE HE POWER. WE CAN STOP HIM, HERE AND NOW.
SONJA, YOU DON'T GET IT. THIS TOWER ABSORBS SO MUCH POWER...AND I'VE FED IT TO HIM. TO SAVE THESE PEOPLE, I'VE GIVEN HIM THE POWER TO KILL THEM ALL.
THERE'S NO STOPPING HIM--
ALL I CAN TRY TO DO IS MINIMIZE THE DAMAGE...

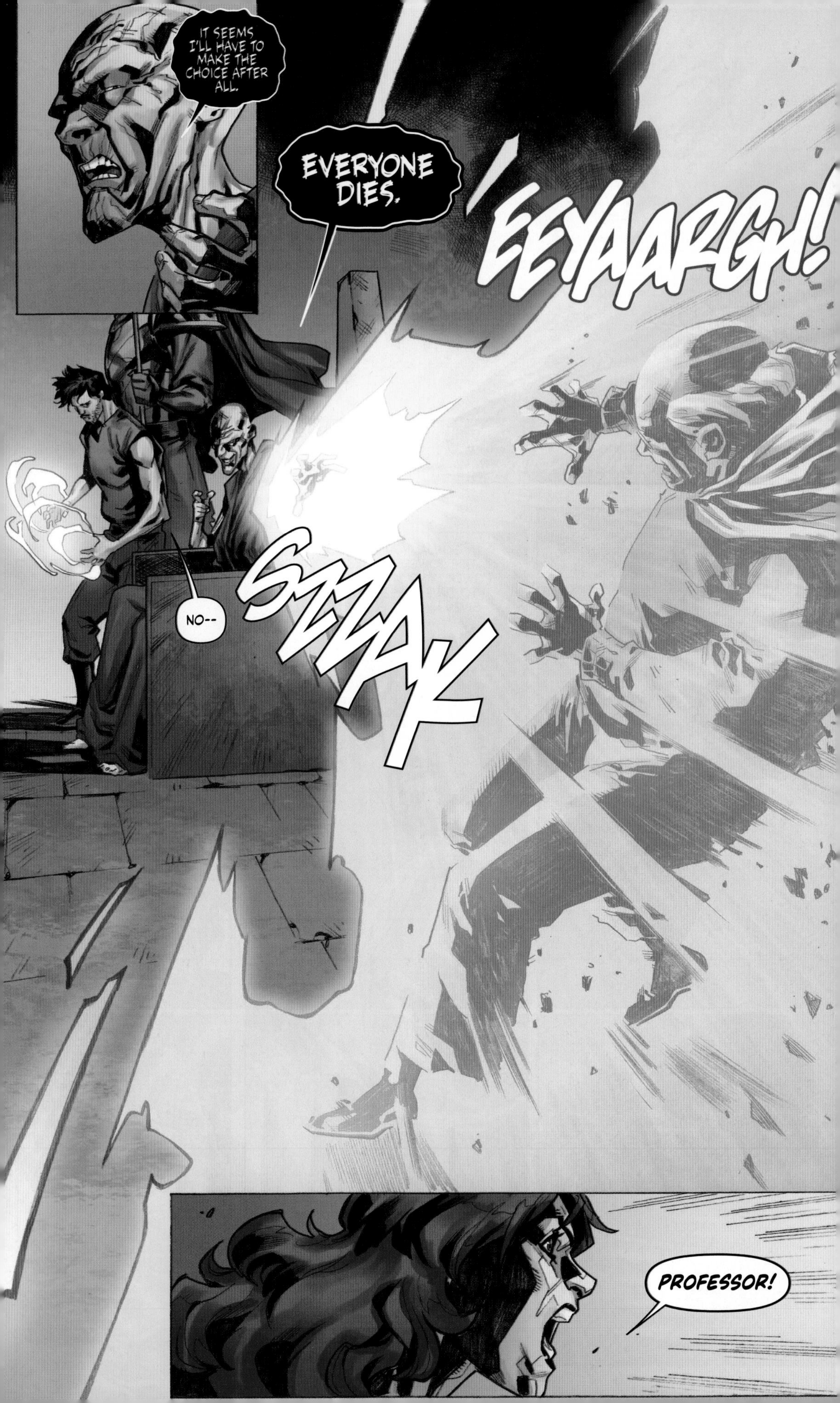
IT SEEMS I'LL HAVE TO MAKE THE CHOICE AFTER ALL.
EVERYONE DIES.
EEYAARGH!
NO--
SZZZAK
PROFESSOR!

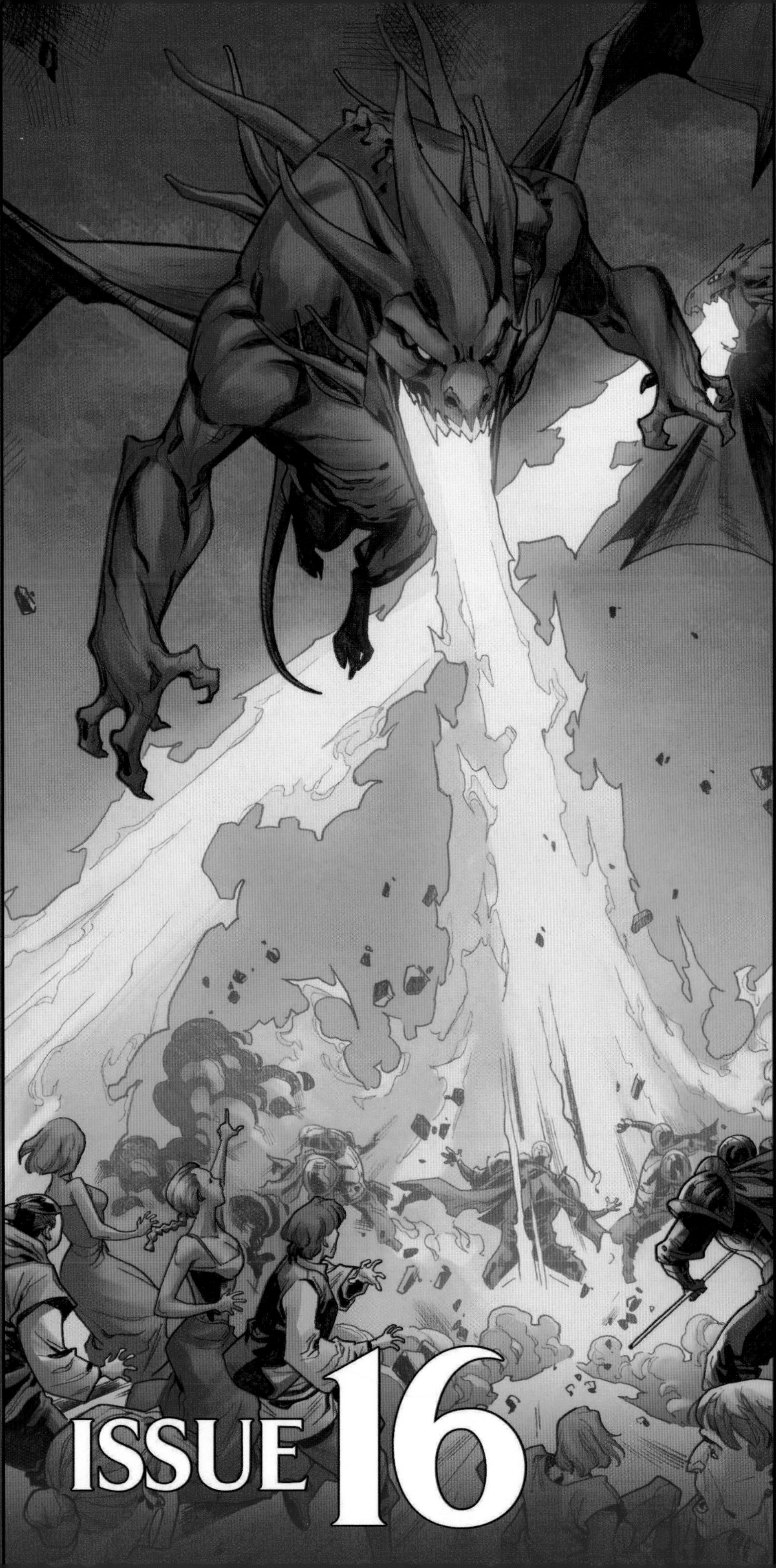
ISSUE 16

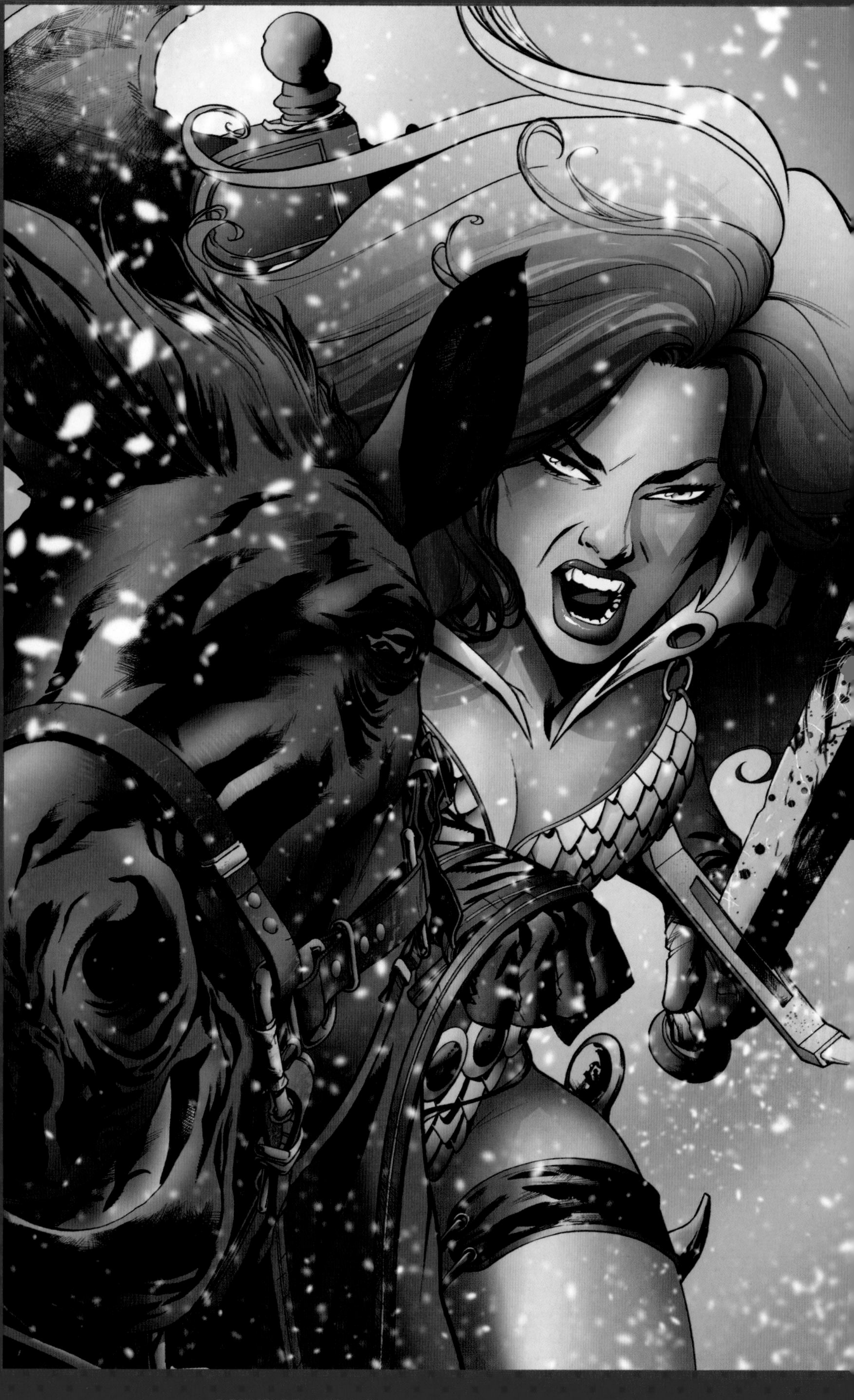

ISSUE #16: COVER ART BY **MIKE McKONE**

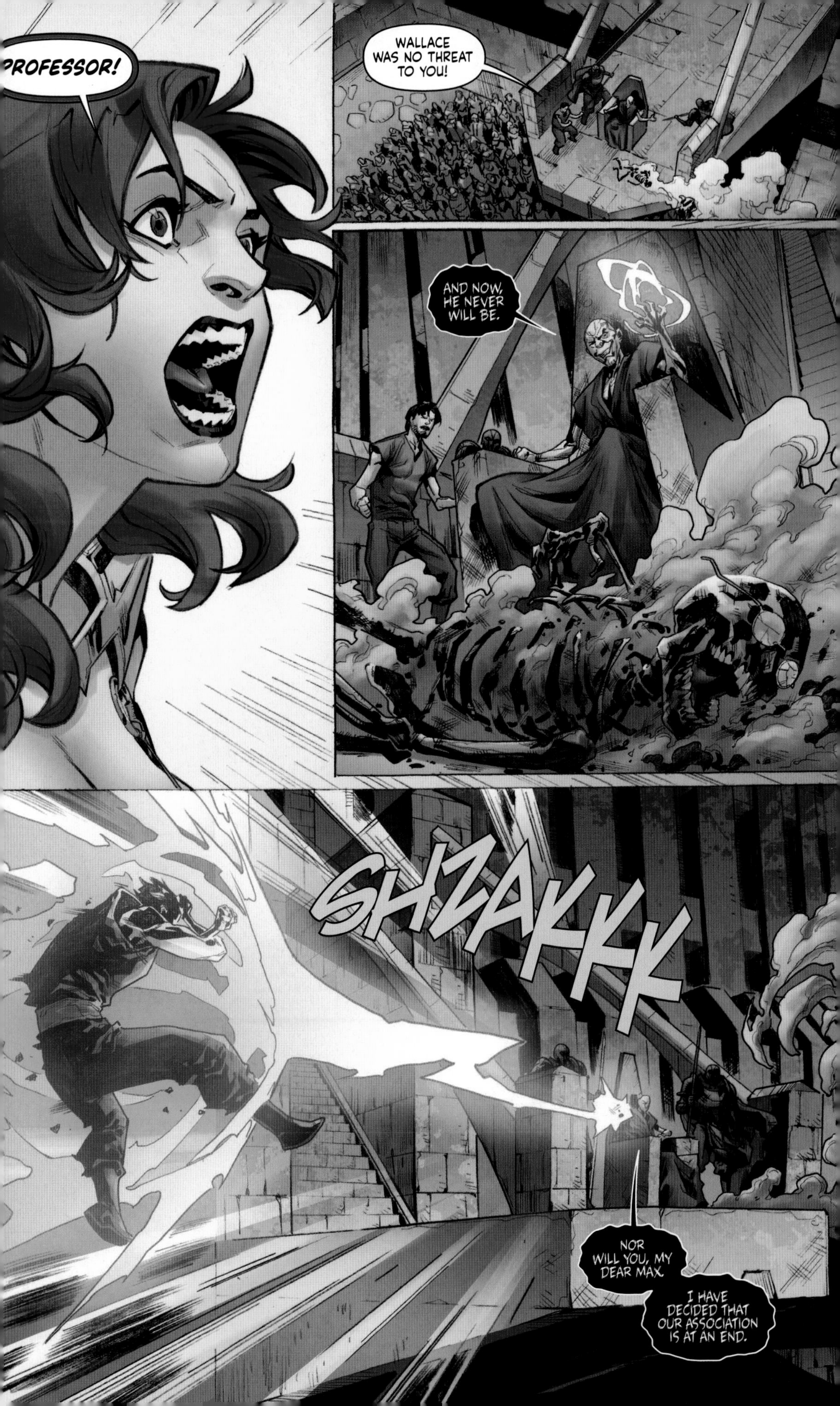
PROFESSOR!
WALLACE WAS NO THREAT TO YOU!
AND NOW, HE NEVER WILL BE.
SHZAKKK
NOR WILL YOU, MY DEAR MAX.
I HAVE DECIDED THAT OUR ASSOCIATION IS AT AN END.

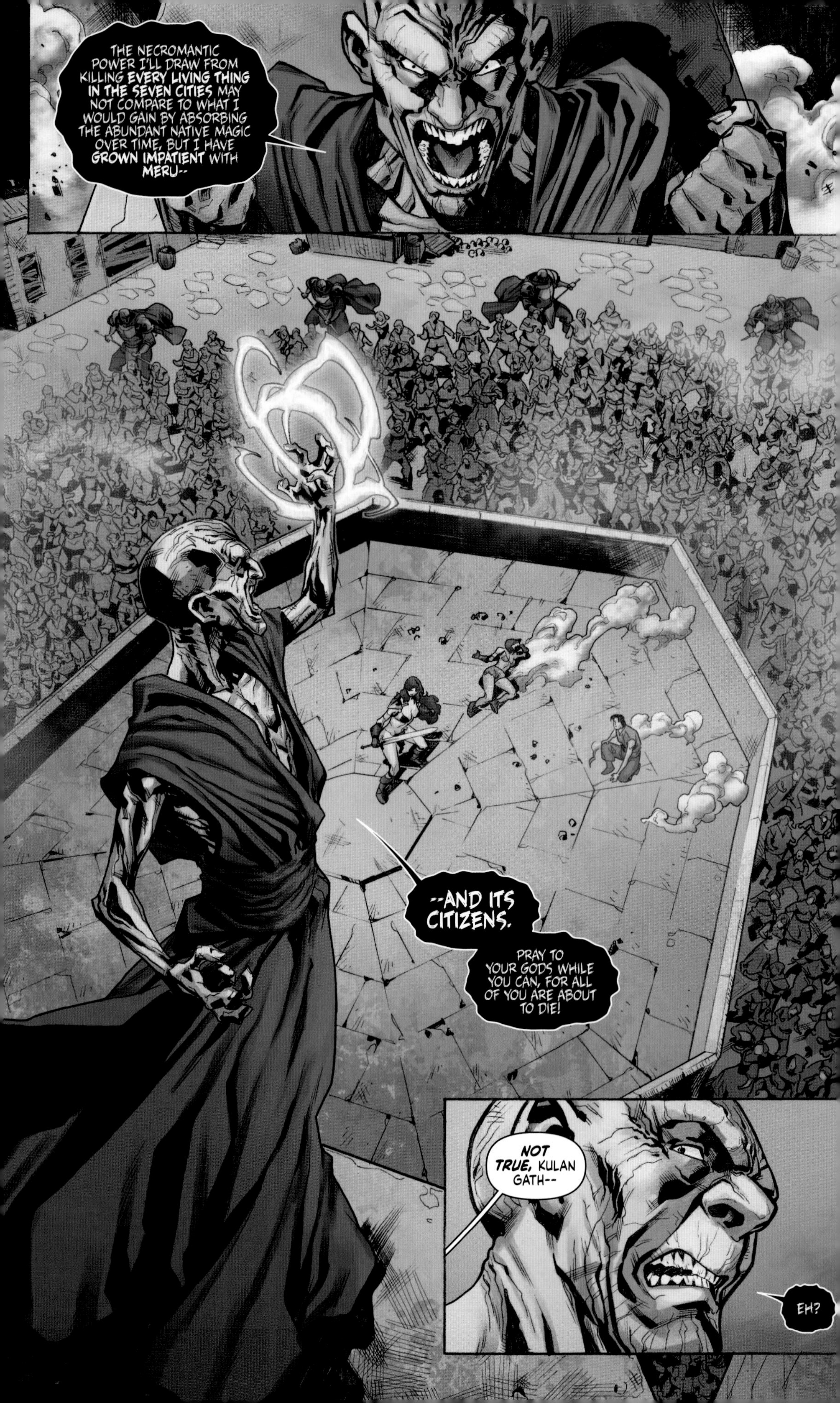
THE NECROMANTIC POWER I'LL DRAW FROM KILLING EVERY LIVING THING IN THE SEVEN CITIES MAY NOT COMPARE TO WHAT I WOULD GAIN BY ABSORBING THE ABUNDANT NATIVE MAGIC OVER TIME, BUT I HAVE GROWN IMPATIENT WITH MERU--
--AND ITS CITIZENS.
PRAY TO YOUR GODS WHILE YOU CAN, FOR ALL OF YOU ARE ABOUT TO DIE!
NOT TRUE, KULAN GATH--
EH?

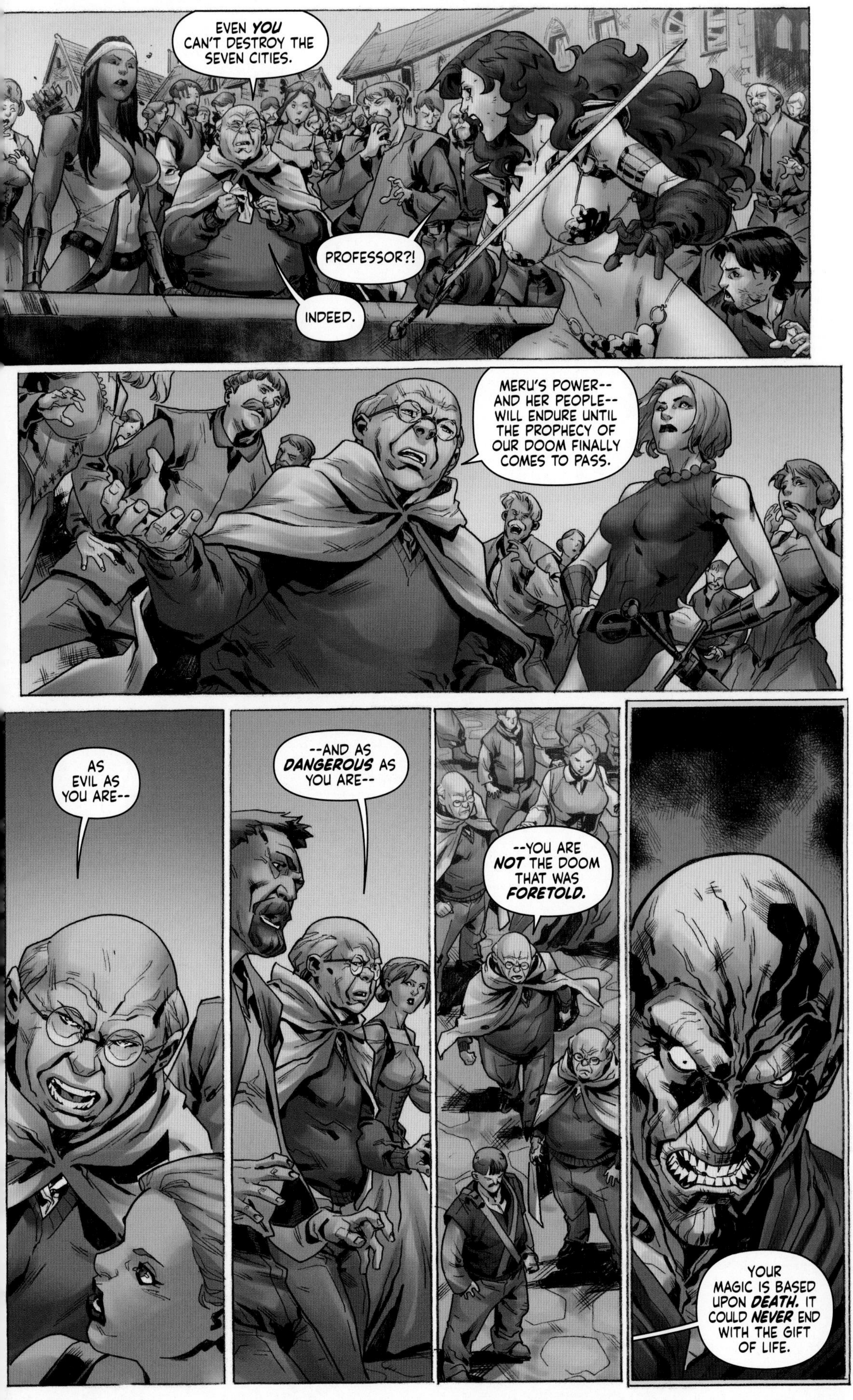
EVEN *YOU* CAN'T DESTROY THE SEVEN CITIES.
PROFESSOR?!
INDEED.
MERU'S POWER-- AND HER PEOPLE-- WILL ENDURE UNTIL THE PROPHECY OF OUR DOOM FINALLY COMES TO PASS.
AS EVIL AS YOU ARE--
--AND AS *DANGEROUS* AS YOU ARE--
--YOU ARE *NOT* THE DOOM THAT WAS *FORETOLD.*
YOUR MAGIC IS BASED UPON *DEATH.* IT COULD *NEVER* END WITH THE GIFT OF LIFE.

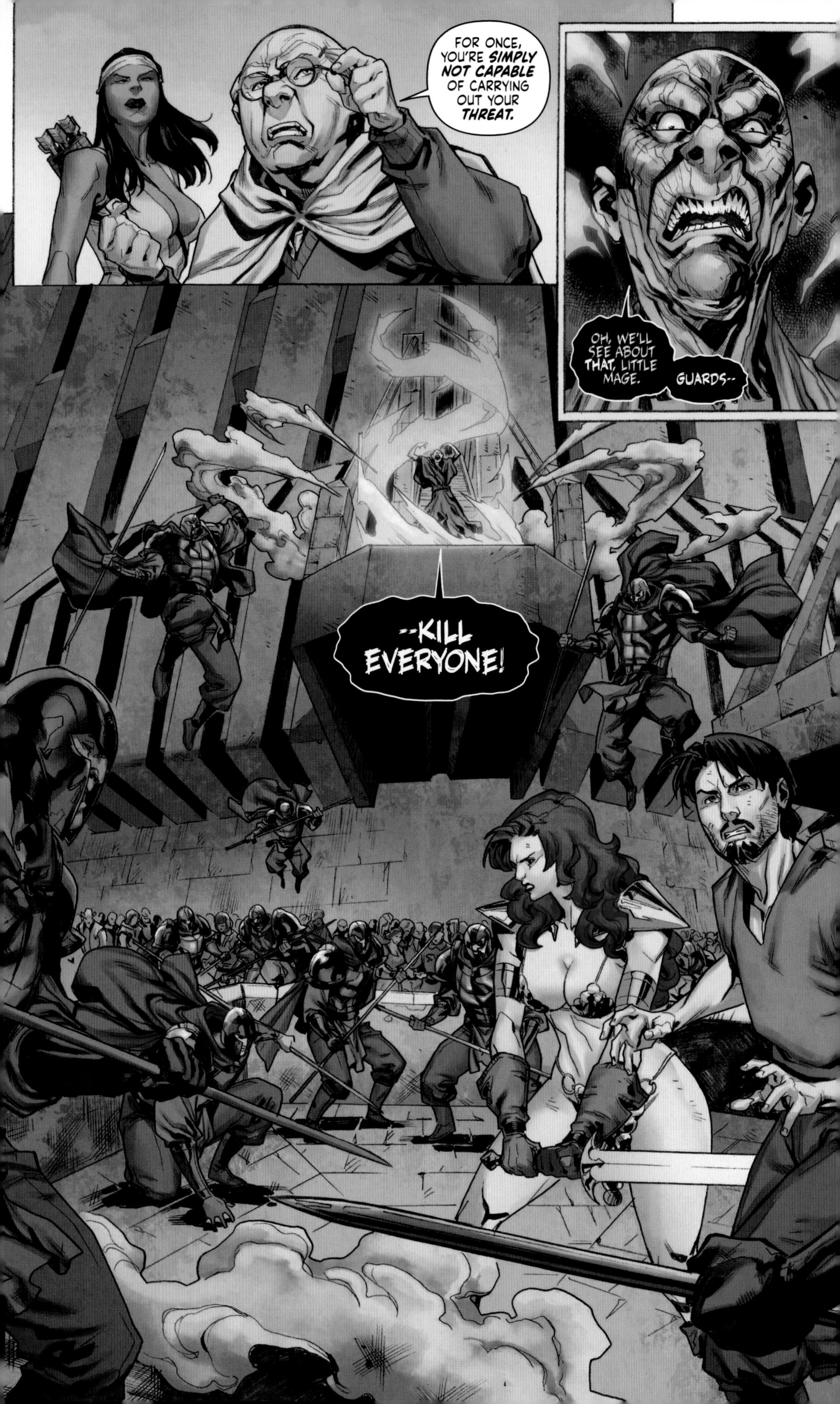
FOR ONCE, YOU'RE *SIMPLY NOT CAPABLE* OF CARRYING OUT YOUR *THREAT.*
OH, WE'LL SEE ABOUT **THAT,** LITTLE MAGE.
GUARDS--
--KILL EVERYONE!

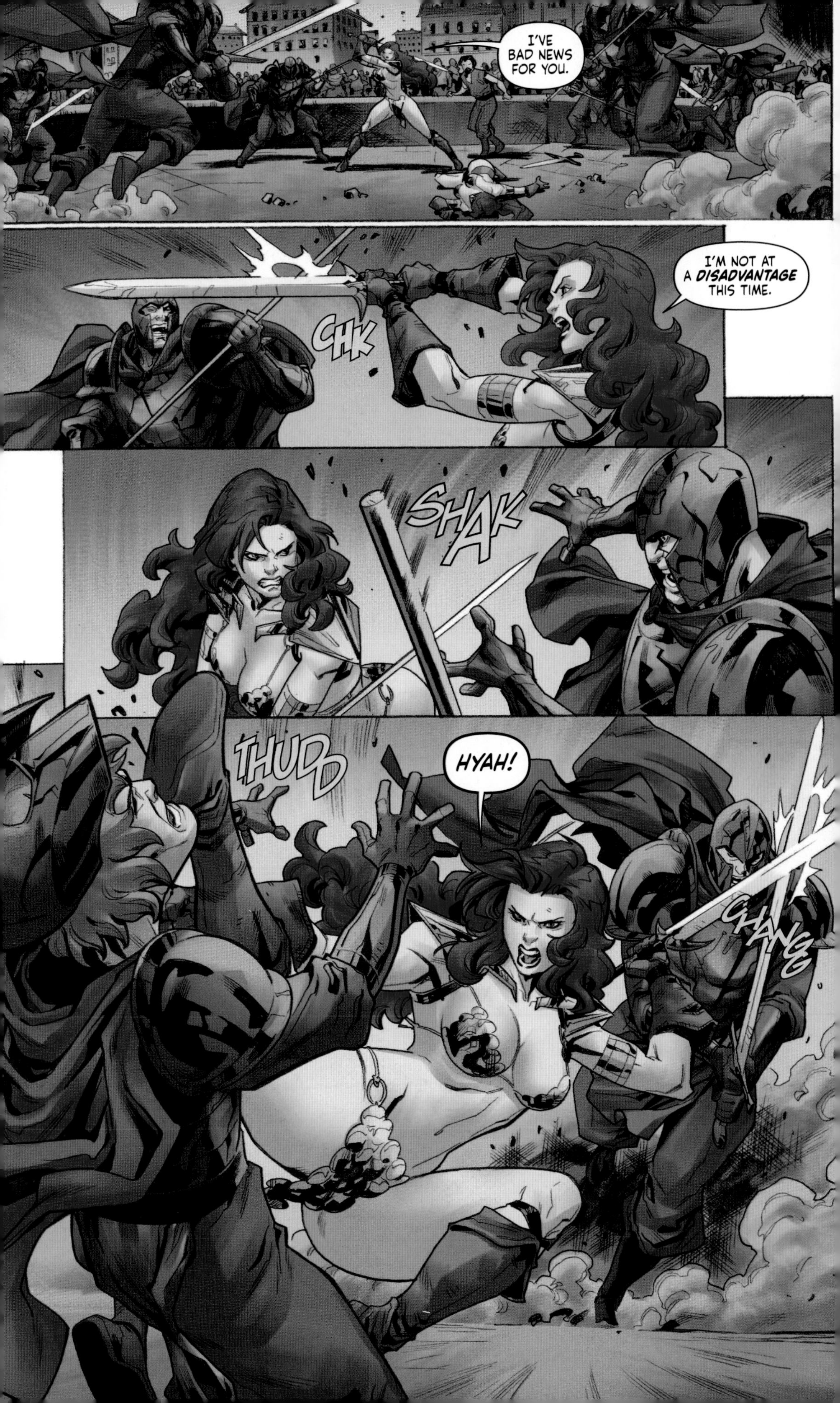

I'VE BAD NEWS FOR YOU.
CHK
I'M NOT AT A *DISADVANTAGE* THIS TIME.
SHAK
THUDD
HYAH!
CHANGG

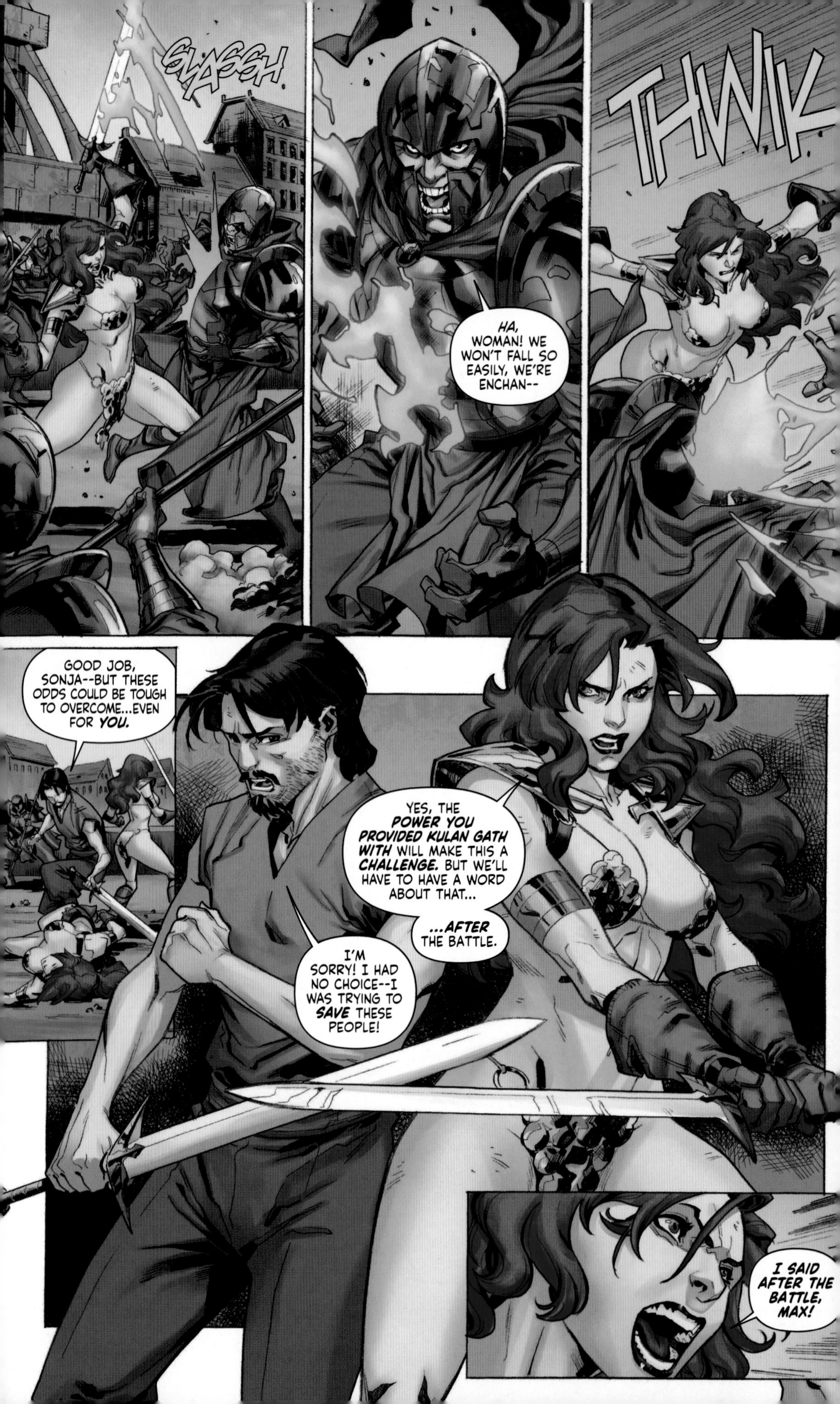
SLASSH
HA, WOMAN! WE WON'T FALL SO EASILY, WE'RE ENCHAN--
THWIK
GOOD JOB, SONJA--BUT THESE ODDS COULD BE TOUGH TO OVERCOME...EVEN FOR YOU.
YES, THE POWER YOU PROVIDED KULAN GATH WITH WILL MAKE THIS A CHALLENGE. BUT WE'LL HAVE TO HAVE A WORD ABOUT THAT...
...AFTER THE BATTLE.
I'M SORRY! I HAD NO CHOICE--I WAS TRYING TO SAVE THESE PEOPLE!
I SAID AFTER THE BATTLE, MAX!

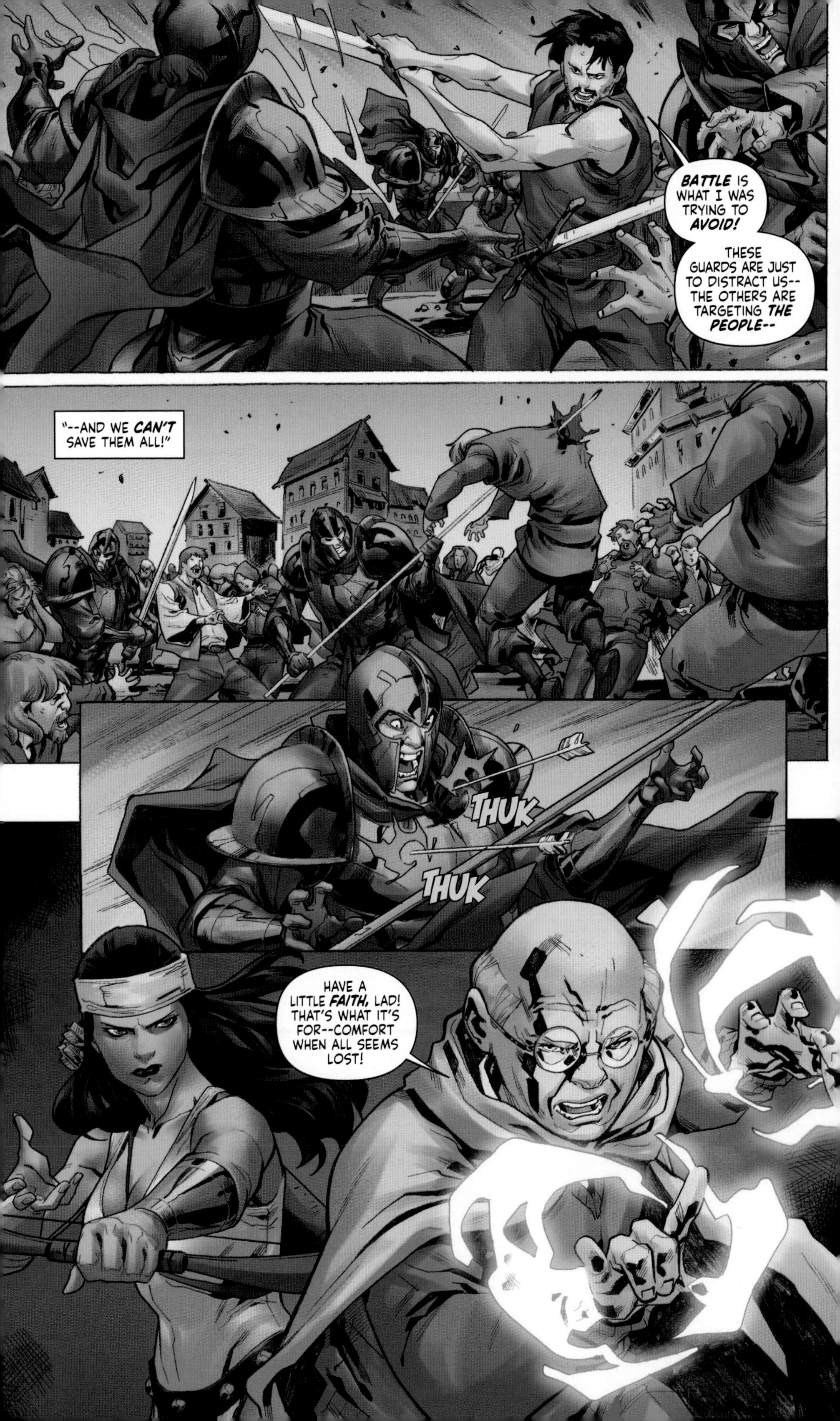
BATTLE IS WHAT I WAS TRYING TO AVOID!
THESE GUARDS ARE JUST TO DISTRACT US-- THE OTHERS ARE TARGETING THE PEOPLE--
"--AND WE CAN'T SAVE THEM ALL!"
THUK
THUK
HAVE A LITTLE FAITH, LAD! THAT'S WHAT IT'S FOR--COMFORT WHEN ALL SEEMS LOST!

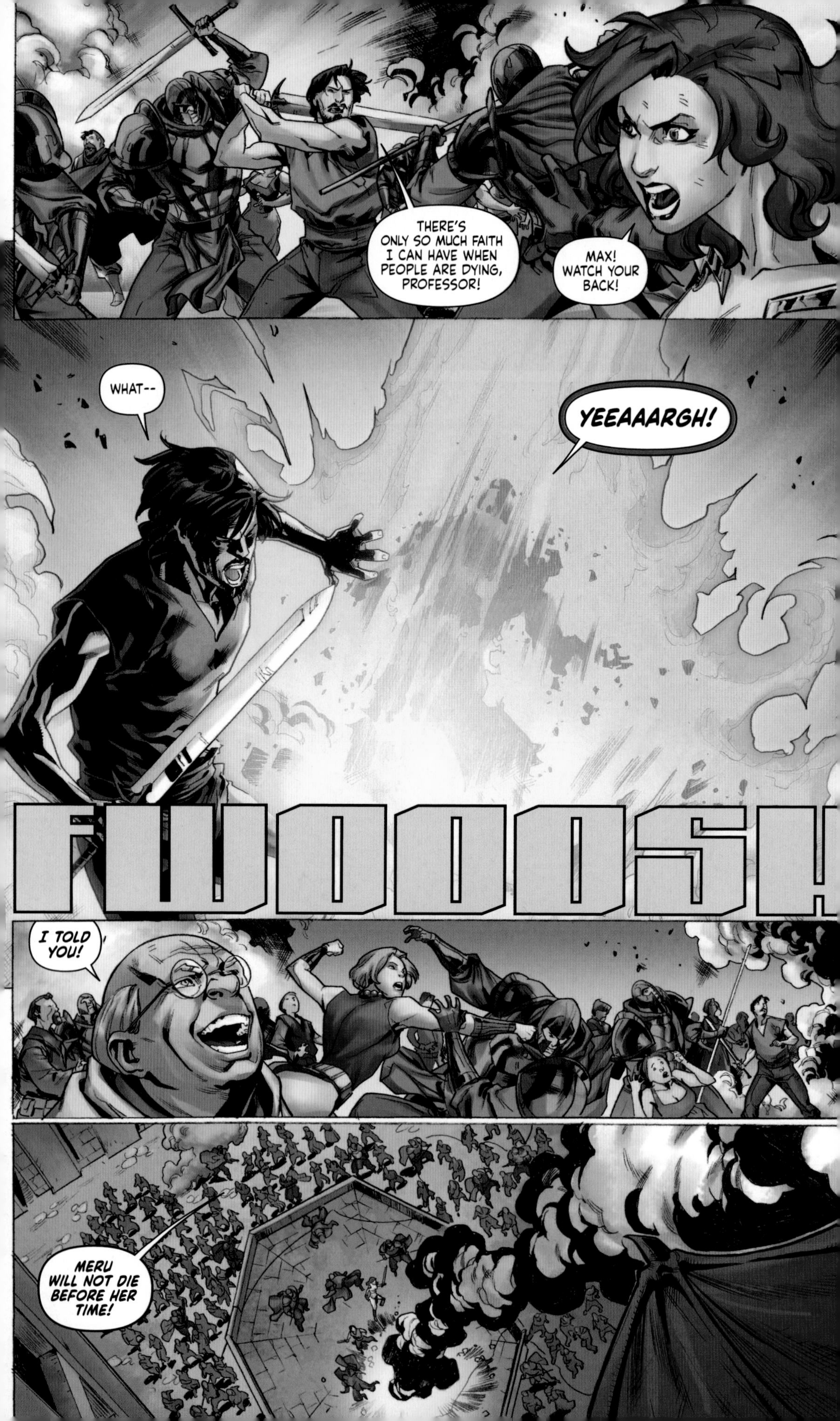

THERE'S ONLY SO MUCH FAITH I CAN HAVE WHEN PEOPLE ARE DYING, PROFESSOR!
MAX! WATCH YOUR BACK!
WHAT--
YEEAAARGH!
FWOOSH
I TOLD YOU!
MERU WILL NOT DIE BEFORE HER TIME!

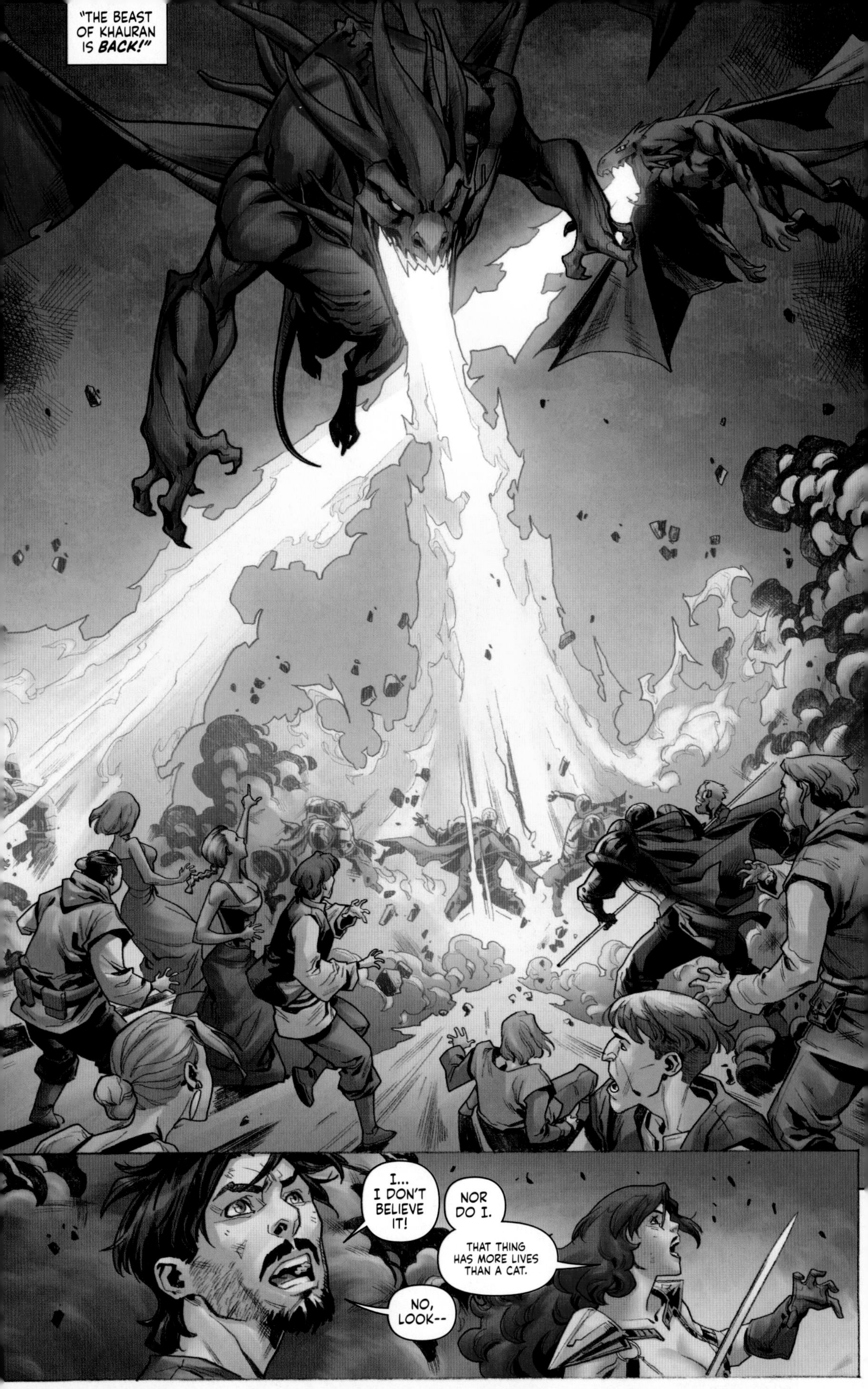
"THE BEAST OF KHAURAN IS BACK!"
I... I DON'T BELIEVE IT!
NOR DO I.
THAT THING HAS MORE LIVES THAN A CAT.
NO, LOOK--

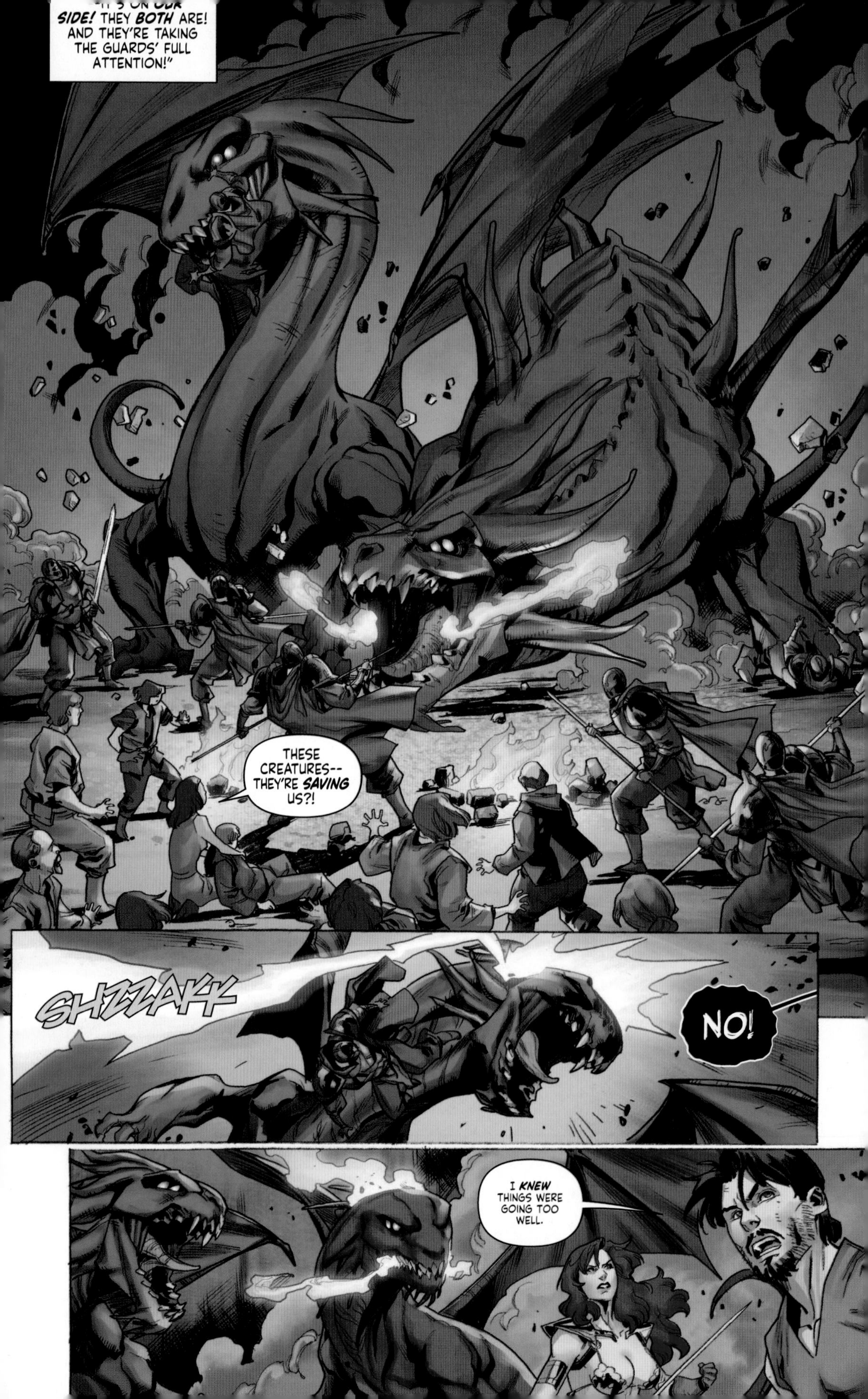
SIDE! THEY BOTH ARE! AND THEY'RE TAKING THE GUARDS' FULL ATTENTION!"
THESE CREATURES-- THEY'RE SAVING US?!
SHZZAKK
NO!
I KNEW THINGS WERE GOING TOO WELL.

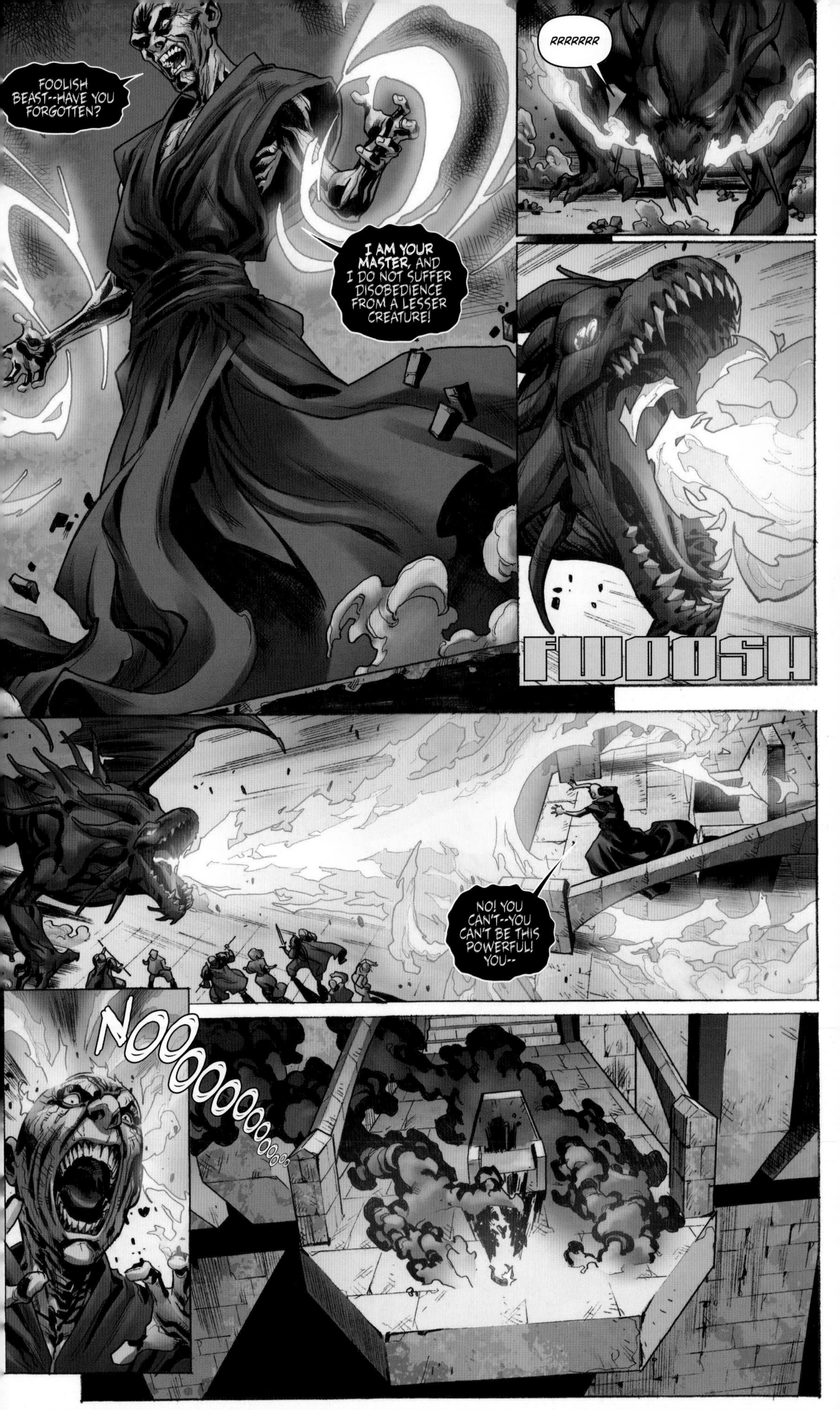
FOOLISH BEAST--HAVE YOU FORGOTTEN?
RRRRRRR
I AM YOUR MASTER, AND I DO NOT SUFFER DISOBEDIENCE FROM A LESSER CREATURE!
FWOOSH
NO! YOU CAN'T--YOU CAN'T BE THIS POWERFUL! YOU--
NOOOOOOOOOooo

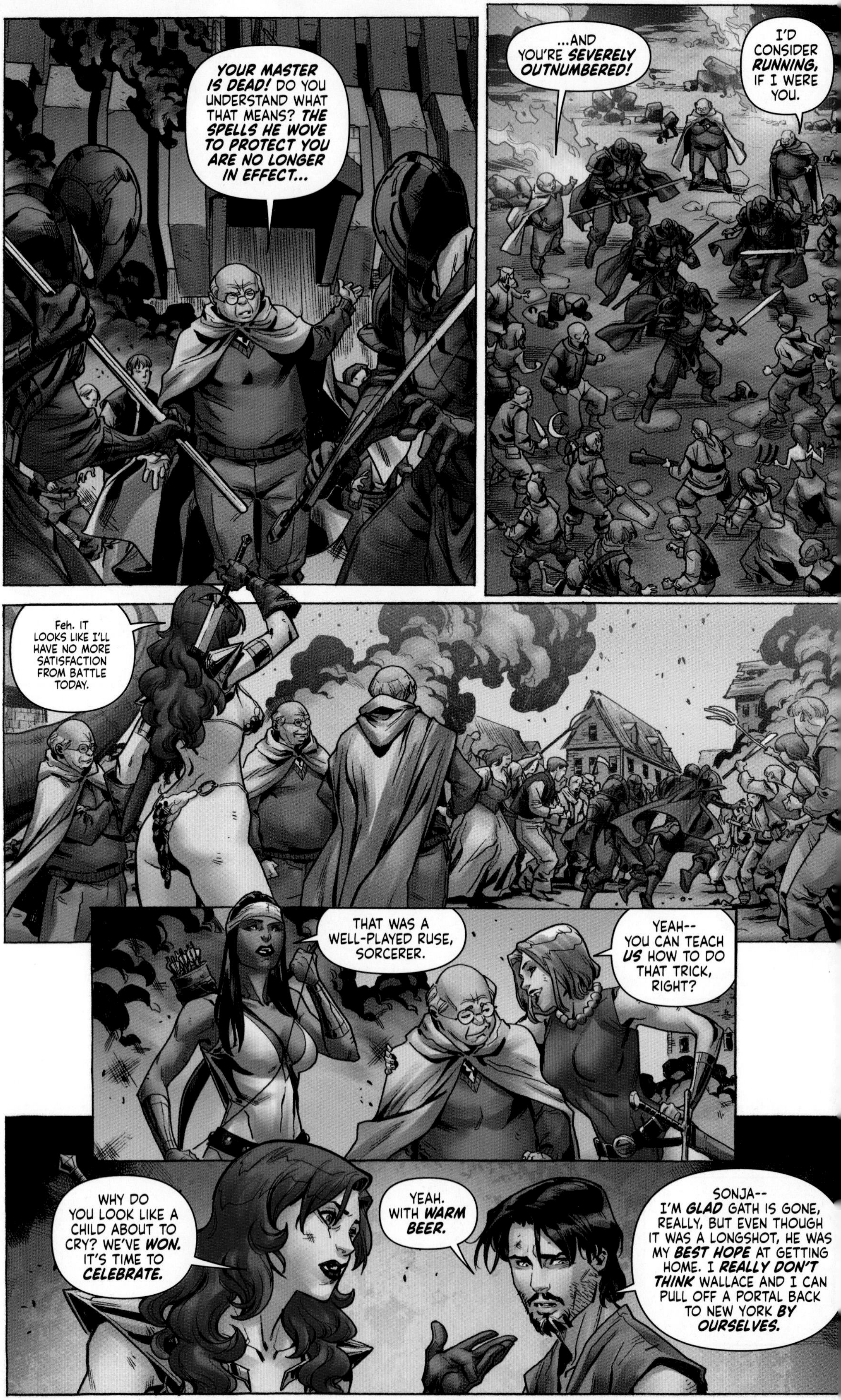
YOUR MASTER IS DEAD! DO YOU UNDERSTAND WHAT THAT MEANS? THE SPELLS HE WOVE TO PROTECT YOU ARE NO LONGER IN EFFECT...
...AND YOU'RE SEVERELY OUTNUMBERED!
I'D CONSIDER RUNNING, IF I WERE YOU.
Feh. IT LOOKS LIKE I'LL HAVE NO MORE SATISFACTION FROM BATTLE TODAY.
THAT WAS A WELL-PLAYED RUSE, SORCERER.
YEAH-- YOU CAN TEACH US HOW TO DO THAT TRICK, RIGHT?
WHY DO YOU LOOK LIKE A CHILD ABOUT TO CRY? WE'VE WON. IT'S TIME TO CELEBRATE.
YEAH. WITH WARM BEER.
SONJA-- I'M GLAD GATH IS GONE, REALLY, BUT EVEN THOUGH IT WAS A LONGSHOT, HE WAS MY BEST HOPE AT GETTING HOME. I REALLY DON'T THINK WALLACE AND I CAN PULL OFF A PORTAL BACK TO NEW YORK BY OURSELVES.

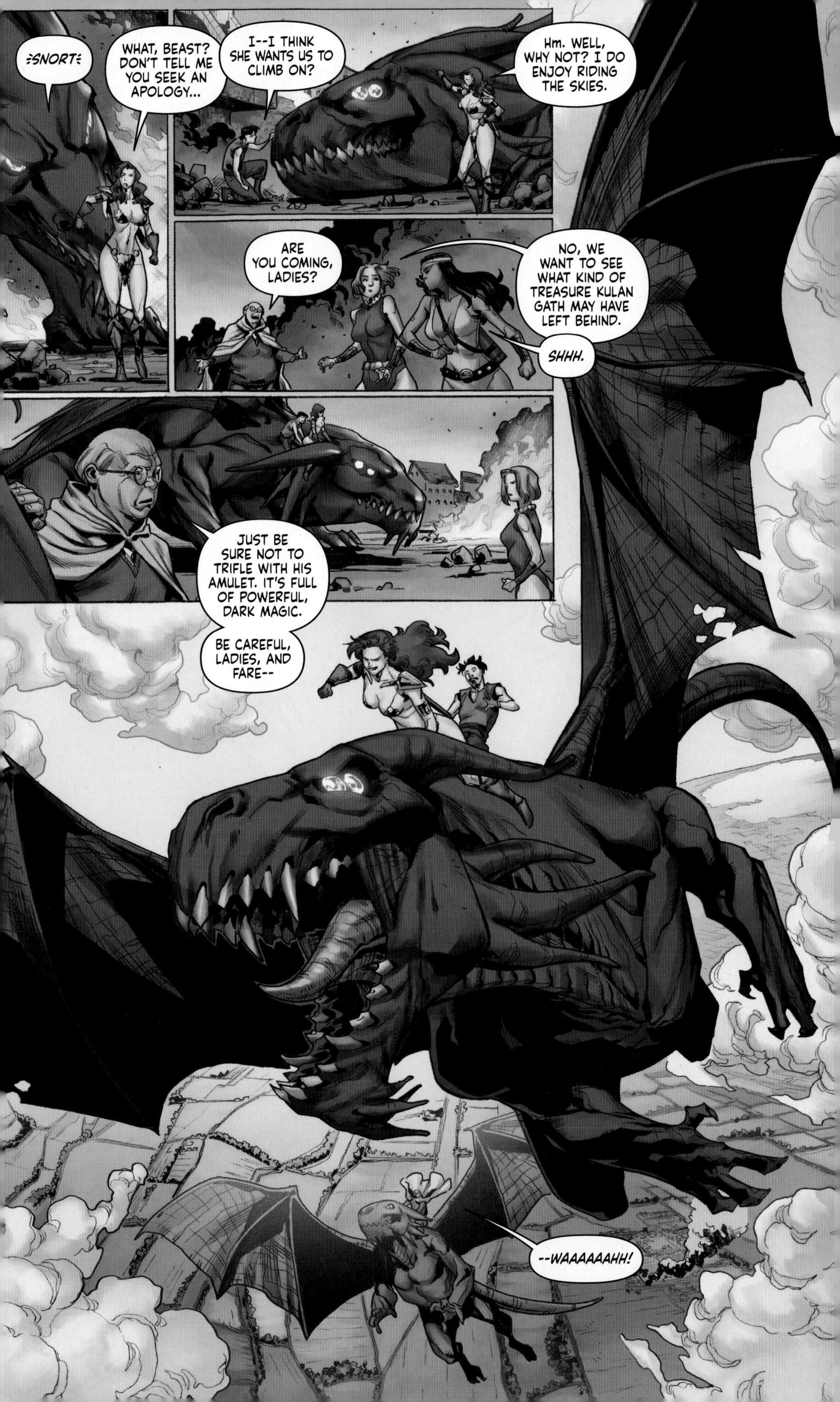

SNORT
WHAT, BEAST? DON'T TELL ME YOU SEEK AN APOLOGY...
I--I THINK SHE WANTS US TO CLIMB ON?
Hm. WELL, WHY NOT? I DO ENJOY RIDING THE SKIES.
ARE YOU COMING, LADIES?
NO, WE WANT TO SEE WHAT KIND OF TREASURE KULAN GATH MAY HAVE LEFT BEHIND.
SHHH.
JUST BE SURE NOT TO TRIFLE WITH HIS AMULET. IT'S FULL OF POWERFUL, DARK MAGIC.
BE CAREFUL, LADIES, AND FARE--
--WAAAAAAHH!

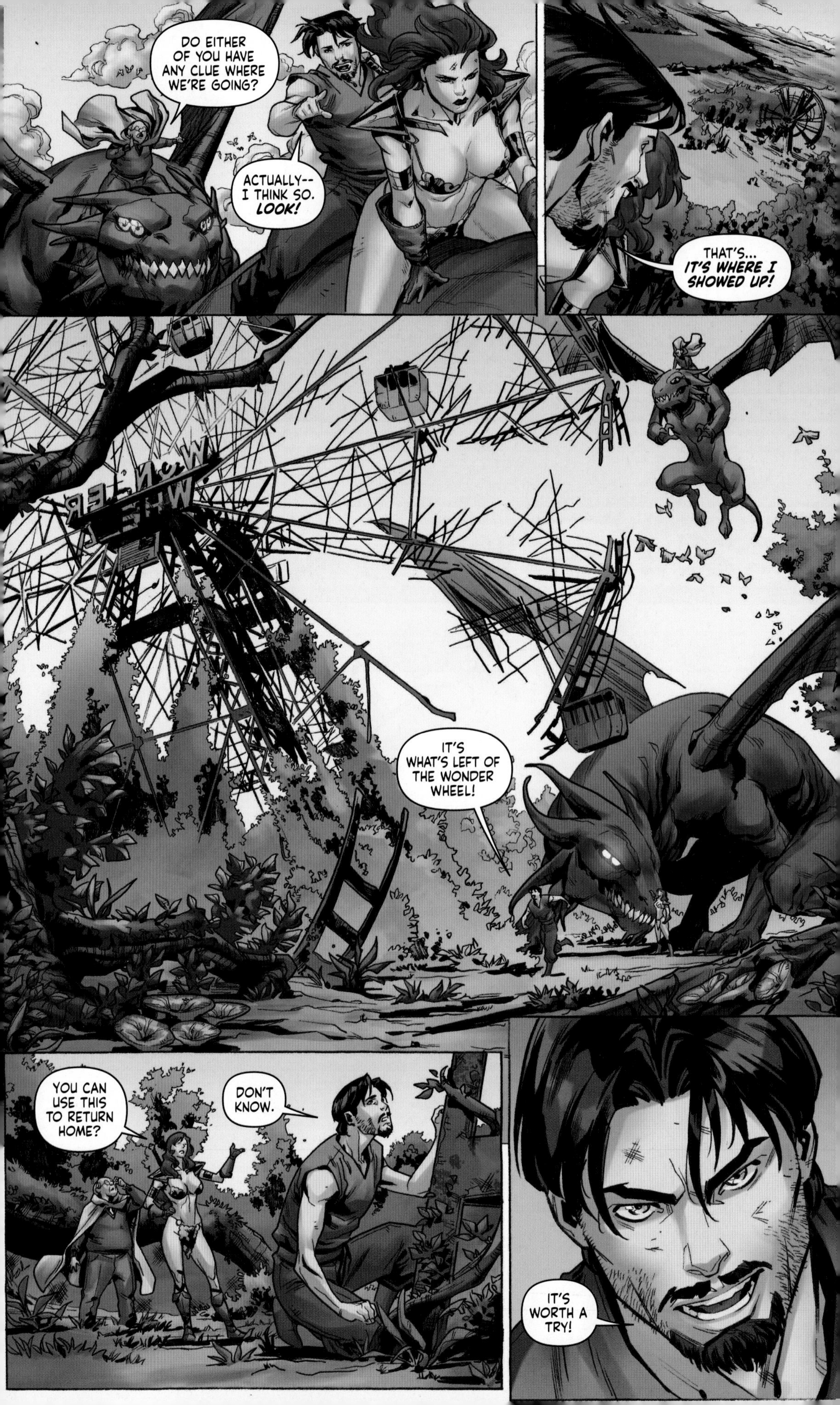
DO EITHER OF YOU HAVE ANY CLUE WHERE WE'RE GOING?
ACTUALLY-- I THINK SO. LOOK!
THAT'S... IT'S WHERE I SHOWED UP!
WONDER WHEEL
IT'S WHAT'S LEFT OF THE WONDER WHEEL!
YOU CAN USE THIS TO RETURN HOME?
DON'T KNOW.
IT'S WORTH A TRY!

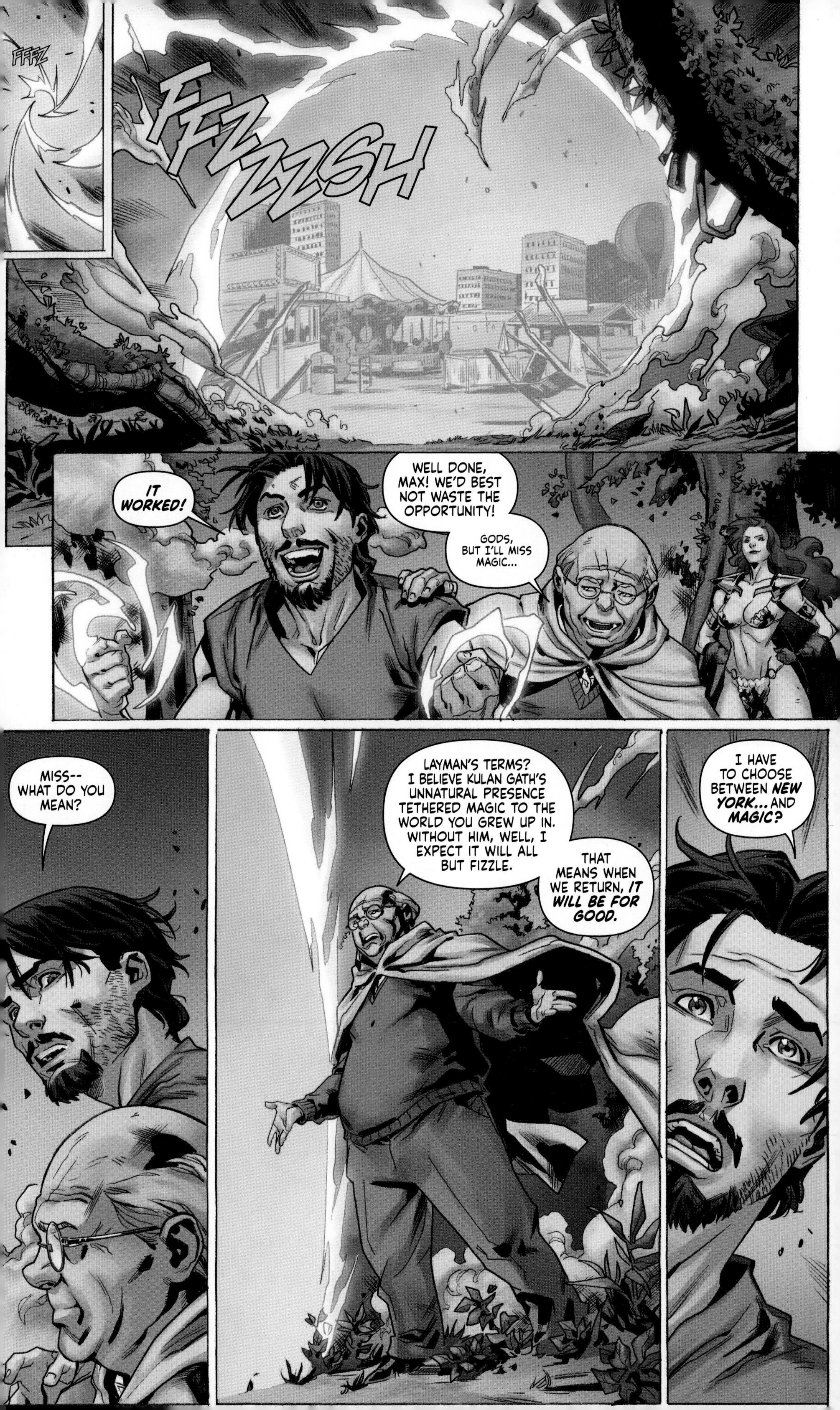
FFFZ
FFZZZSH
IT WORKED!
WELL DONE, MAX! WE'D BEST NOT WASTE THE OPPORTUNITY!
GODS, BUT I'LL MISS MAGIC...
MISS-- WHAT DO YOU MEAN?
LAYMAN'S TERMS? I BELIEVE KULAN GATH'S UNNATURAL PRESENCE TETHERED MAGIC TO THE WORLD YOU GREW UP IN. WITHOUT HIM, WELL, I EXPECT IT WILL ALL BUT FIZZLE.
THAT MEANS WHEN WE RETURN, IT WILL BE FOR GOOD.
I HAVE TO CHOOSE BETWEEN NEW YORK...AND MAGIC?

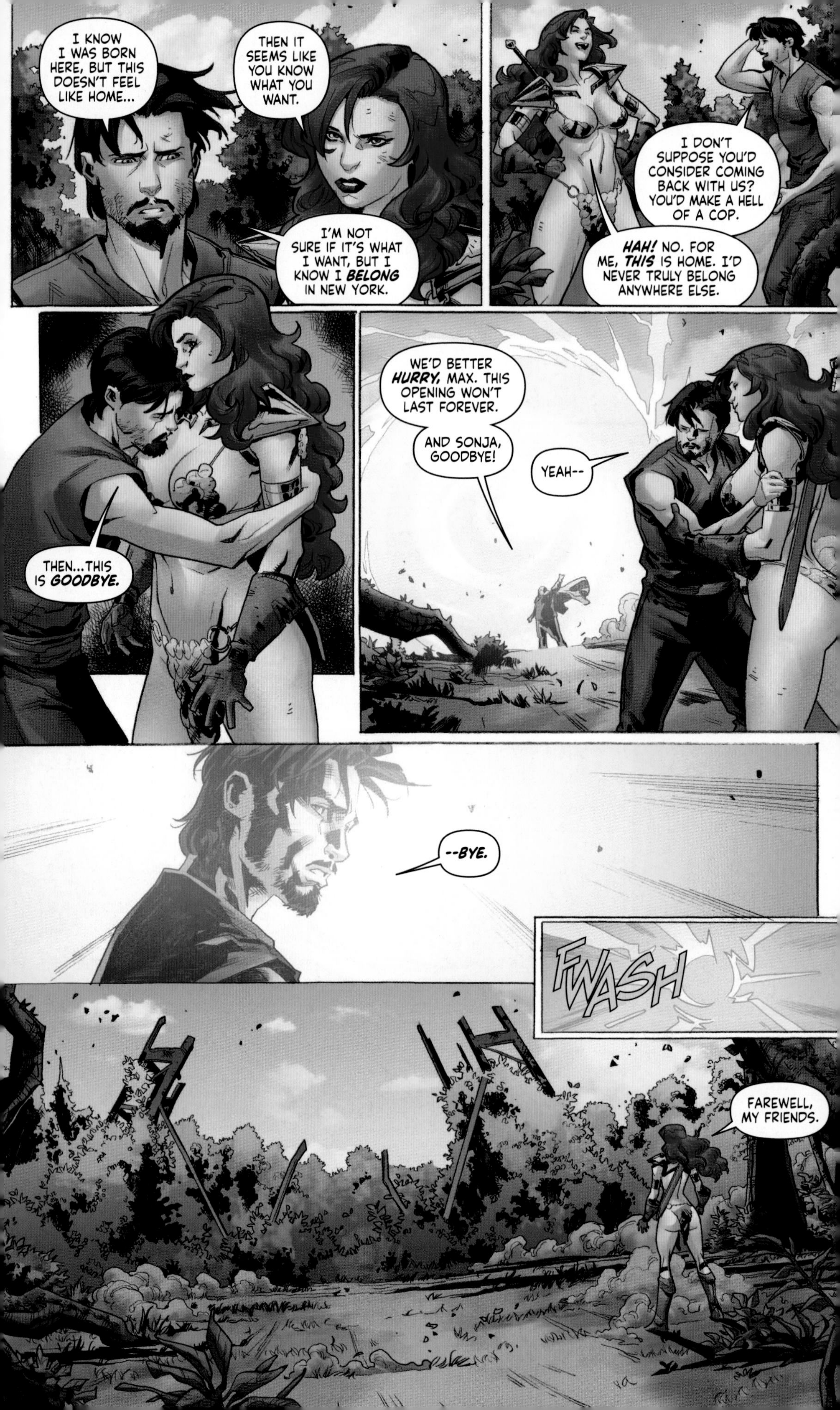

I KNOW I WAS BORN HERE, BUT THIS DOESN'T FEEL LIKE HOME...
THEN IT SEEMS LIKE YOU KNOW WHAT YOU WANT.
I'M NOT SURE IF IT'S WHAT I WANT, BUT I KNOW I **BELONG** IN NEW YORK.
I DON'T SUPPOSE YOU'D CONSIDER COMING BACK WITH US? YOU'D MAKE A HELL OF A COP.
HAH! NO. FOR ME, **THIS** IS HOME. I'D NEVER TRULY BELONG ANYWHERE ELSE.
THEN...THIS IS **GOODBYE.**
WE'D BETTER **HURRY,** MAX. THIS OPENING WON'T LAST FOREVER.
AND SONJA, GOODBYE!
YEAH--
--**BYE.**
FWASH
FAREWELL, MY FRIENDS.

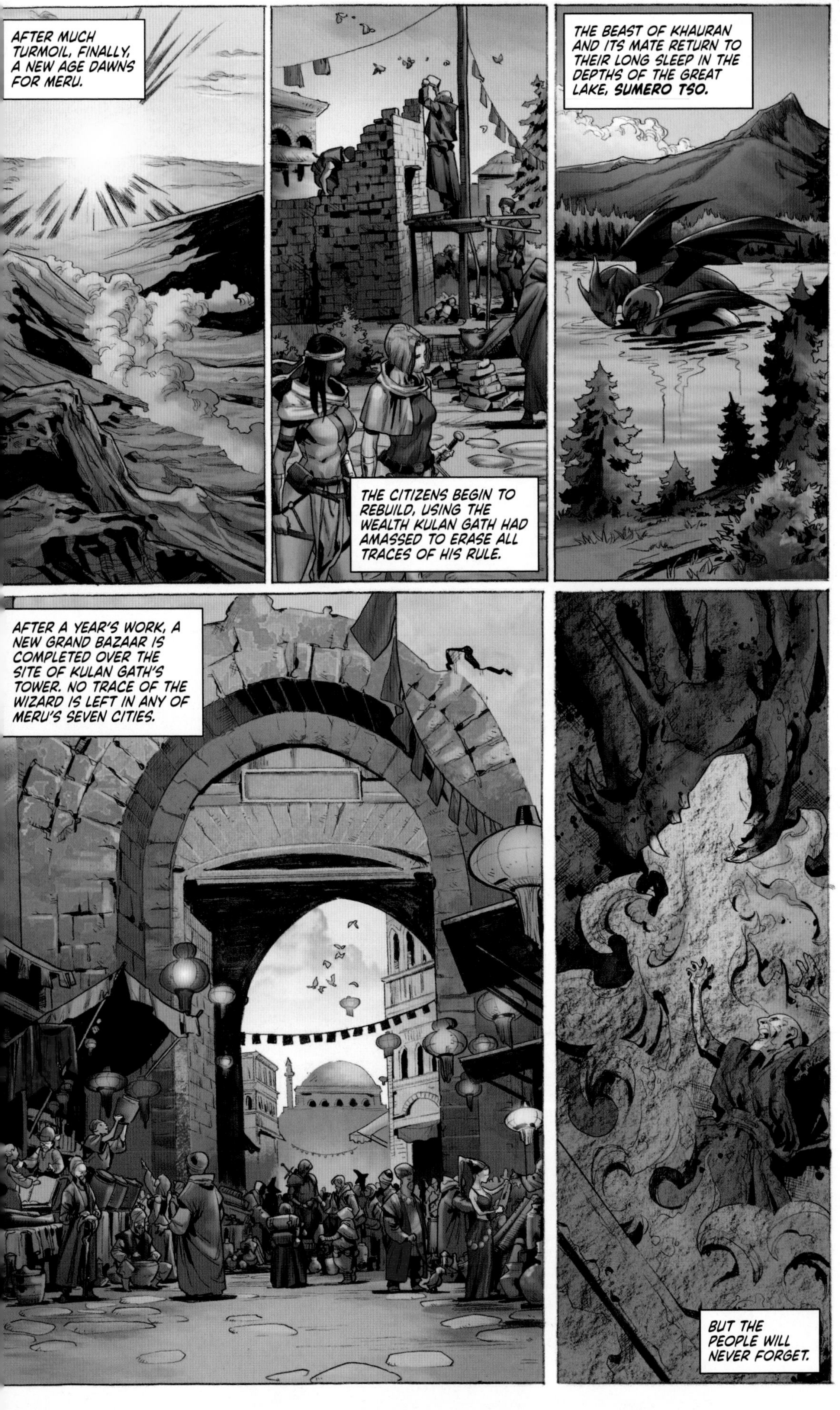
AFTER MUCH TURMOIL, FINALLY, A NEW AGE DAWNS FOR MERU.
THE CITIZENS BEGIN TO REBUILD, USING THE WEALTH KULAN GATH HAD AMASSED TO ERASE ALL TRACES OF HIS RULE.
THE BEAST OF KHAURAN AND ITS MATE RETURN TO THEIR LONG SLEEP IN THE DEPTHS OF THE GREAT LAKE, SUMERO TSO.
AFTER A YEAR'S WORK, A NEW GRAND BAZAAR IS COMPLETED OVER THE SITE OF KULAN GATH'S TOWER. NO TRACE OF THE WIZARD IS LEFT IN ANY OF MERU'S SEVEN CITIES.
BUT THE PEOPLE WILL NEVER FORGET.

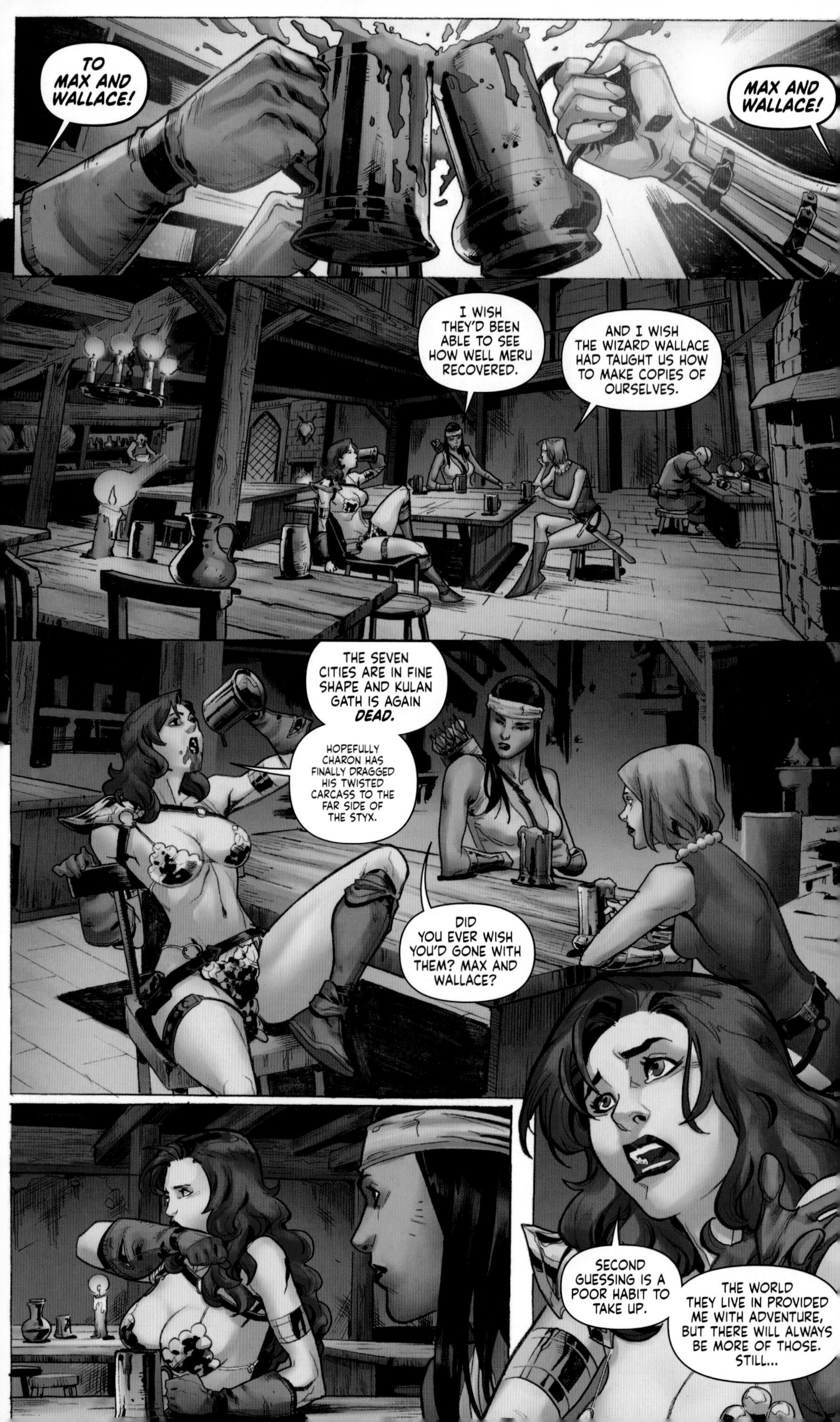
TO MAX AND WALLACE!
MAX AND WALLACE!
I WISH THEY'D BEEN ABLE TO SEE HOW WELL MERU RECOVERED.
AND I WISH THE WIZARD WALLACE HAD TAUGHT US HOW TO MAKE COPIES OF OURSELVES.
THE SEVEN CITIES ARE IN FINE SHAPE AND KULAN GATH IS AGAIN DEAD.
HOPEFULLY CHARON HAS FINALLY DRAGGED HIS TWISTED CARCASS TO THE FAR SIDE OF THE STYX.
DID YOU EVER WISH YOU'D GONE WITH THEM? MAX AND WALLACE?
SECOND GUESSING IS A POOR HABIT TO TAKE UP.
THE WORLD THEY LIVE IN PROVIDED ME WITH ADVENTURE, BUT THERE WILL ALWAYS BE MORE OF THOSE. STILL...

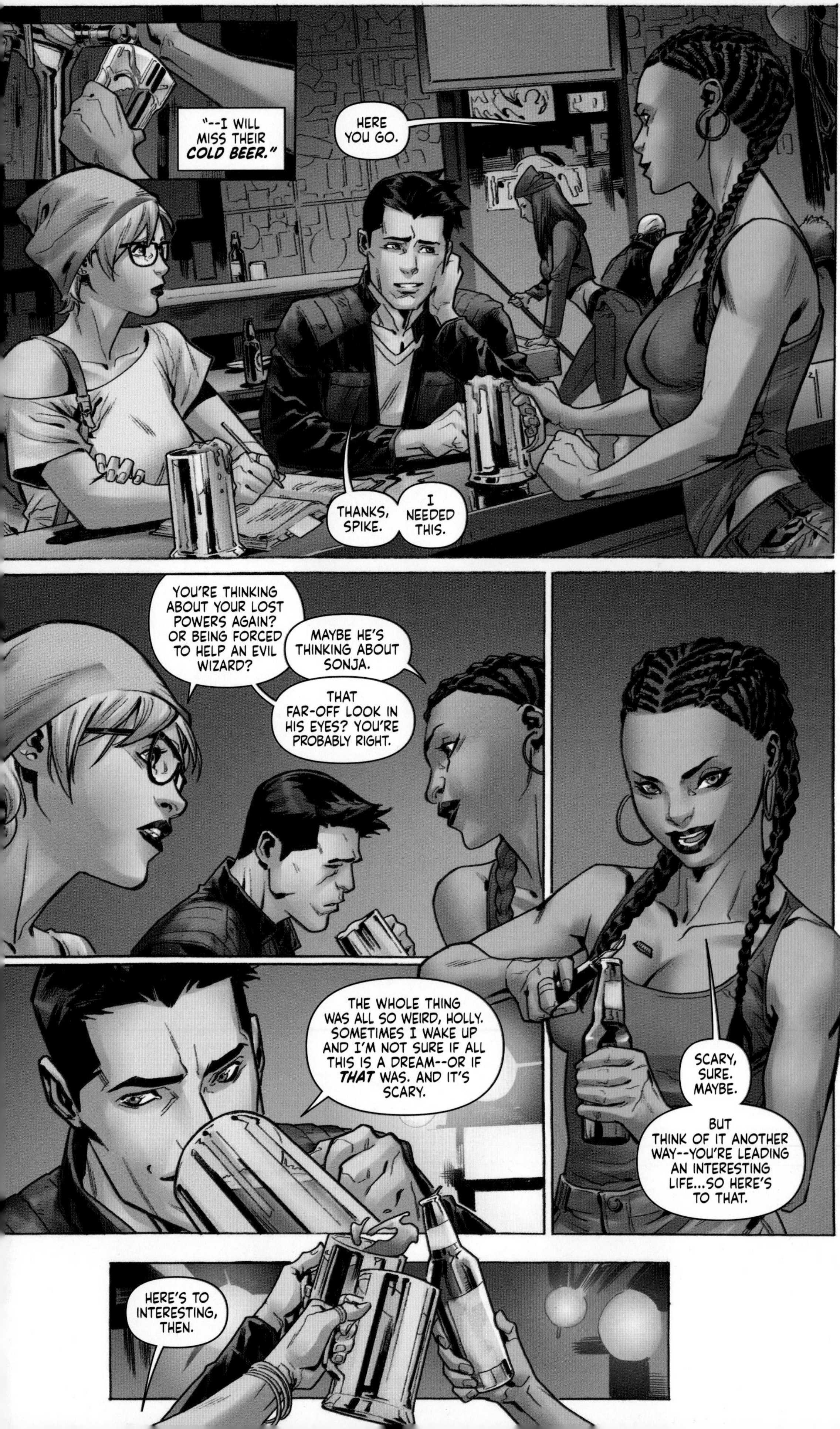
"--I WILL MISS THEIR *COLD BEER."*
HERE YOU GO.
THANKS, SPIKE.
I NEEDED THIS.
YOU'RE THINKING ABOUT YOUR LOST POWERS AGAIN? OR BEING FORCED TO HELP AN EVIL WIZARD?
MAYBE HE'S THINKING ABOUT SONJA.
THAT FAR-OFF LOOK IN HIS EYES? YOU'RE PROBABLY RIGHT.
THE WHOLE THING WAS ALL SO WEIRD, HOLLY. SOMETIMES I WAKE UP AND I'M NOT SURE IF ALL THIS IS A DREAM--OR IF *THAT* WAS. AND IT'S SCARY.
SCARY, SURE. MAYBE.
BUT THINK OF IT ANOTHER WAY--YOU'RE LEADING AN INTERESTING LIFE...SO HERE'S TO THAT.
HERE'S TO INTERESTING, THEN.

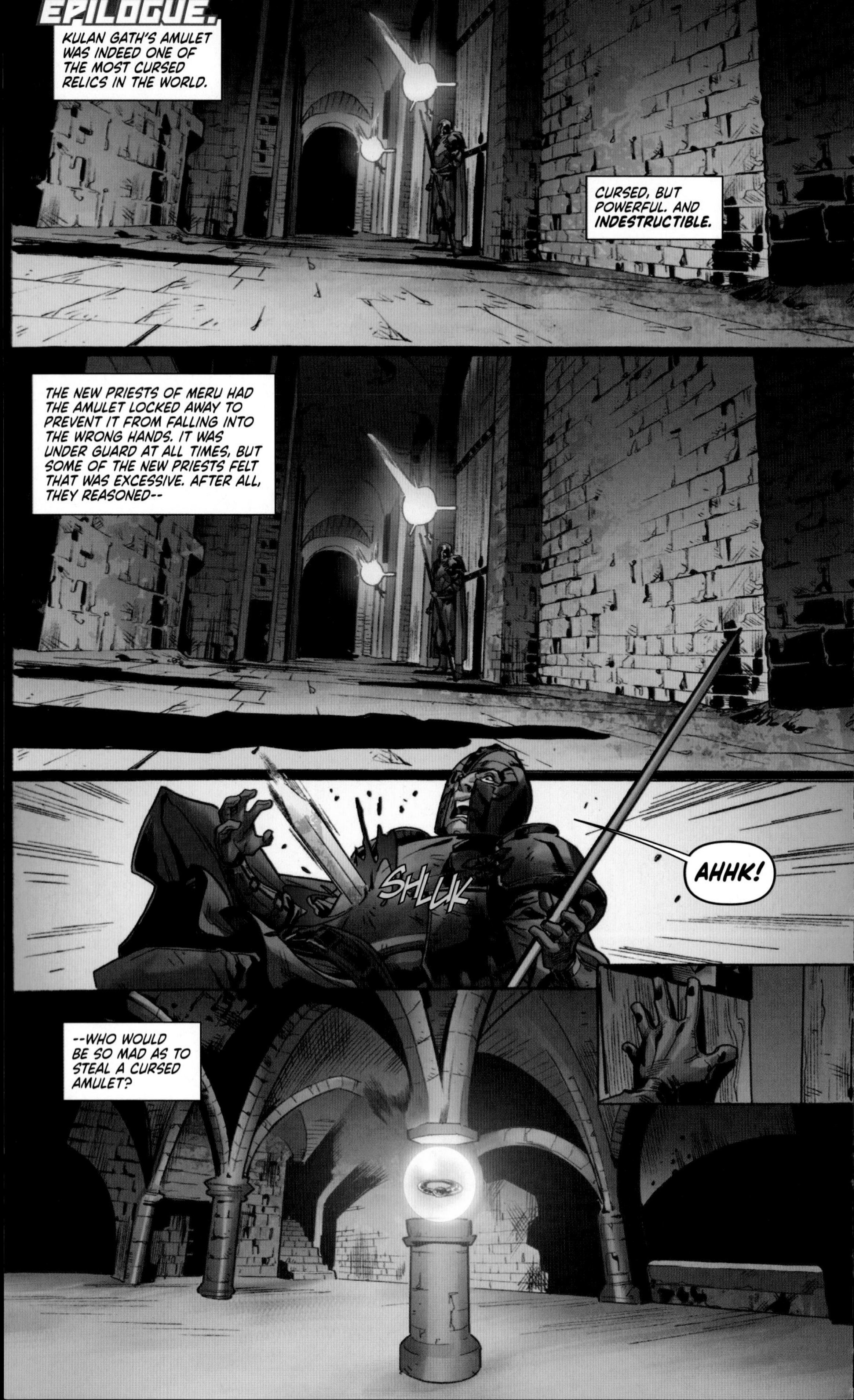
EPILOGUE:
KULAN GATH'S AMULET WAS INDEED ONE OF THE MOST CURSED RELICS IN THE WORLD.
CURSED, BUT POWERFUL. AND INDESTRUCTIBLE.
THE NEW PRIESTS OF MERU HAD THE AMULET LOCKED AWAY TO PREVENT IT FROM FALLING INTO THE WRONG HANDS. IT WAS UNDER GUARD AT ALL TIMES, BUT SOME OF THE NEW PRIESTS FELT THAT WAS EXCESSIVE. AFTER ALL, THEY REASONED--
AHHK!
SHLUK
--WHO WOULD BE SO MAD AS TO STEAL A CURSED AMULET?

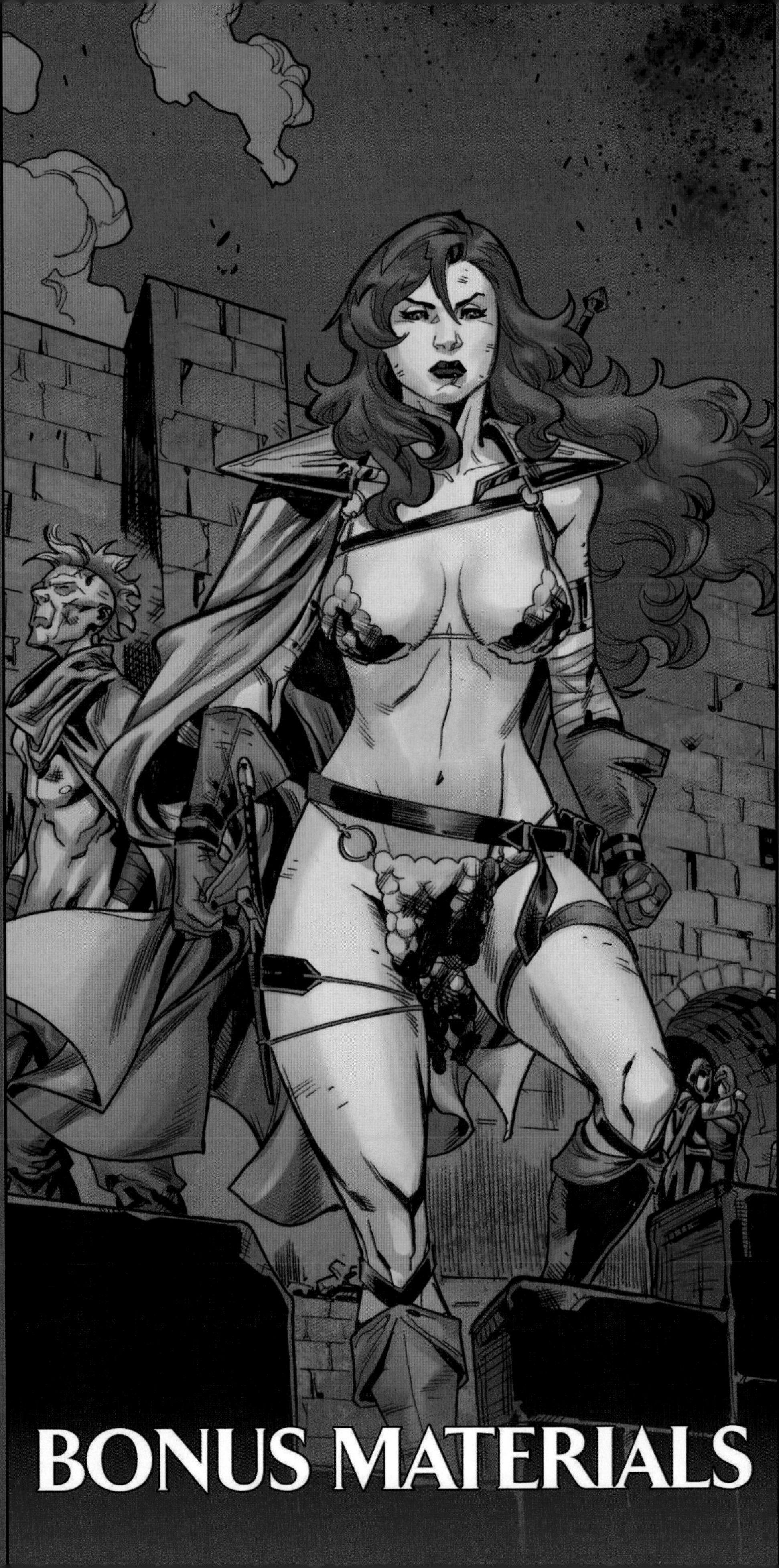

BONUS MATERIALS

COVER GALLERY

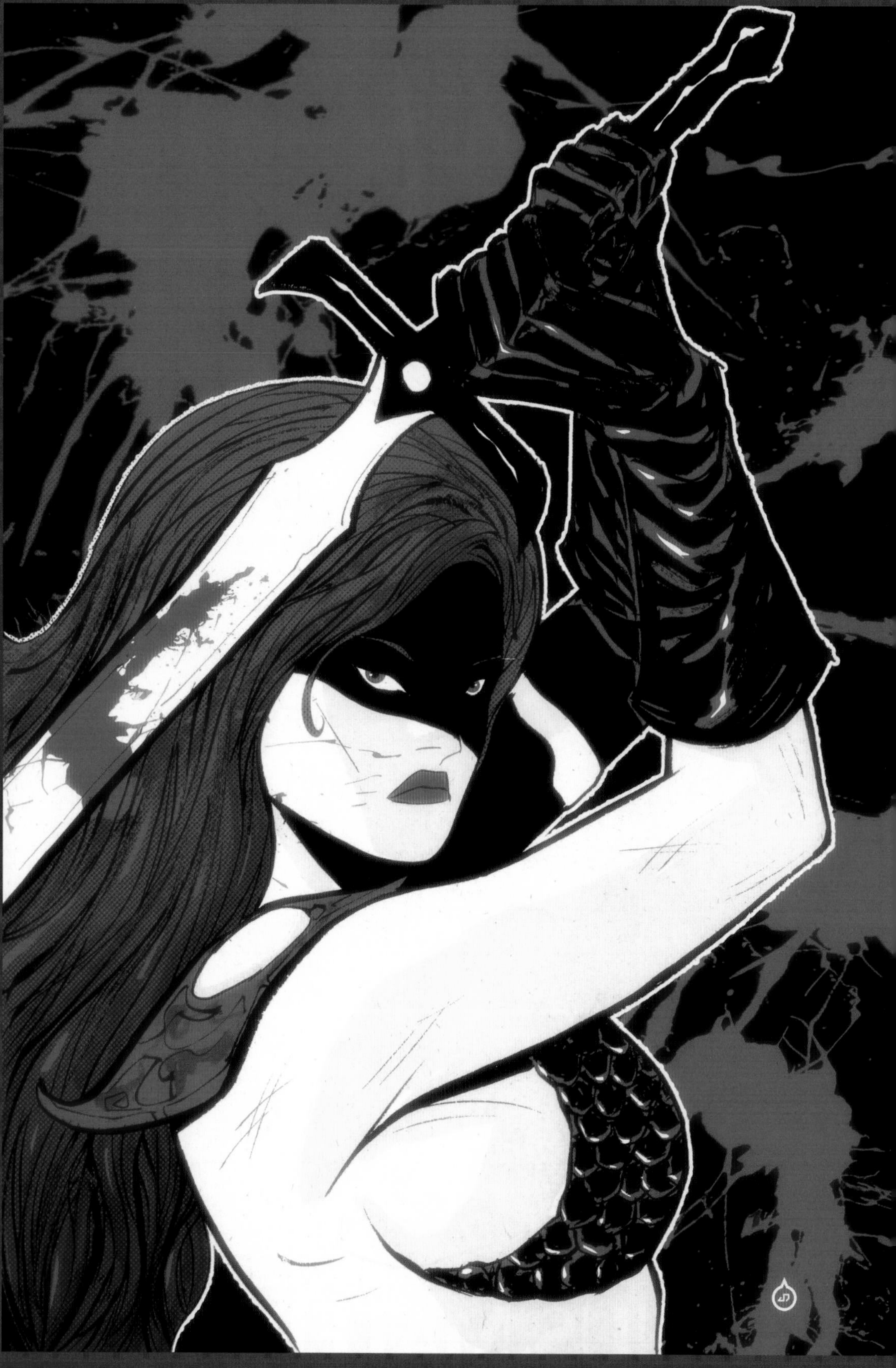

ISSUE #12: COVER ART BY JUAN DOE

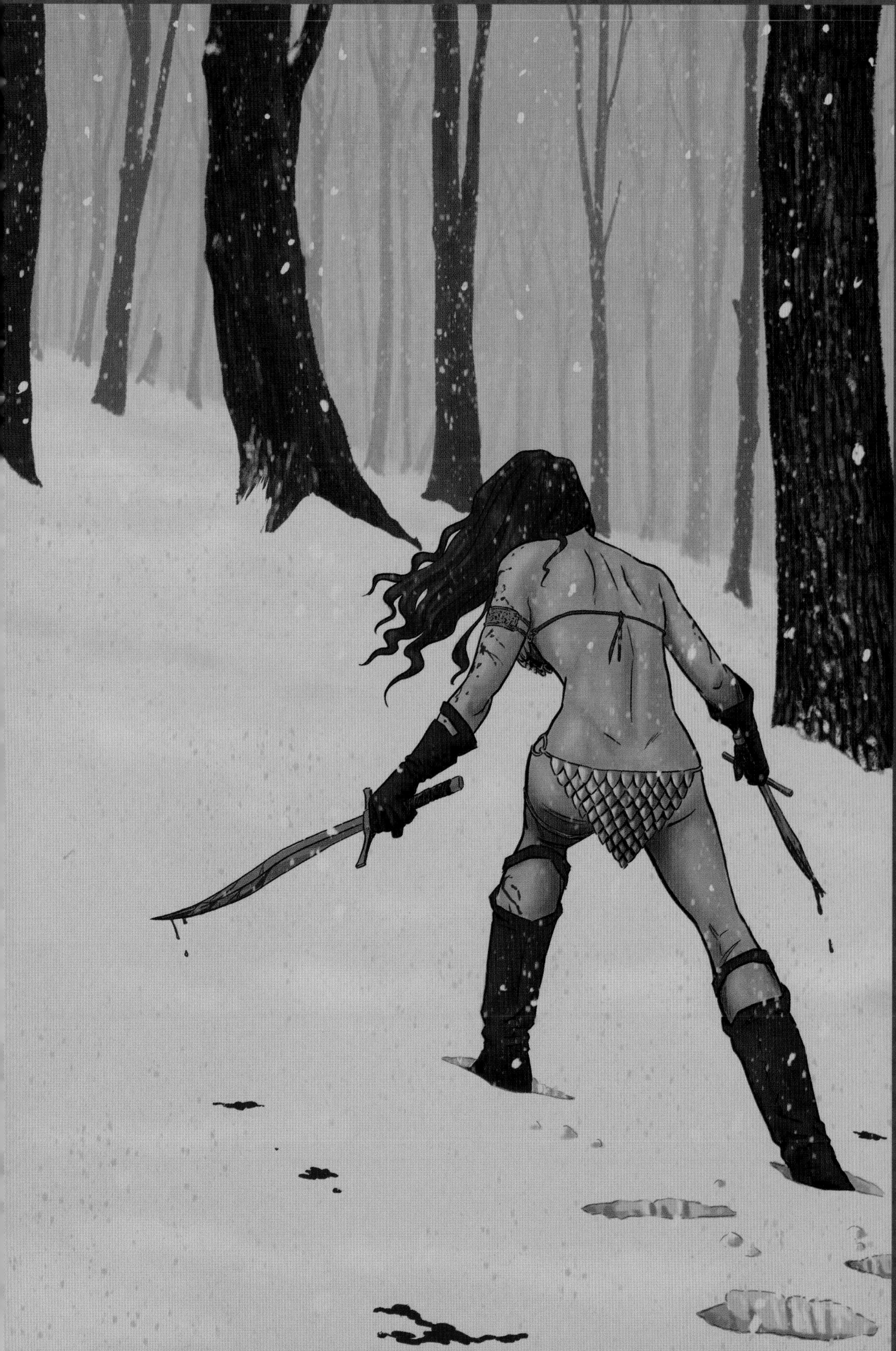

ISSUE #12: COVER ART BY **PIA GUERRA**

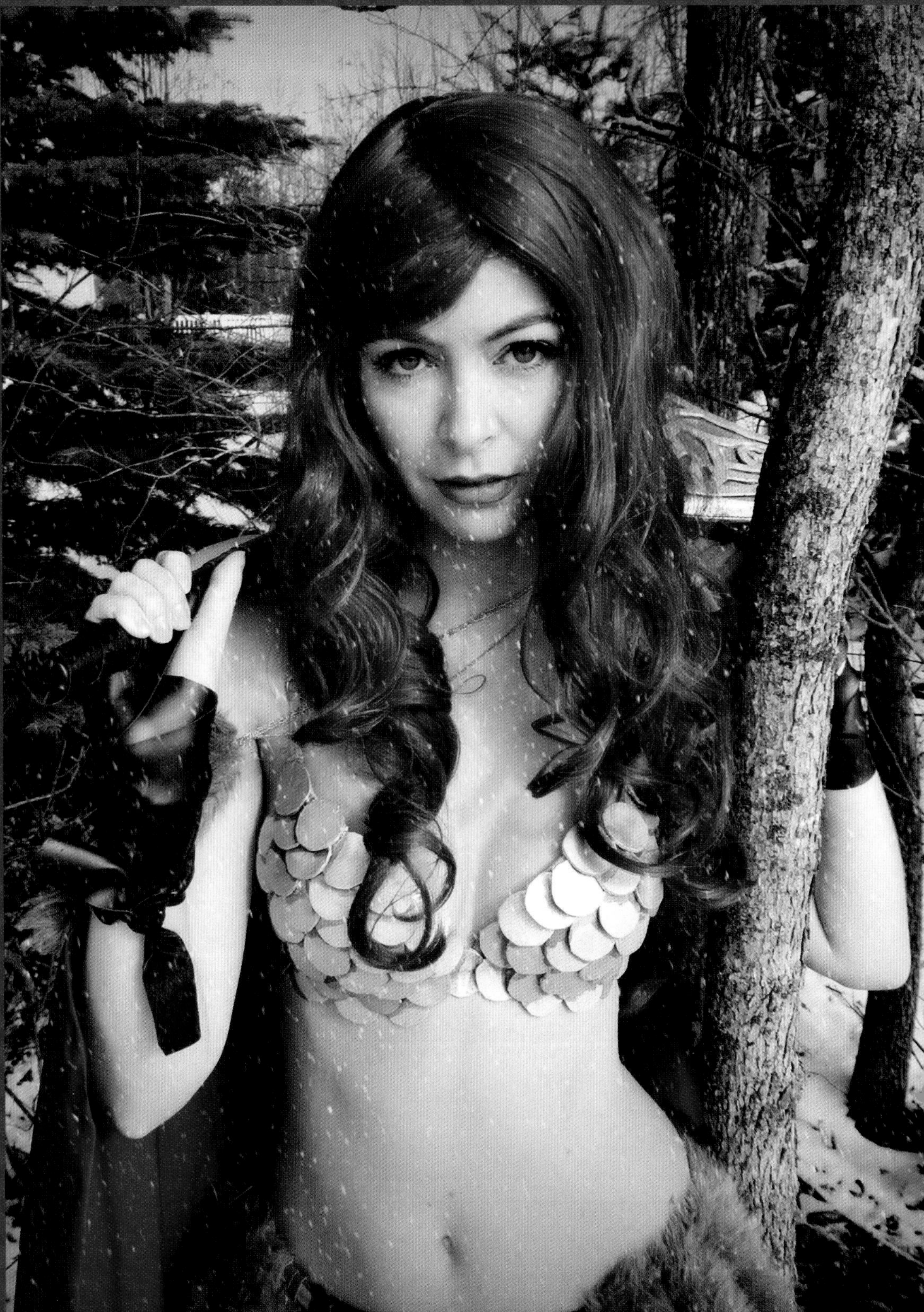

ISSUE #12: COSPLAY VARIANT
MODEL: CASABELLA (TWITTER: @CASABELLACOSPLAY), PHOTOGRAPHER: TL PHOTOGRAPHY

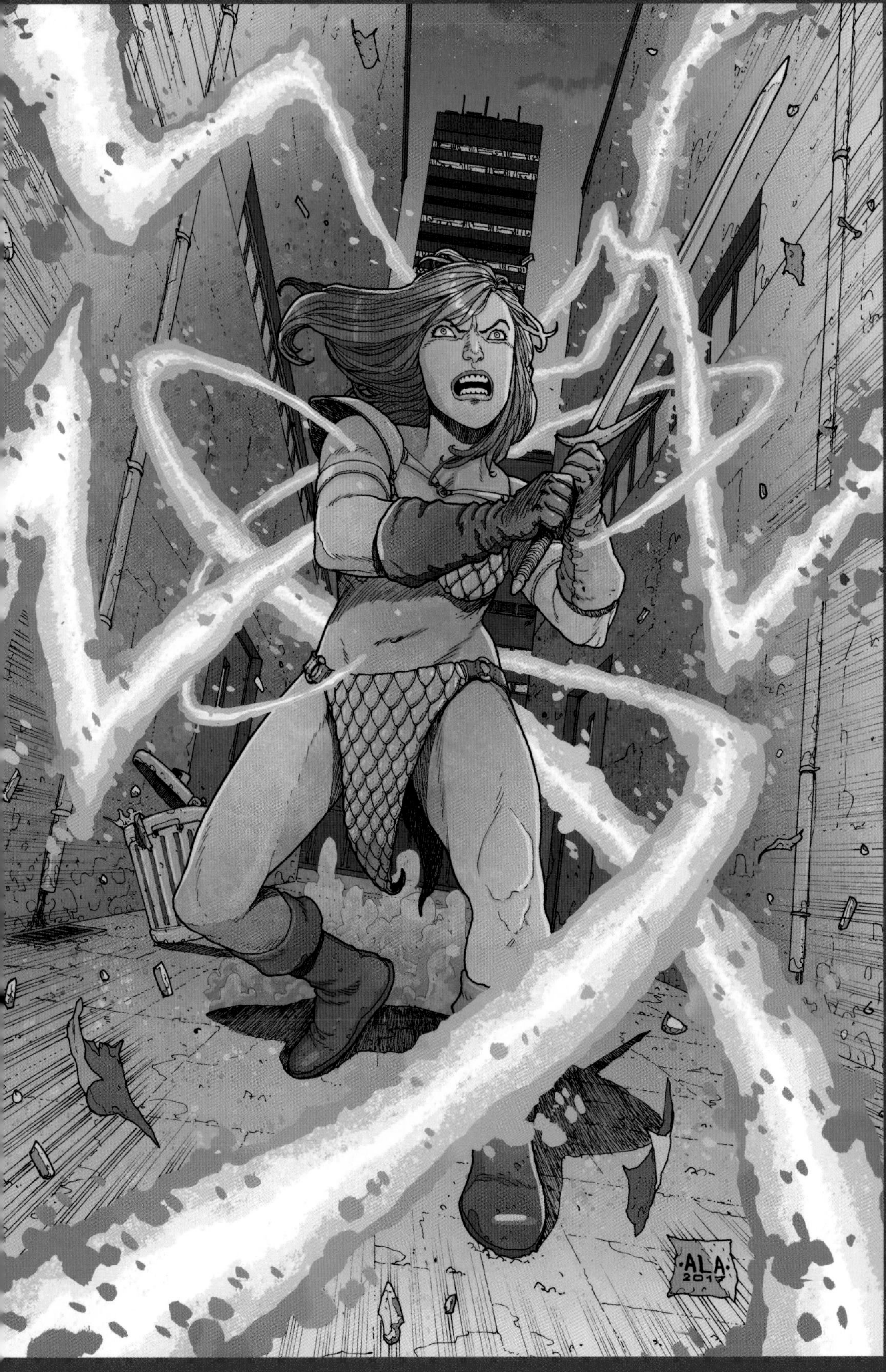
ALA
2017

ISSUE #12: COVER ART BY **ANDRE LIMA ARAUJO**

COVER GALLERY

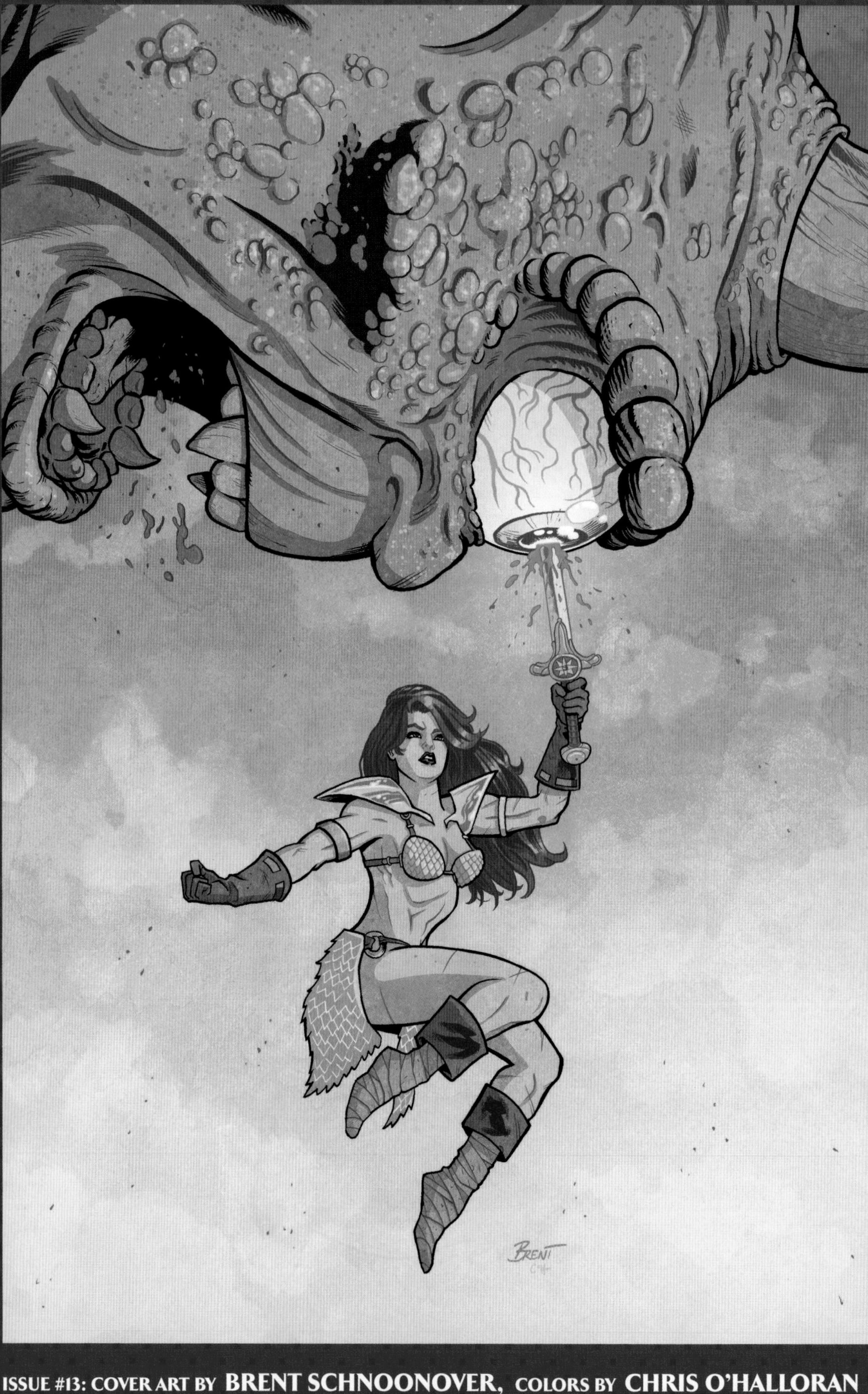
BRENT

ISSUE #13: COVER ART BY **BRENT SCHNOONOVER,** COLORS BY **CHRIS O'HALLORAN**

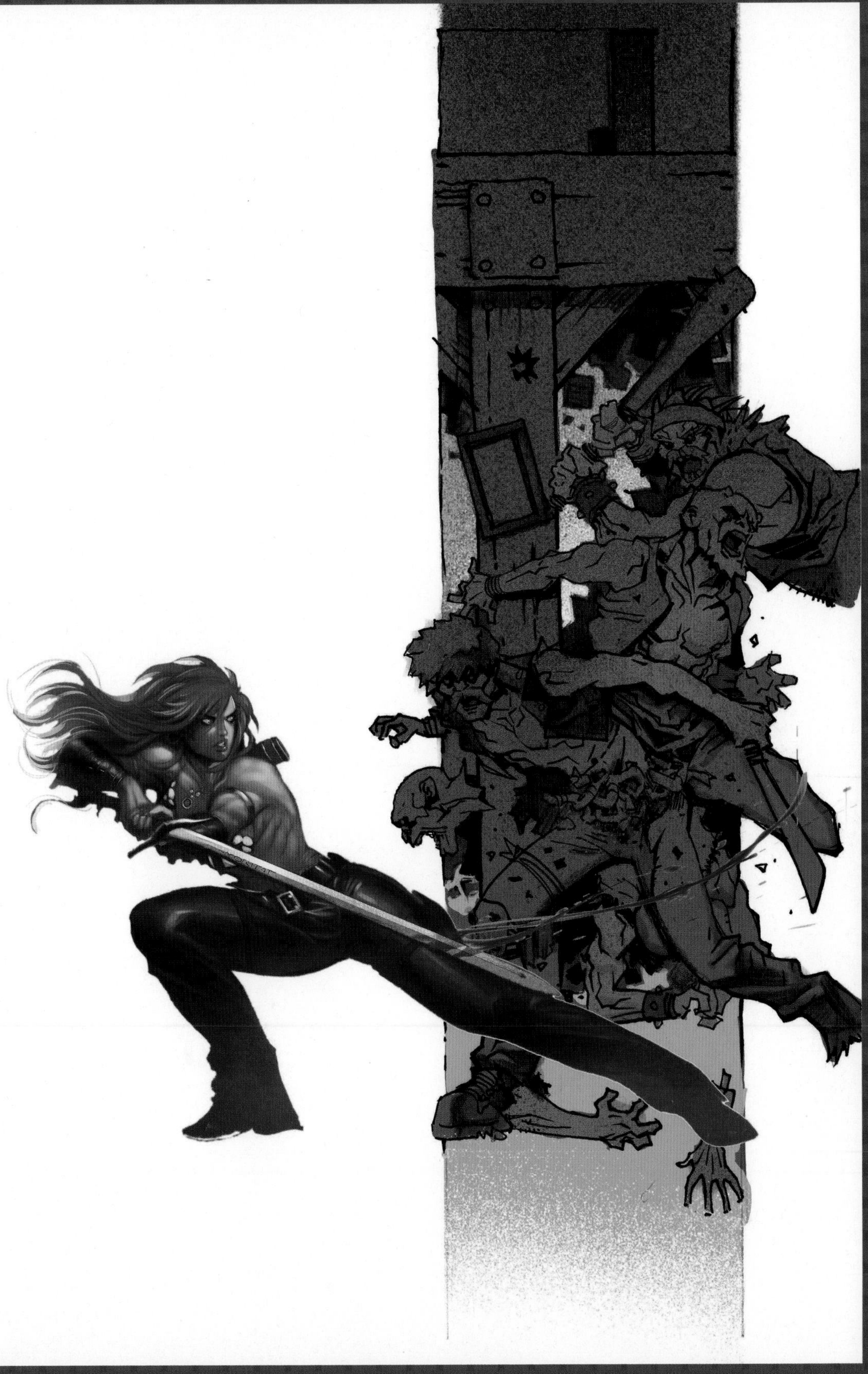

ISSUE #13: COVER ART BY **MORITAT**

COVER GALLERY

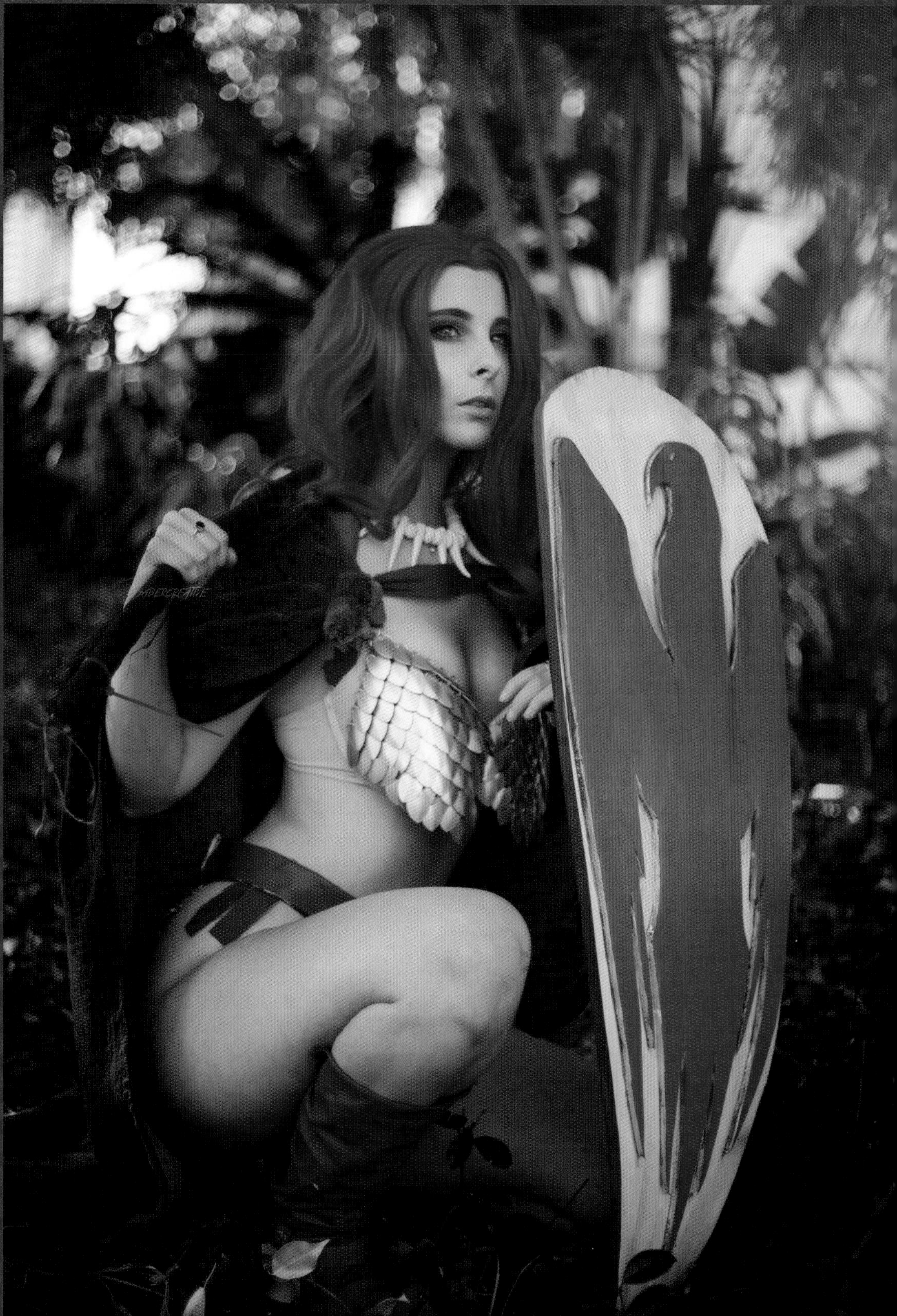

ISSUE #13: COSPLAY VARIANT
MODEL: CATHIE SNELGROVE (INSTAGRAM: @SABERCREATIVE), PHOTOGRAPHER: JACOB SCHULTZ

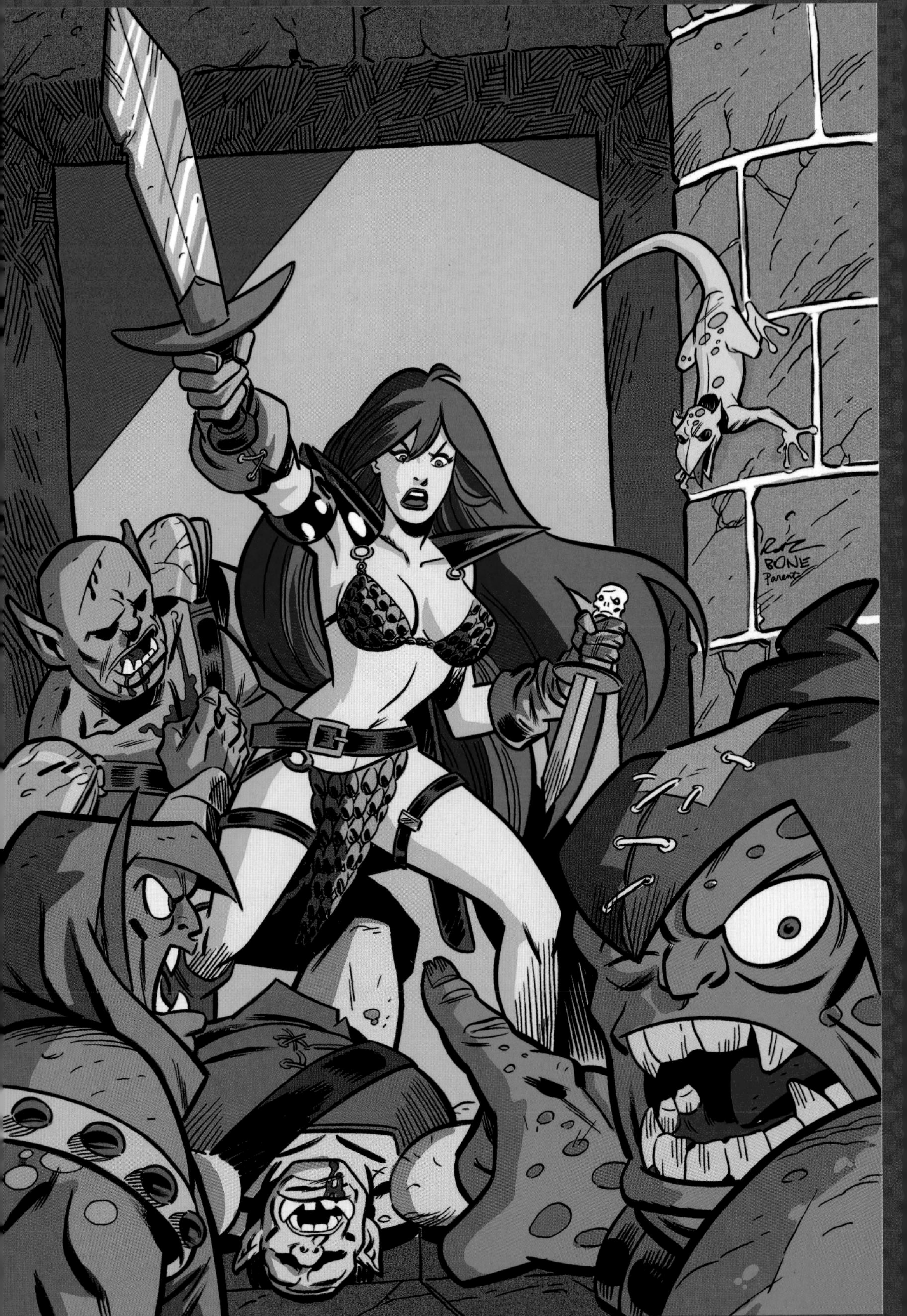

ISSUE #13: COVER ART BY **FERNANDO RUIZ, J. BONE, DAN PARENT**

COVER GALLERY

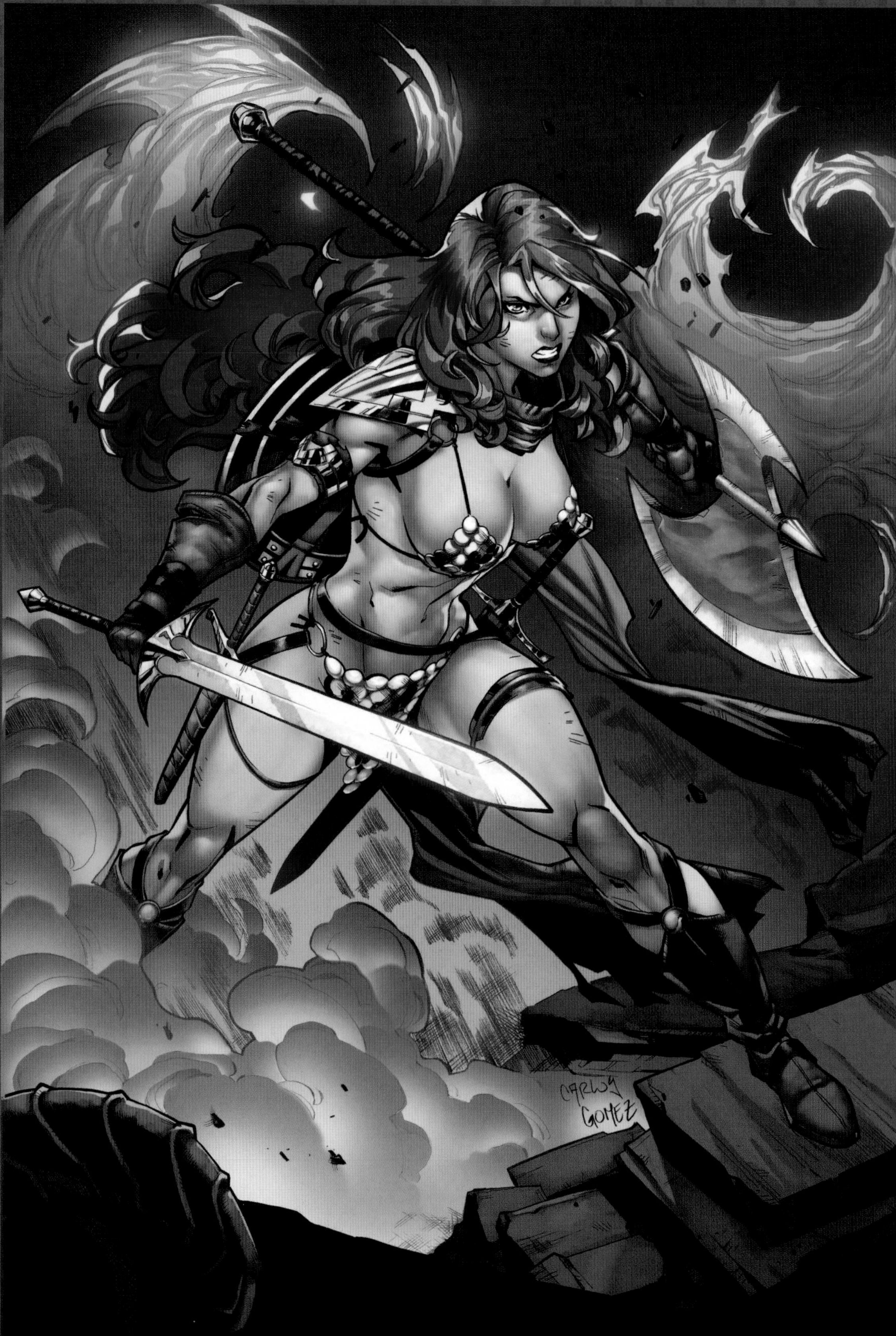
CARLOS
GOMEZ

ISSUE #14: COVER ART BY **CARLOS GOMEZ**

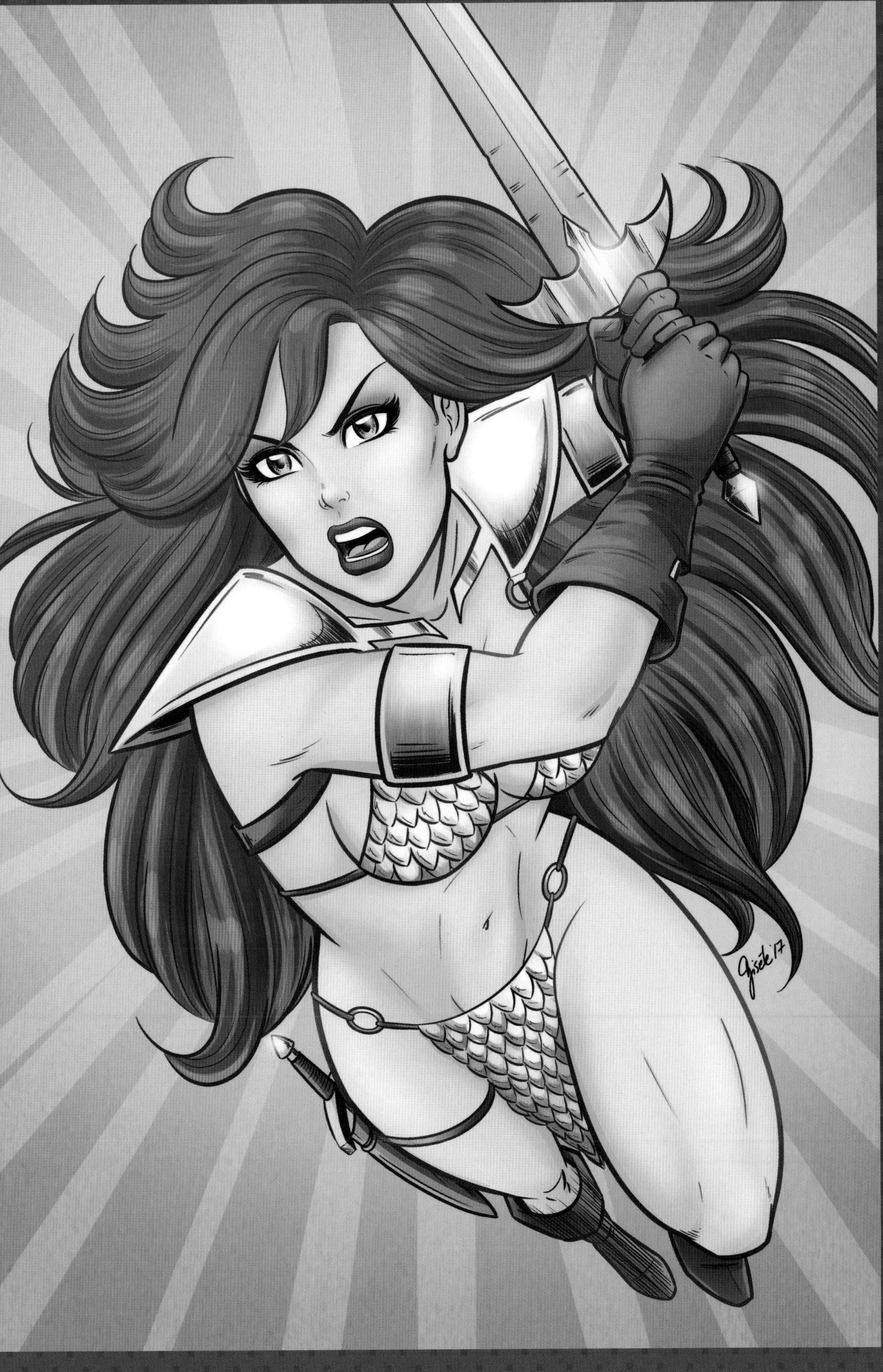

ISSUE #14: COVER ART BY **GISELE LAGACE**

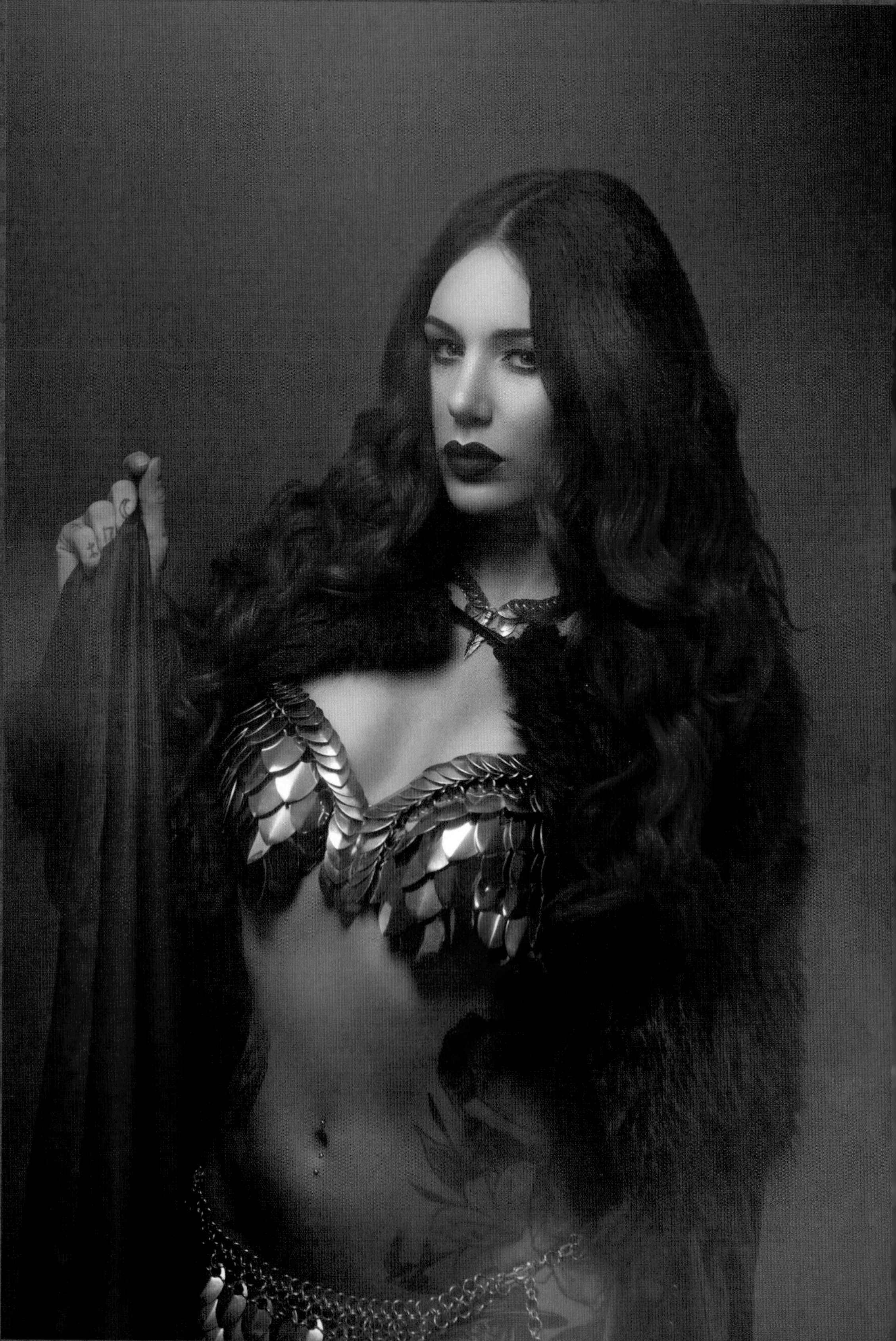

ISSUE #14: COSPLAY VARIANT
MODEL: CERVENA FOX (INSTAGRAM: @CERVENAFOX), PHOTOGRAPHER: KEELY WEIS

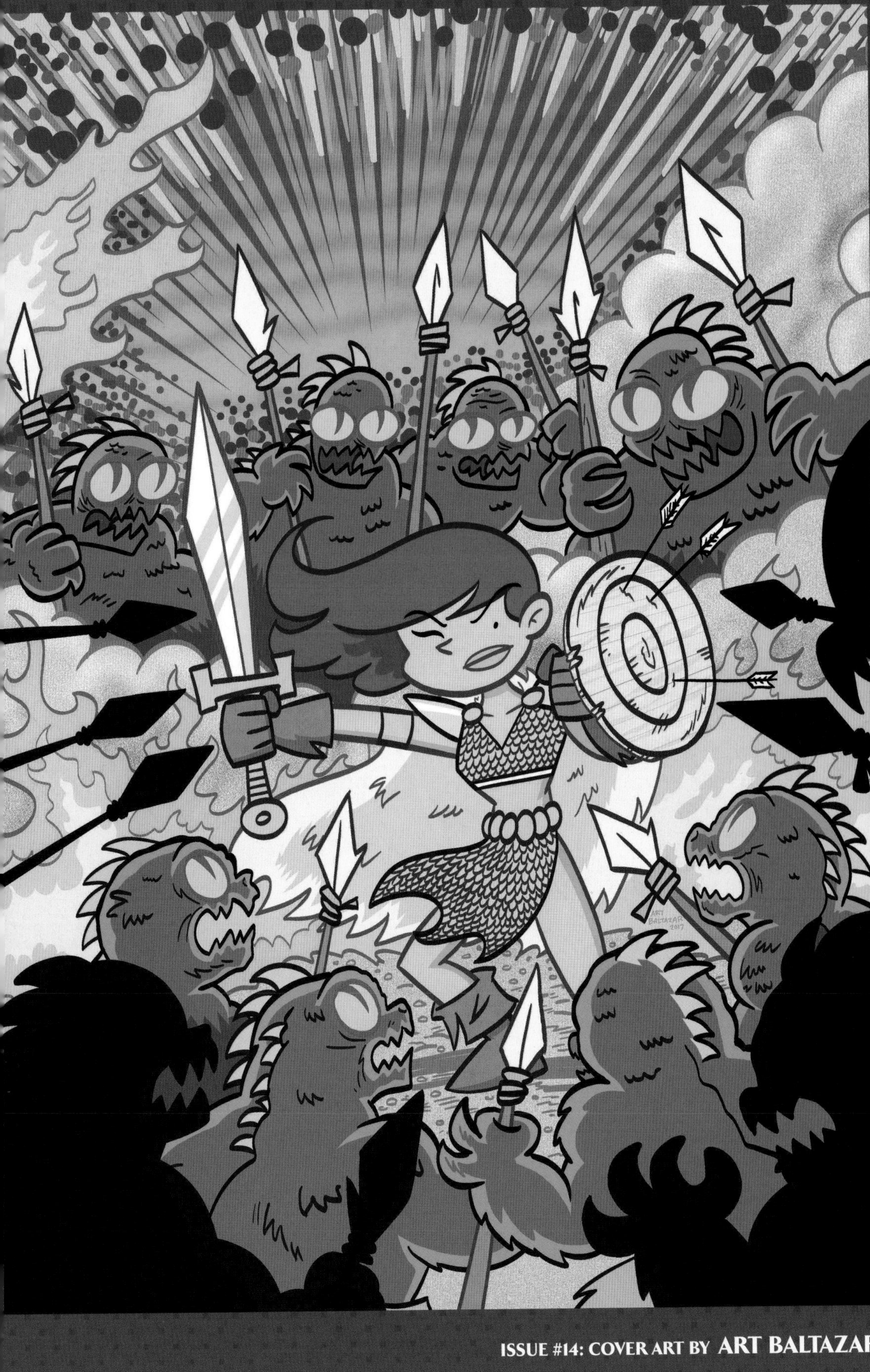

ISSUE #14: COVER ART BY **ART BALTAZAR**

COVER GALLERY

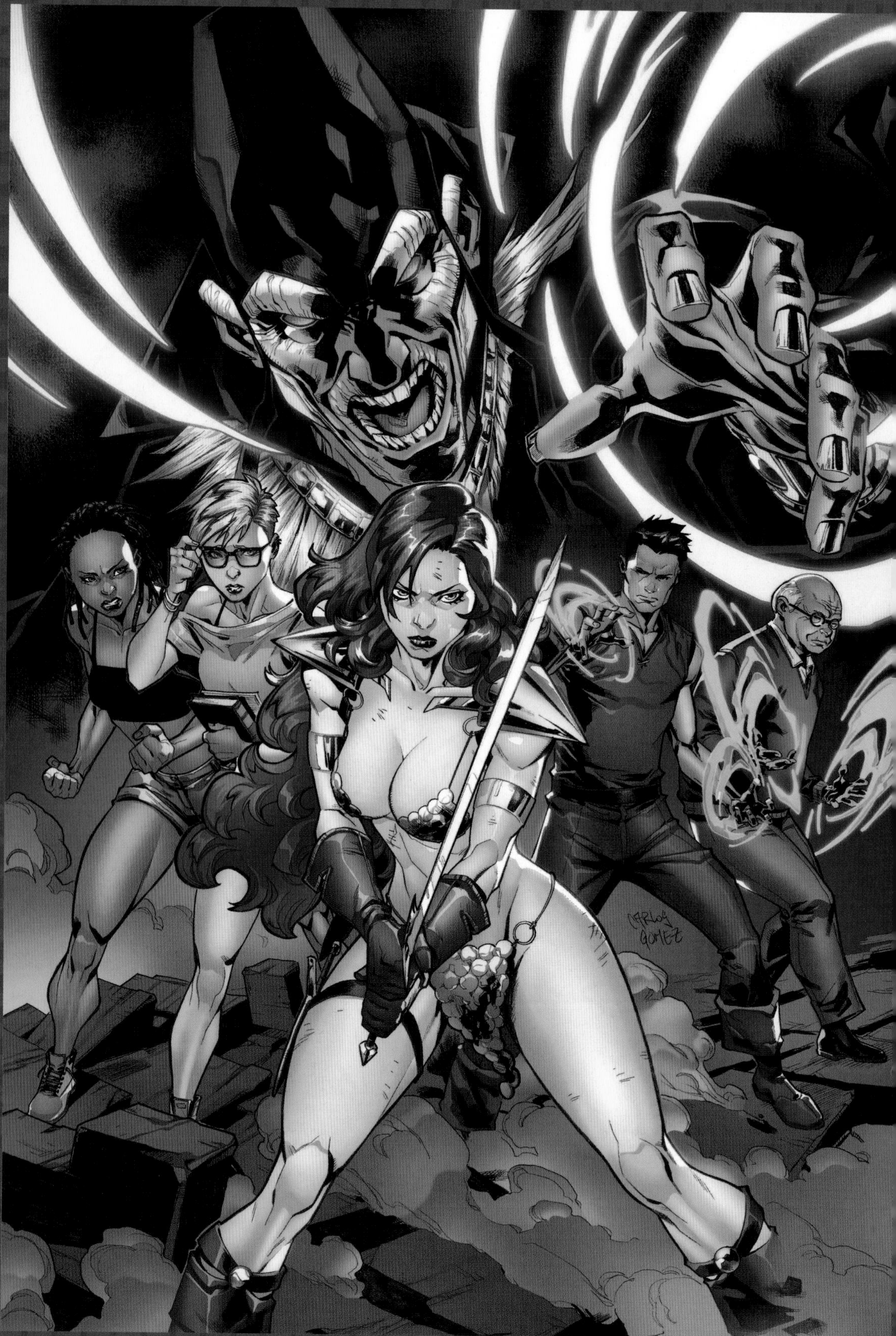
CARLOS
GOMEZ

ISSUE #15: COVER ART BY **CARLOS GOMEZ**

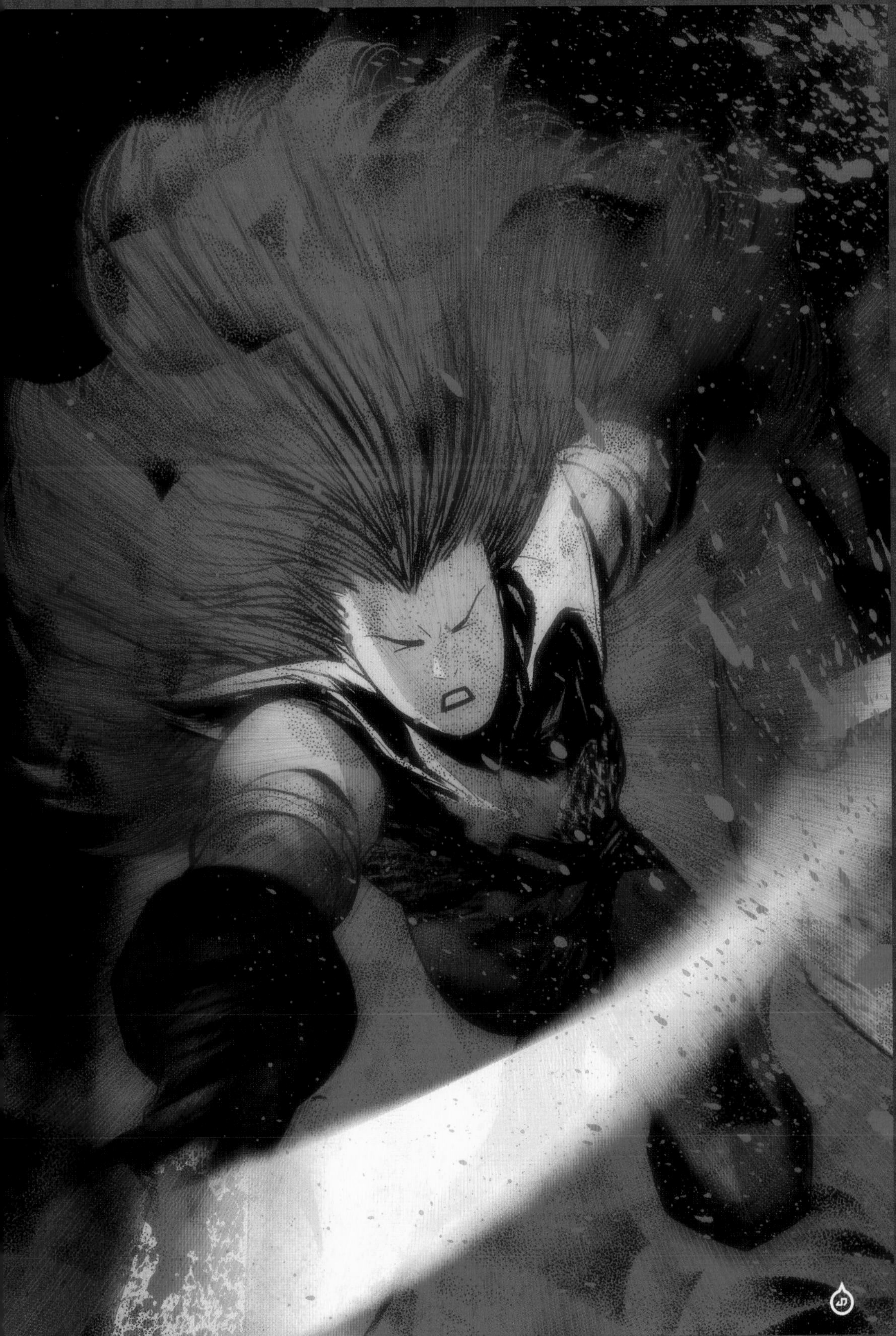

ISSUE #15: COVER ART BY JUAN DOE

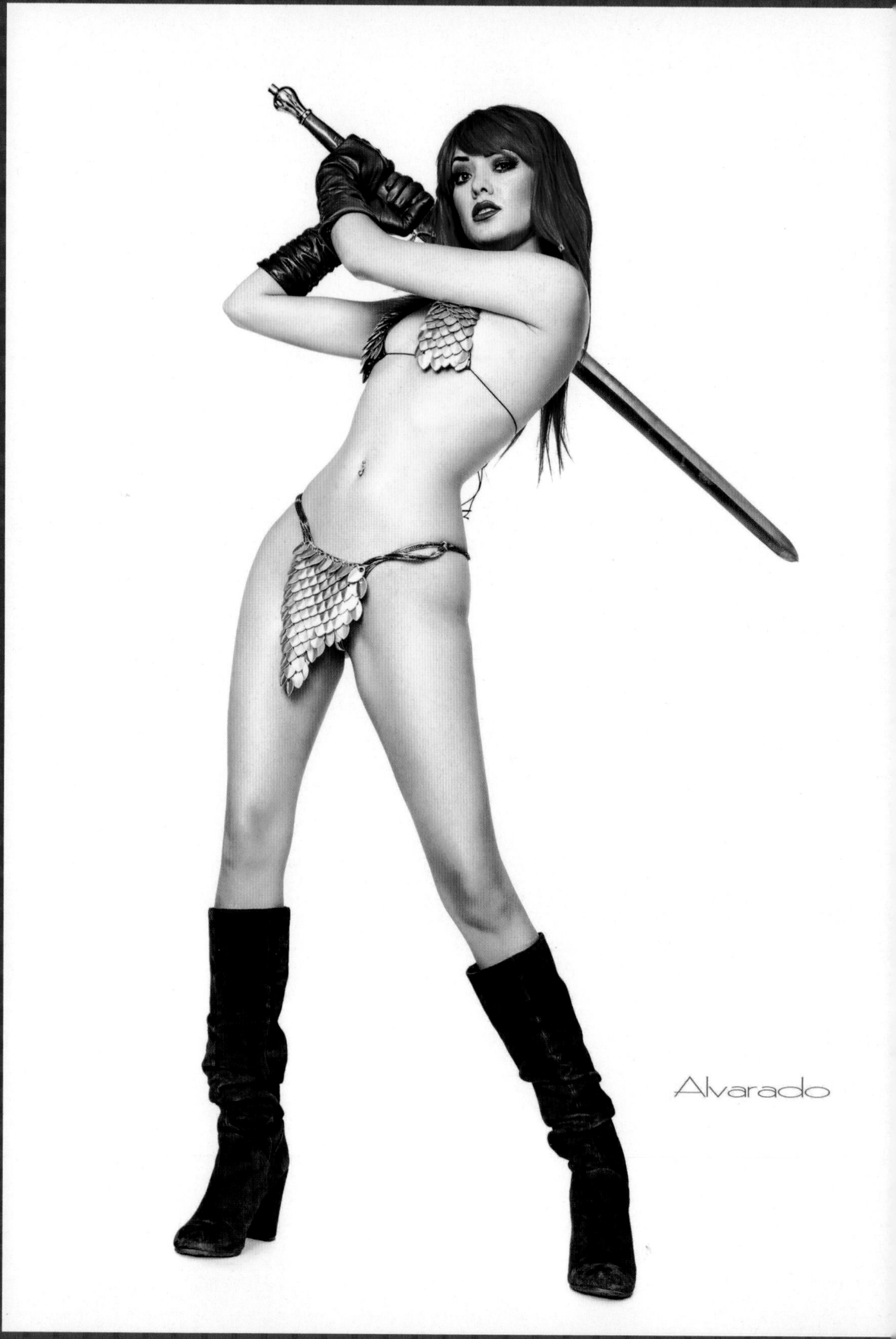
Alvarado

ISSUE #15: COSPLAY VARIANT
MODEL: JOANIE BROSAS (TWITTER: @JOANIEBROSAS), PHOTOGRAPHER: ALVARADO (INSTAGRAM: @ALVARADO)

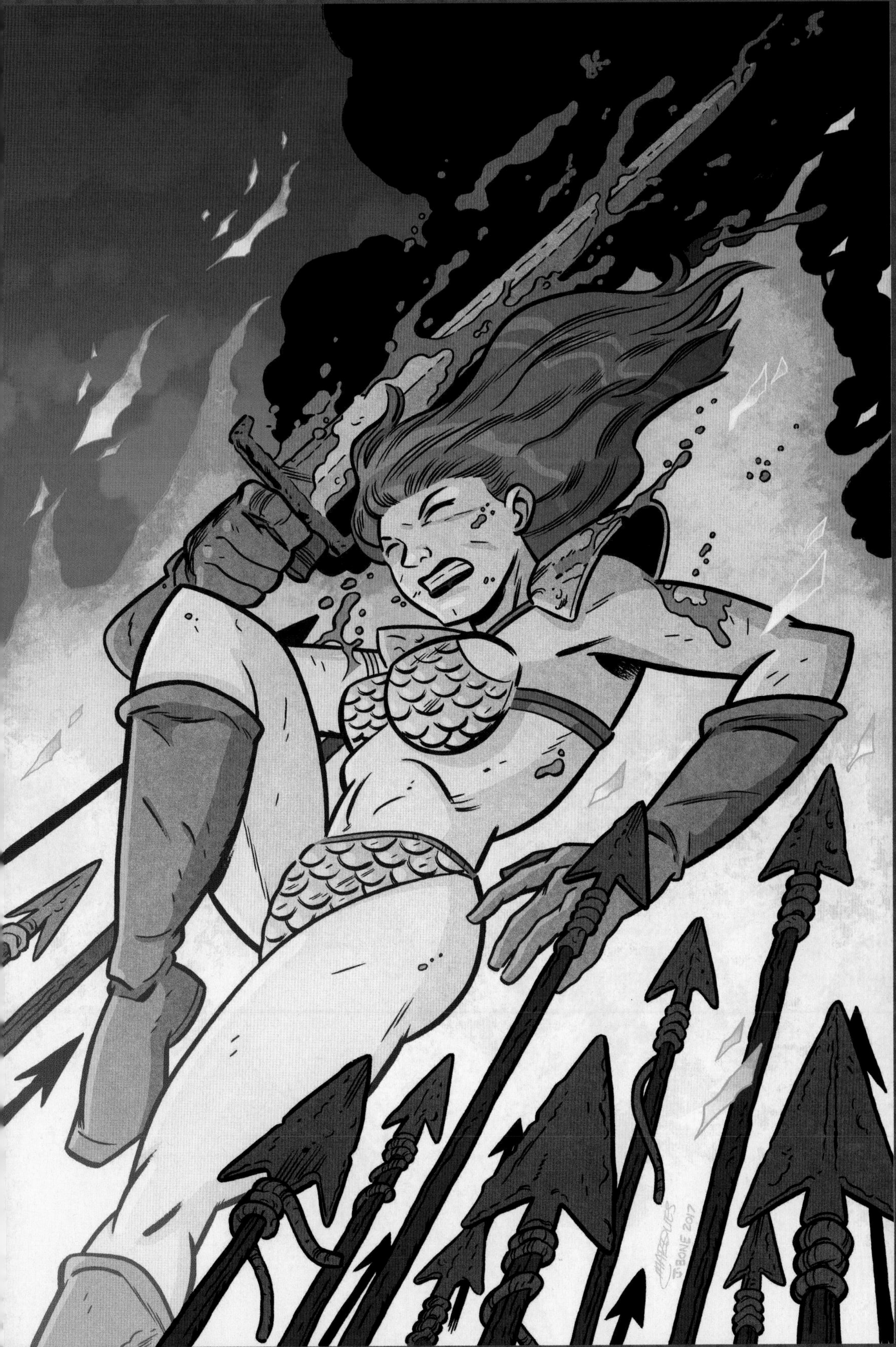
MARQUES
J. BONE 2017

ISSUE #15: COVER ART BY **ANTHONY MARQUES,** COLORS BY **J. BONE**

COVER GALLERY

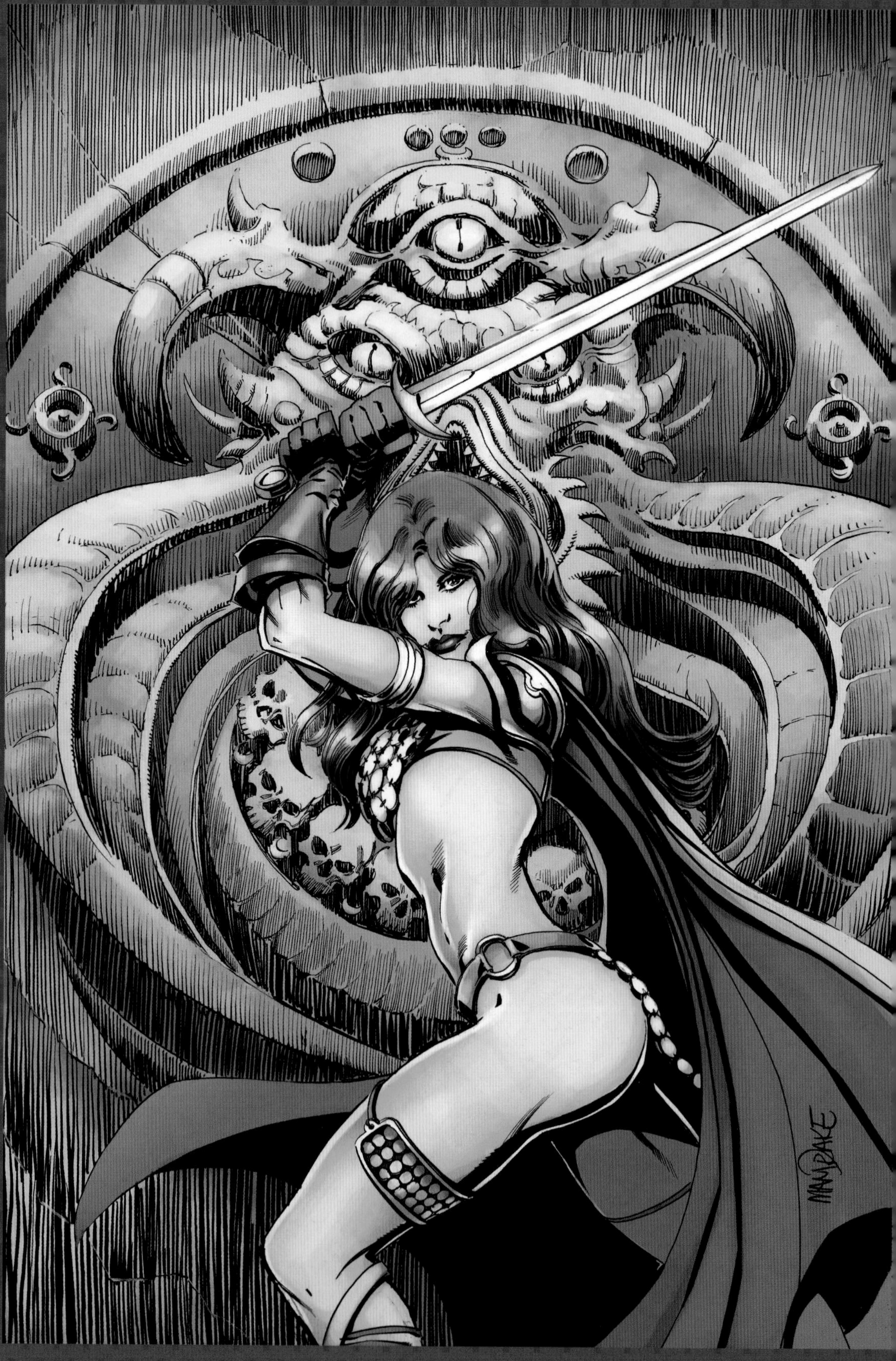

ISSUE #16: COVER ART BY **TOM MANDRAKE**

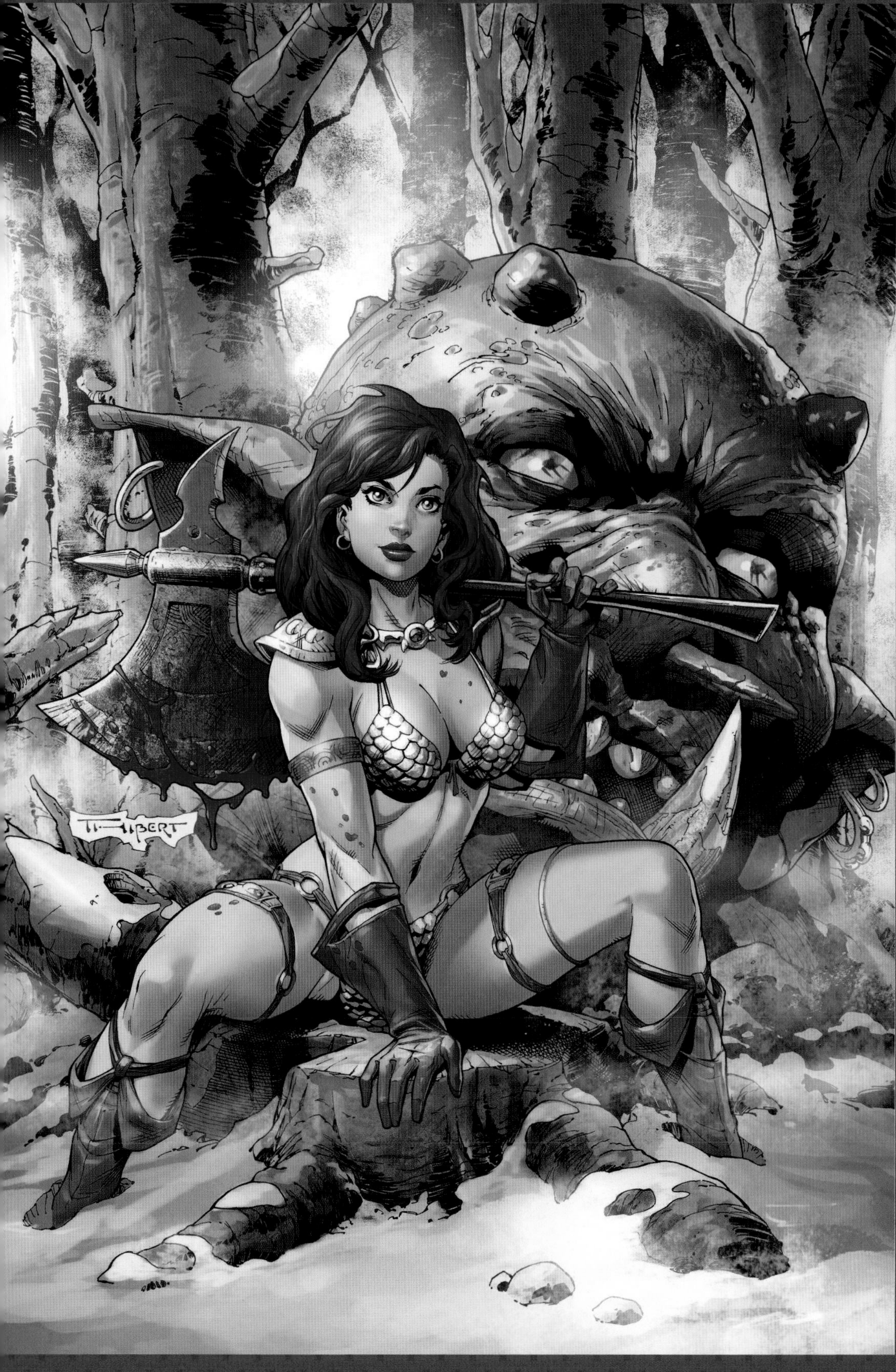

ISSUE #16: COVER ART BY **ART THILBERT**

COVER GALLERY

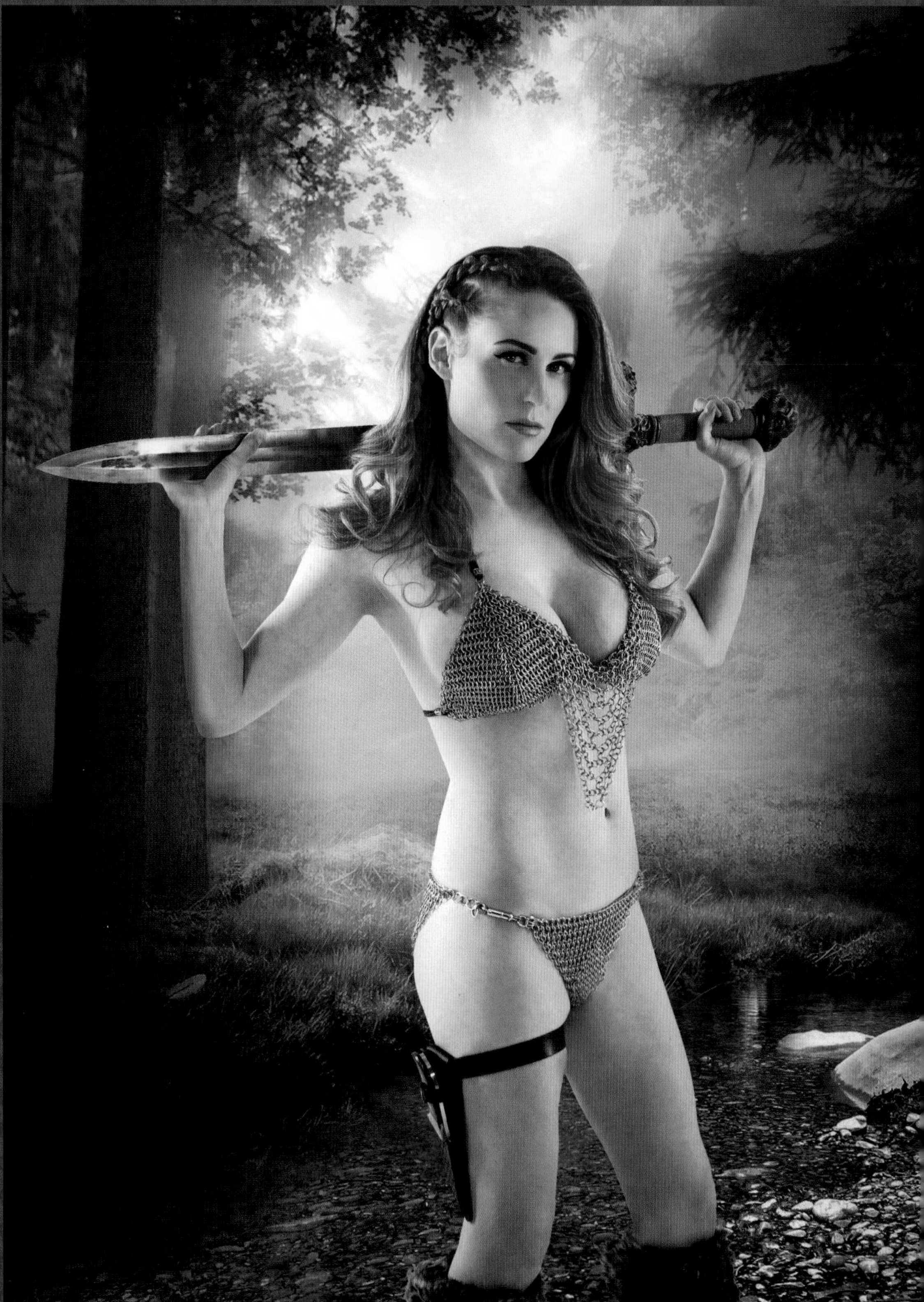

ISSUE #16: COSPLAY VARIANT
MODEL: SHANNON KINGSTON (INSTAGRAM: @THEREALREDSONJA),
PHOTOGRAPHER: GUY IORIO (INSTAGRAM: @GUYIORIO)

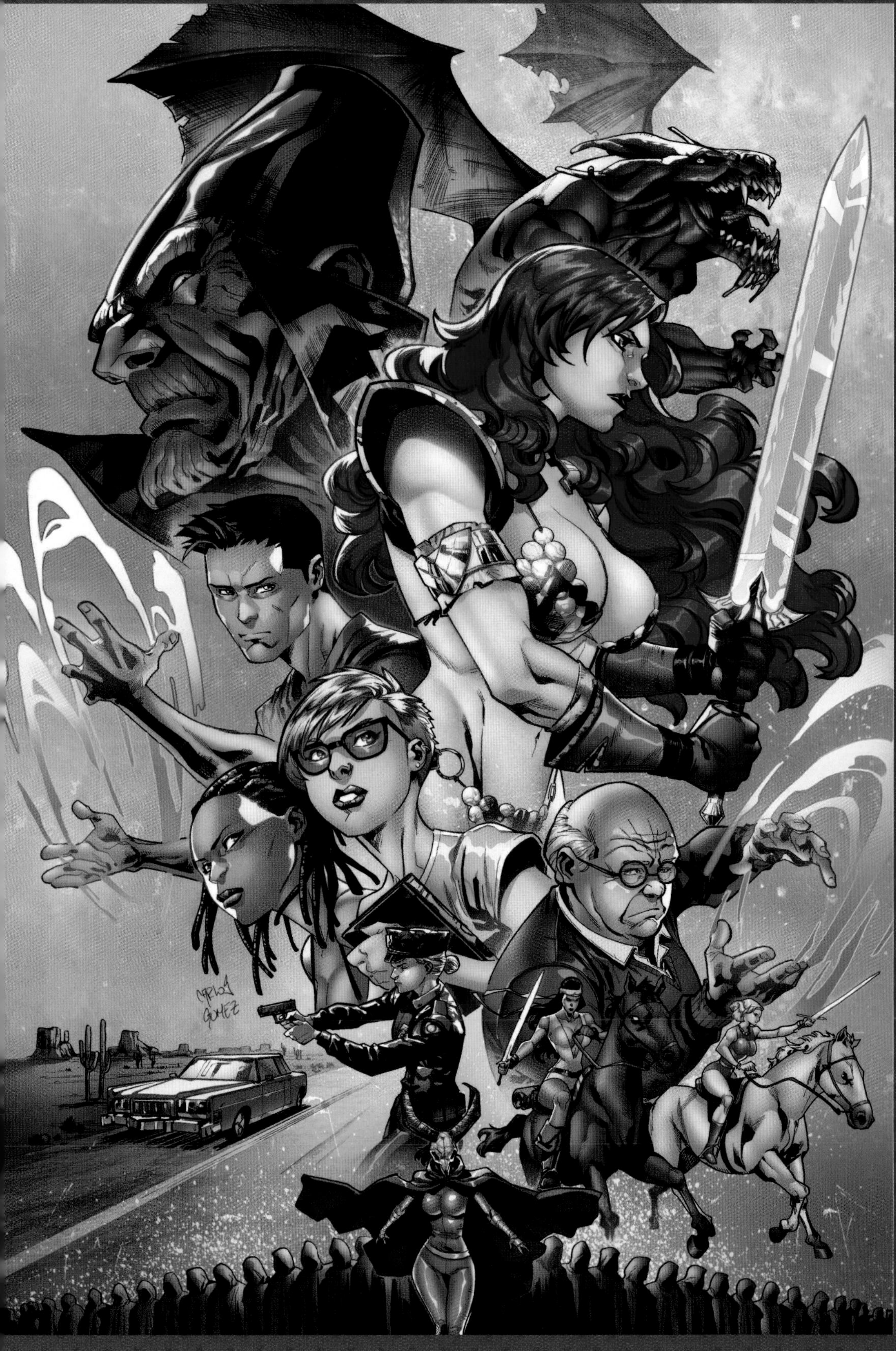

CARLOS GOMEZ

ISSUE #16: COVER ART BY **CARLOS GOMEZ**

RED SONJA FAN ARTIST SPOTLIGHT

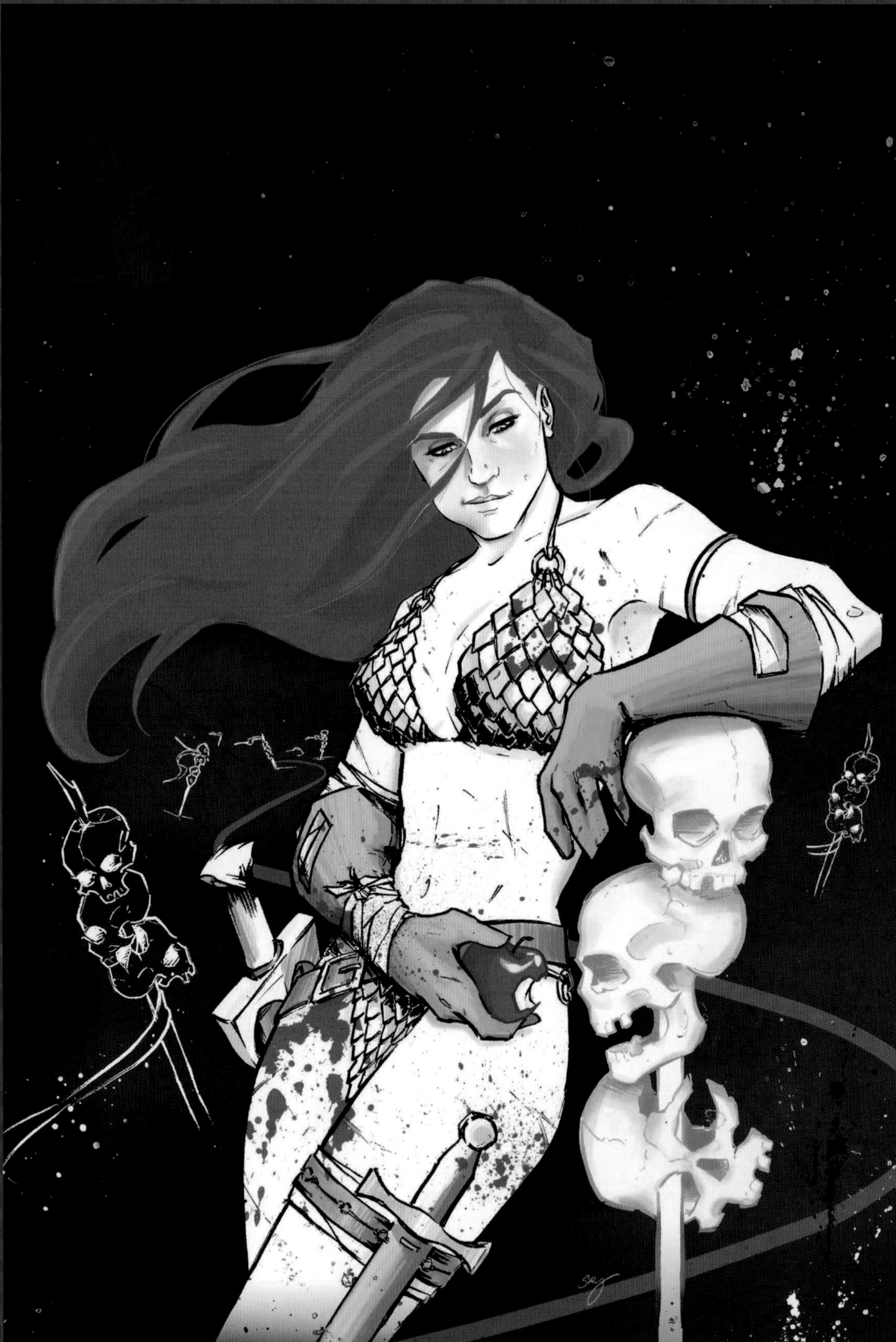

ART BY **SKYLAR PATRIDGE**

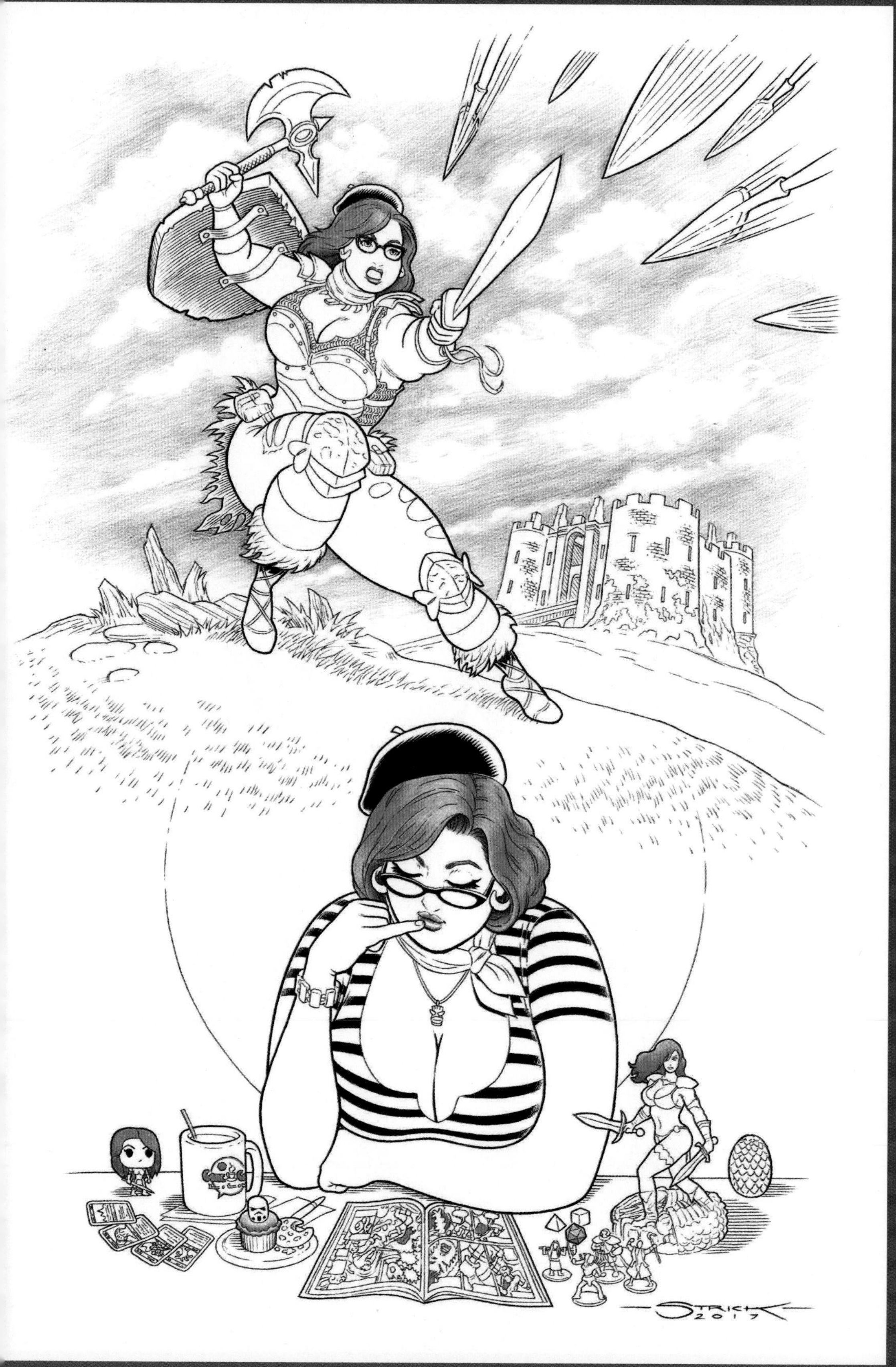
STRICK
2017

ART BY **DANIEL STRICKLAND**

RED SONJA FAN ARTIST SPOTLIGHT

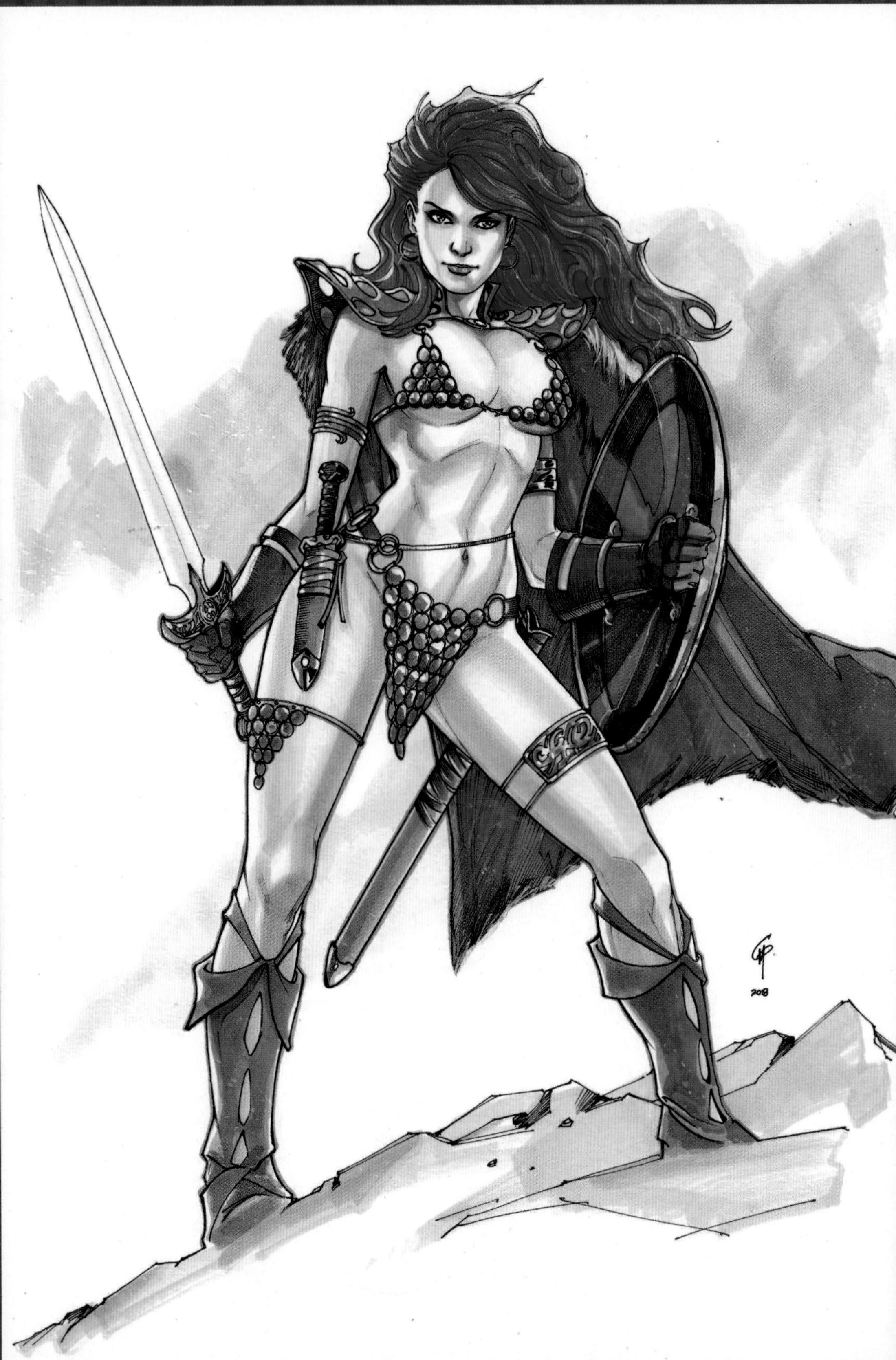

ART BY **GARRIE GASTONNY**

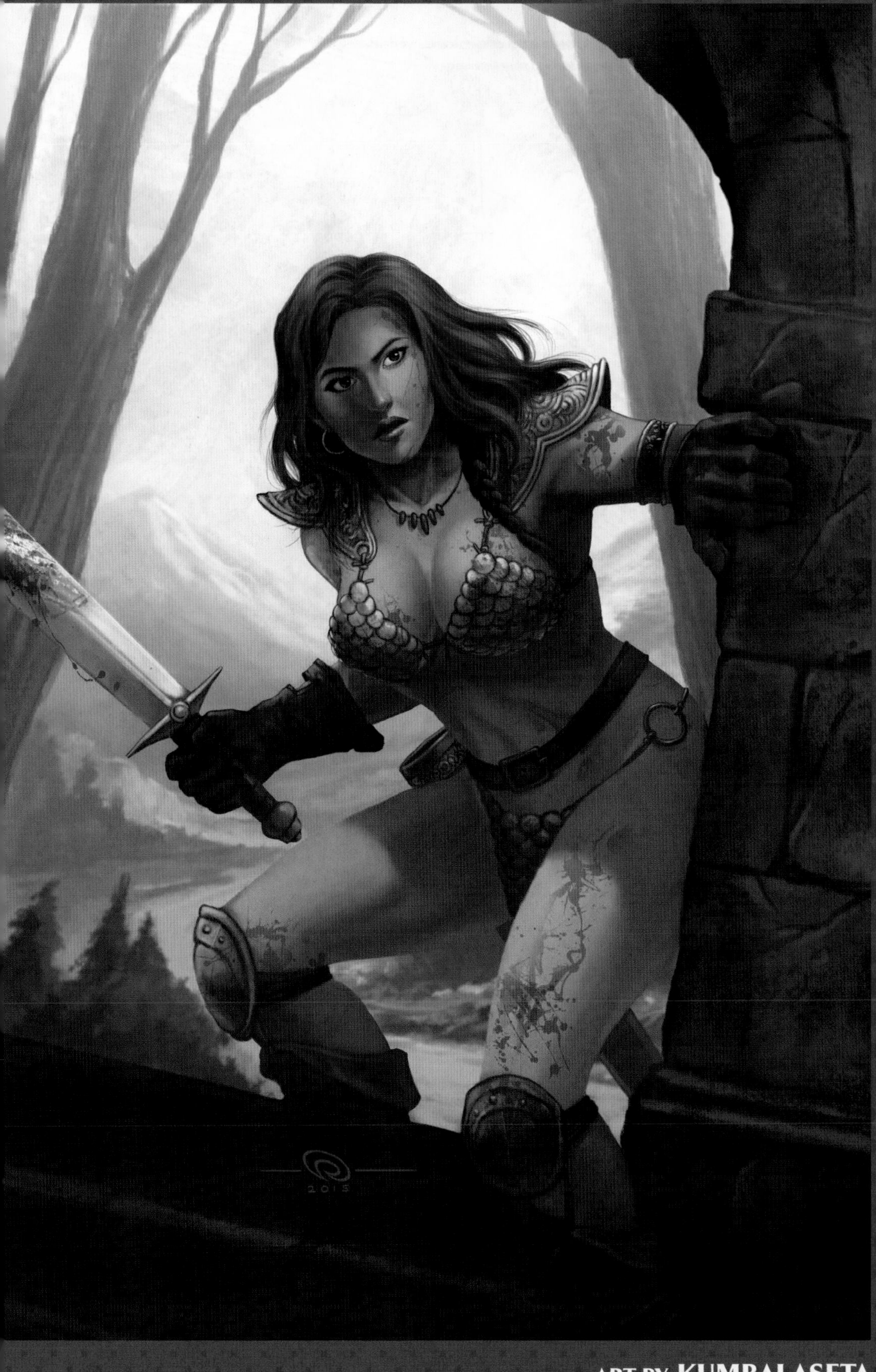
2015

ART BY **KUMBALASETA**

RED SONJA FAN ARTIST SPOTLIGHT

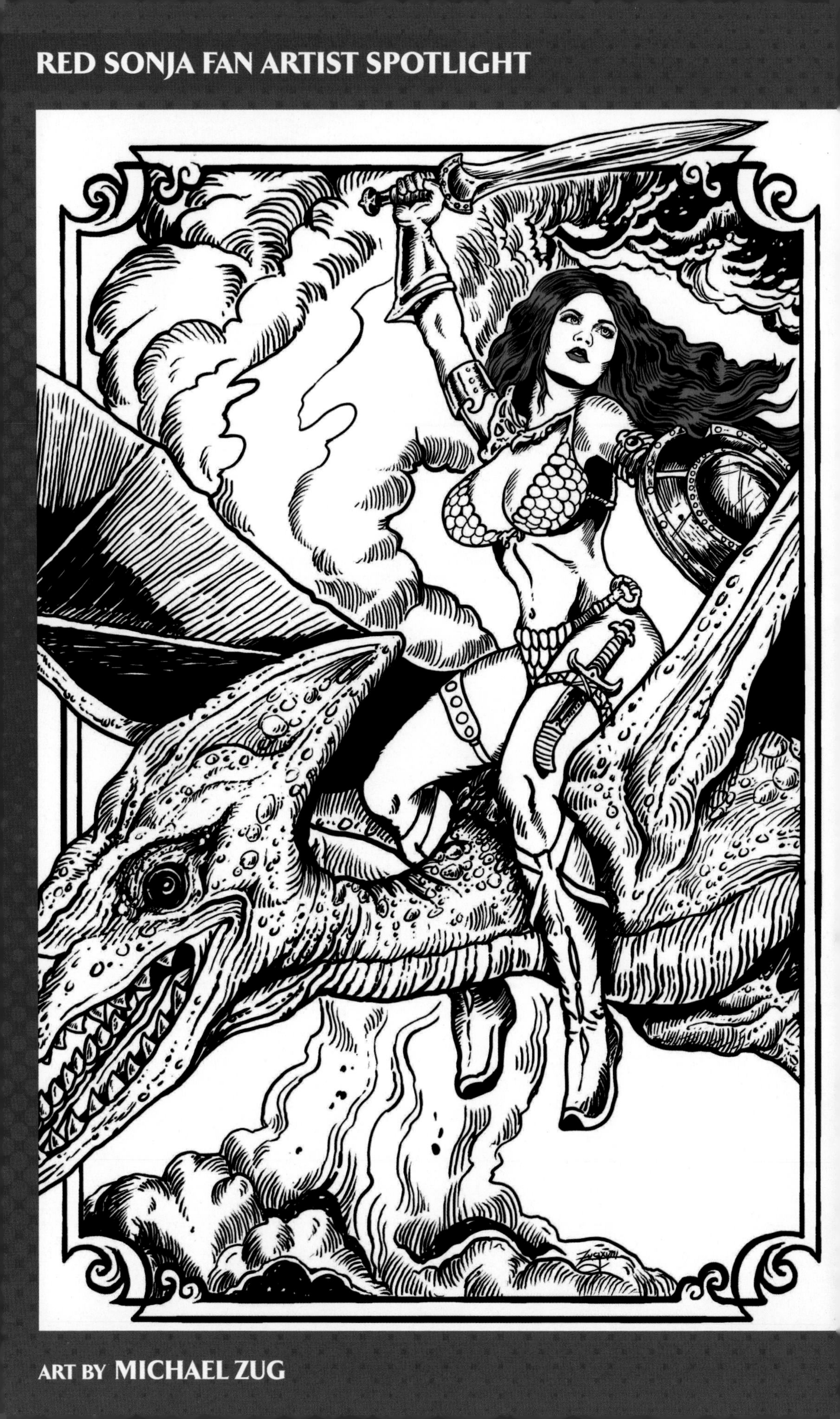

ART BY **MICHAEL ZUG**

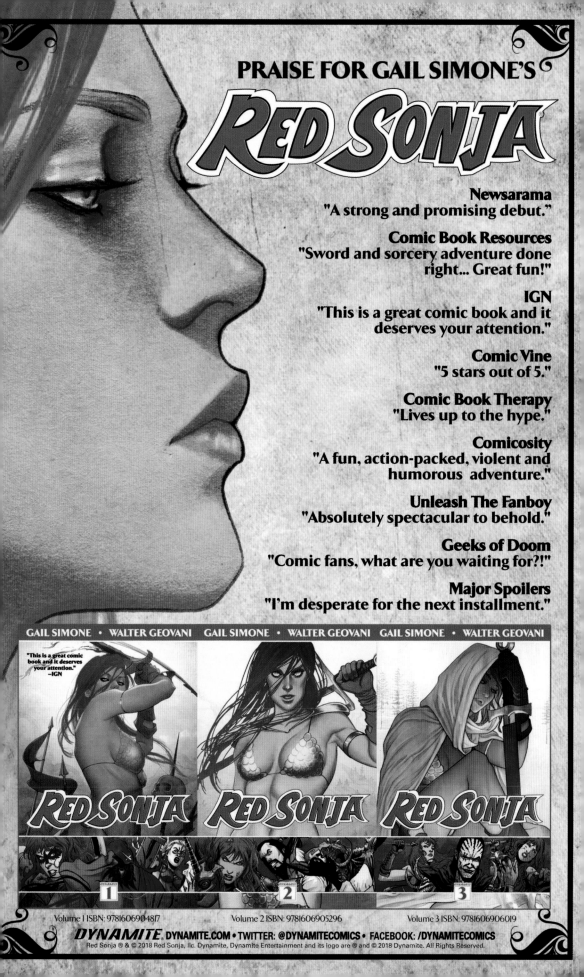

PRAISE FOR GAIL SIMONE'S
RED SONJA

Newsarama
"A strong and promising debut."

Comic Book Resources
"Sword and sorcery adventure done right... Great fun!"

IGN
"This is a great comic book and it deserves your attention."

Comic Vine
"5 stars out of 5."

Comic Book Therapy
"Lives up to the hype."

Comicosity
"A fun, action-packed, violent and humorous adventure."

Unleash The Fanboy
"Absolutely spectacular to behold."

Geeks of Doom
"Comic fans, what are you waiting for?!"

Major Spoilers
"I'm desperate for the next installment."

GAIL SIMONE • WALTER GEOVANI   GAIL SIMONE • WALTER GEOVANI   GAIL SIMONE • WALTER GEOVANI

"This is a great comic book and it deserves your attention." —IGN

1   **2**   **3**

Volume 1 ISBN: 9781606904817   Volume 2 ISBN: 9781606905296   Volume 3 ISBN: 9781606906019

DYNAMITE DYNAMITE.COM • TWITTER: @DYNAMITECOMICS • FACEBOOK: /DYNAMITECOMICS

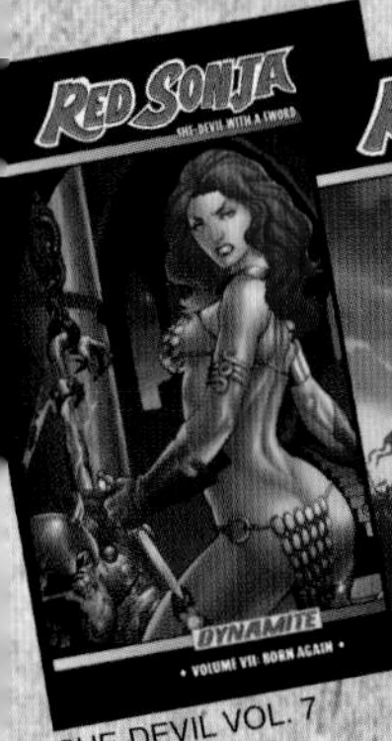
RED SONJA
SHE-DEVIL WITH A SWORD
DYNAMITE
VOLUME VII: BORN AGAIN
SHE-DEVIL VOL. 7
9781606900116

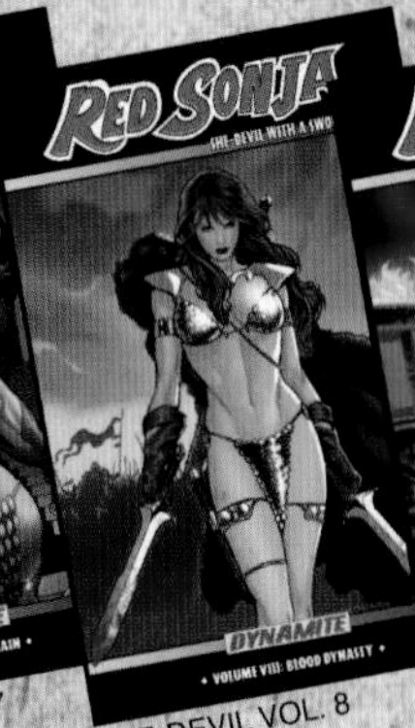
RED SONJA
SHE-DEVIL WITH A SWORD
DYNAMITE
VOLUME VIII: BLOOD DYNASTY
SHE-DEVIL VOL. 8
9781606900635

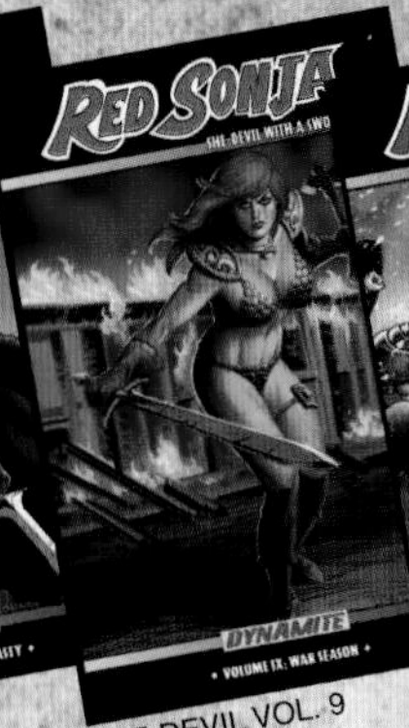
RED SONJA
SHE-DEVIL WITH A SWORD
DYNAMITE
VOLUME IX: WAR SEASON
SHE-DEVIL VOL. 9
9781606901120

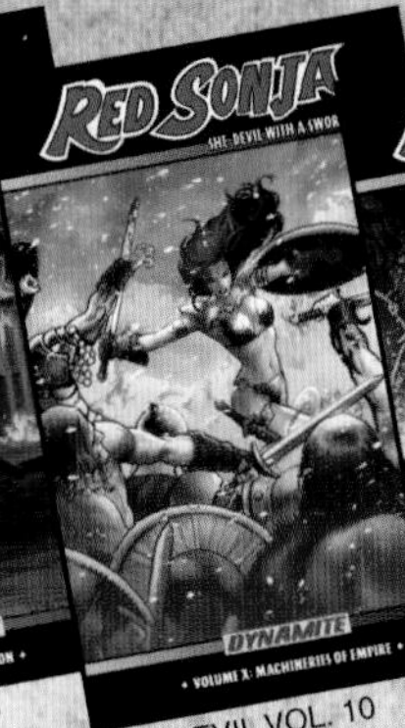
RED SONJA
SHE-DEVIL WITH A SWORD
DYNAMITE
VOLUME X: MACHINERIES OF EMPIRE
SHE-DEVIL VOL. 10
9781606903162

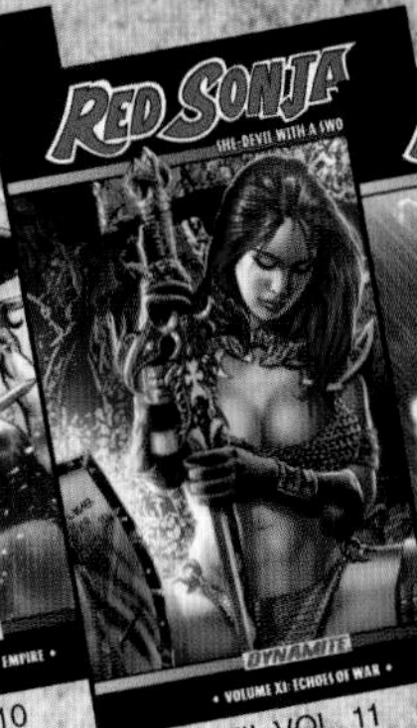
RED SONJA
SHE-DEVIL WITH A SWORD
DYNAMITE
VOLUME XI: ECHOES OF WAR
SHE-DEVIL VOL. 11
9781606904091

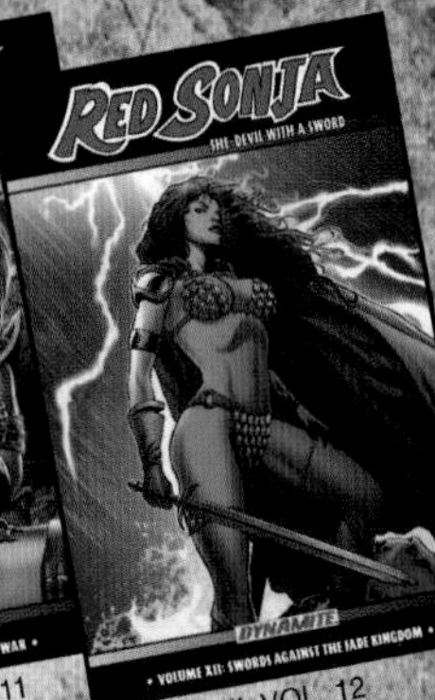
RED SONJA
SHE-DEVIL WITH A SWORD
DYNAMITE
VOLUME XII: SWORDS AGAINST THE JADE KINGDOM
SHE-DEVIL VOL. 12
9781606904428

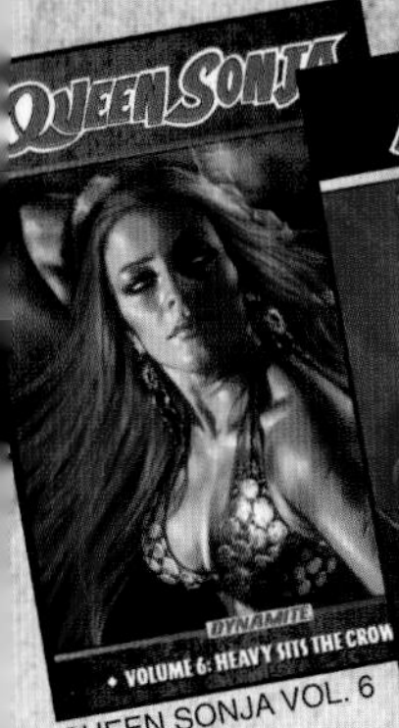
QUEEN SONJA
DYNAMITE
VOLUME 6: HEAVY SITS THE CROW
QUEEN SONJA VOL. 6
9781606904022

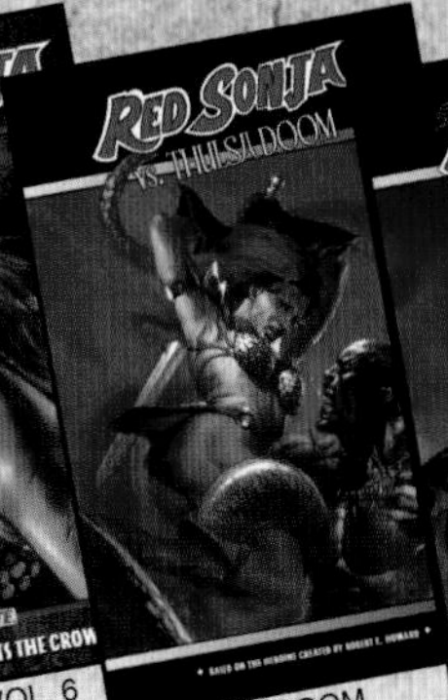
RED SONJA
vs. THULSA DOOM
vs THULSA DOOM
9781933305967

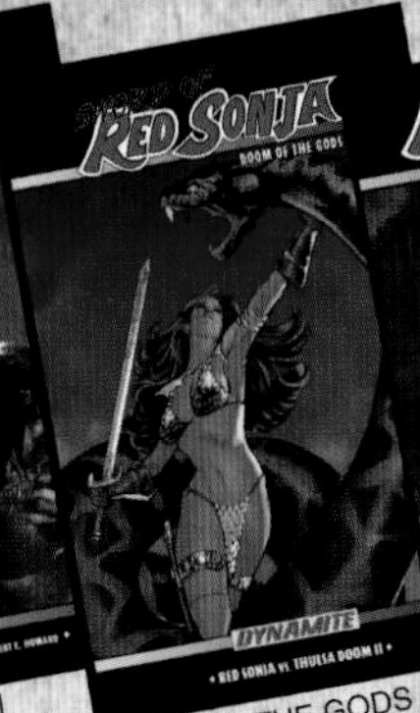
RED SONJA
DOOM OF THE GODS
DYNAMITE
RED SONJA vs. THULSA DOOM II
DOOM OF THE GODS
vs THULSA DOOM II
9781933305769

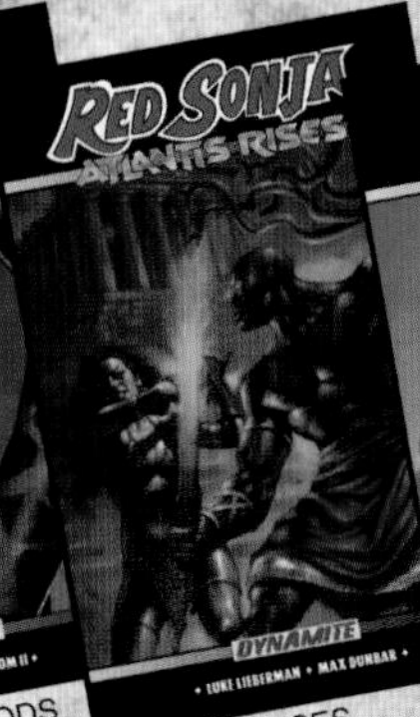
RED SONJA
ATLANTIS RISES
DYNAMITE
LUKE LIEBERMAN • MAX DUNBAR
ATLANTIS RISES
9781606903940

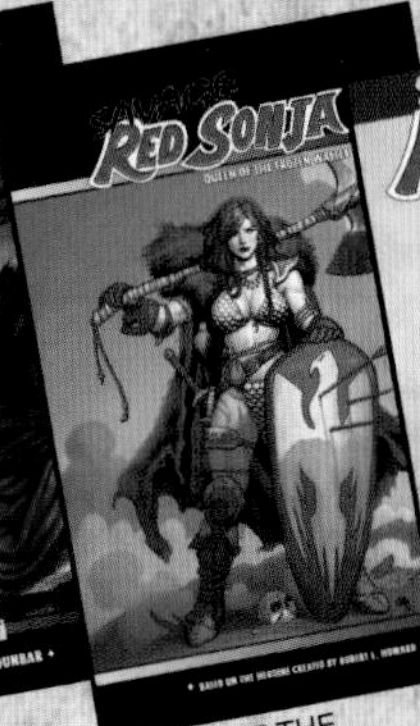
RED SONJA
QUEEN OF THE
FROZZEN WASTES
9781933305387

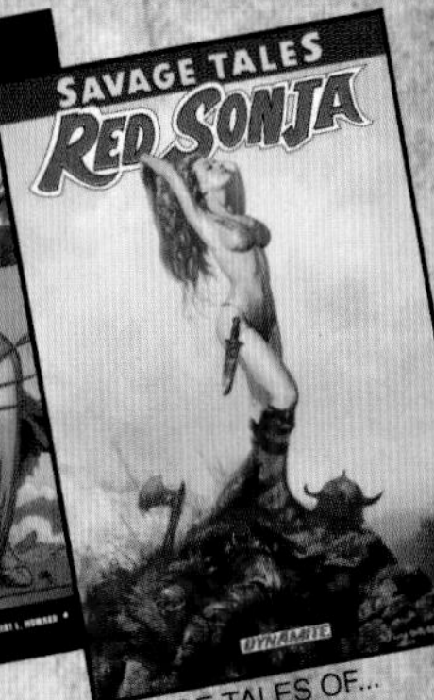
SAVAGE TALES
RED SONJA
DYNAMITE
SAVAGE TALES OF...
9781606900819

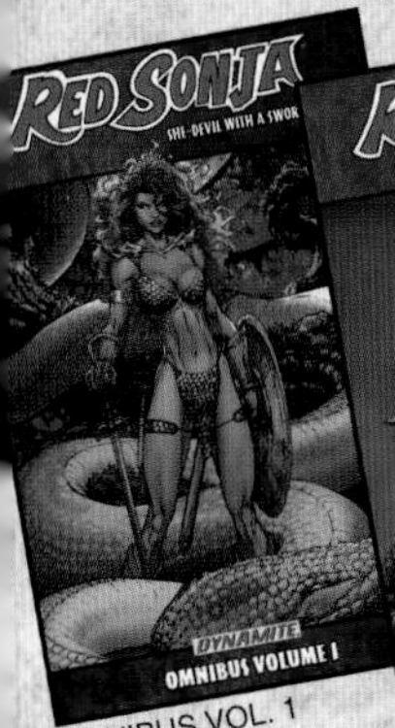
RED SONJA
DYNAMITE
OMNIBUS VOLUME I
OMNIBUS VOL. 1
9781606901014

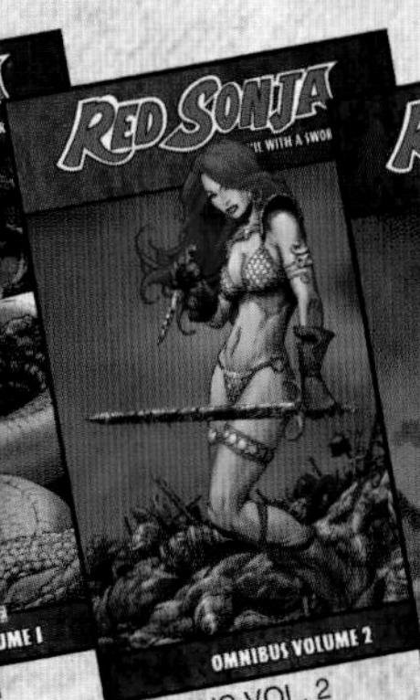
RED SONJA
OMNIBUS VOLUME 2
OMNIBUS VOL. 2
9781606902318

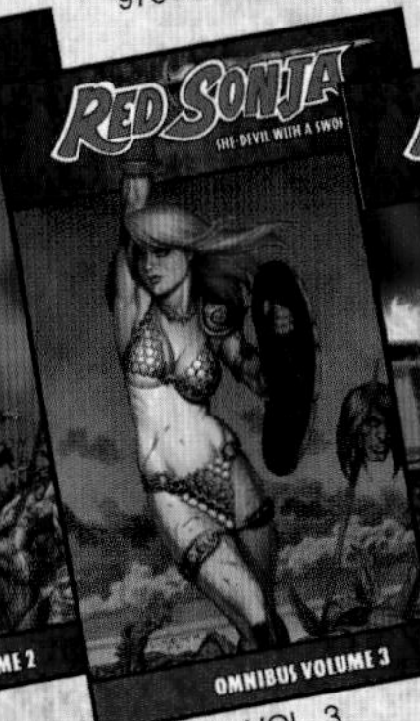
RED SONJA
SHE-DEVIL WITH A SWORD
OMNIBUS VOLUME 3
OMNIBUS VOL. 3
9781606903445

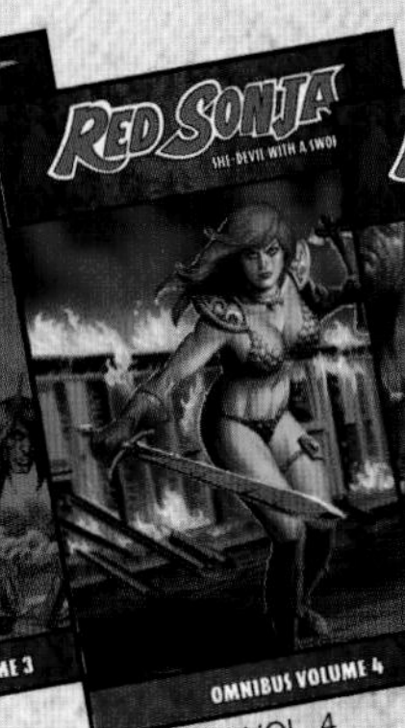
RED SONJA
OMNIBUS VOLUME 4
OMNIBUS VOL. 4
9781606904251

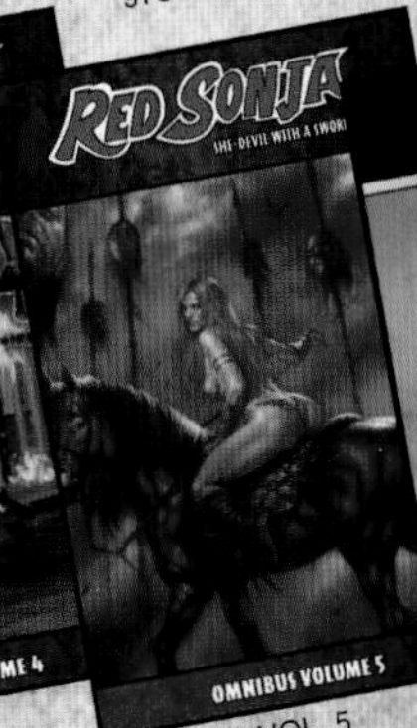
RED SONJA
OMNIBUS VOLUME 5
OMNIBUS VOL. 5
9781606904886

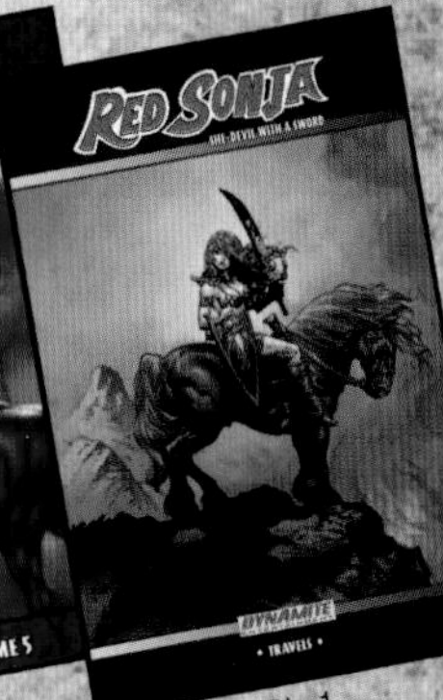
RED SONJA
SHE-DEVIL WITH A SWORD
DYNAMITE
TRAVELS
TRAVELS VOL. 1
9781933305202

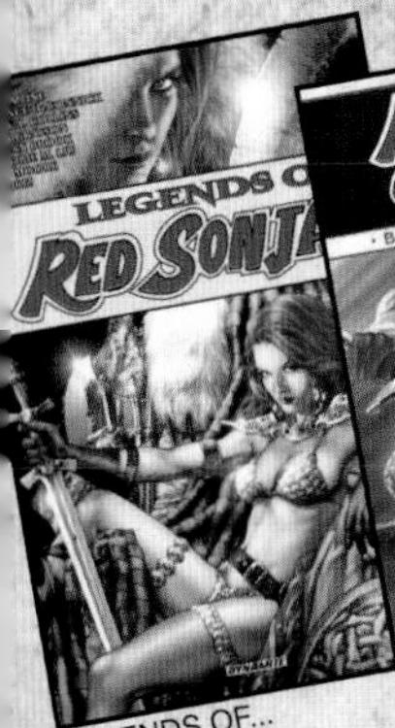
LEGENDS OF
RED SONJA
DYNAMITE
LEGENDS OF...
9781606905258

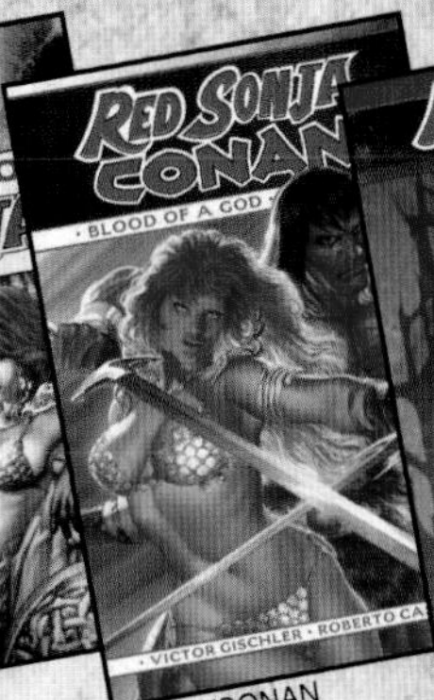
RED SONJA
CONAN
BLOOD OF A GOD
VICTOR GISCHLER • ROBERTO CA
SONJA/CONAN
9781606908211

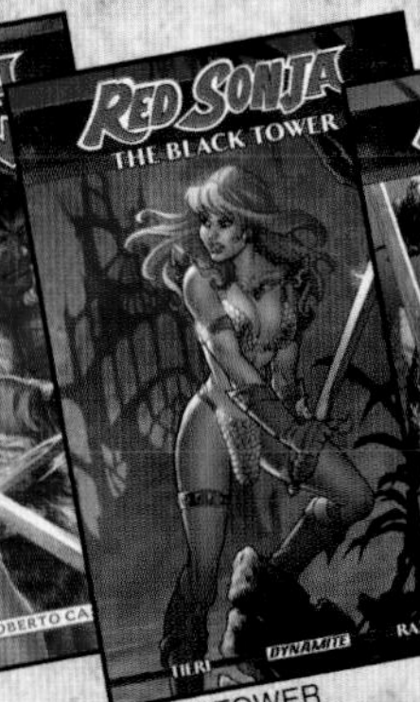
RED SONJA
THE BLACK TOWER
TIERI
DYNAMITE
BLACK TOWER
9781606907924

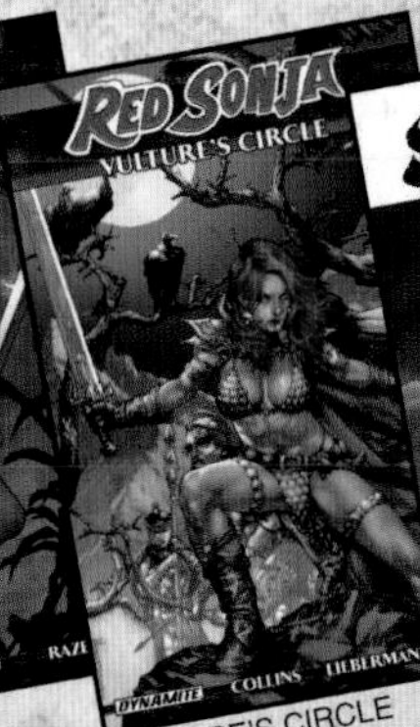
RED SONJA
VULTURE'S CIRCLE
DYNAMITE
COLLINS
LIEBERMAN
VULTURE'S CIRCLE
9781606908020

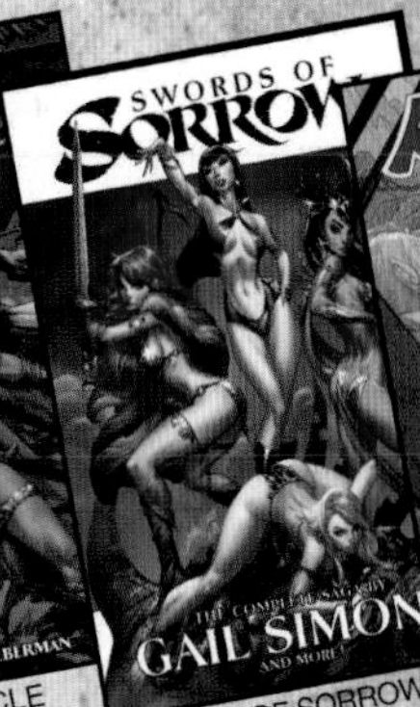
SWORDS OF
SORROW
GAIL SIMONE
AND MORE
SWORDS OF SORROW
9781606908068

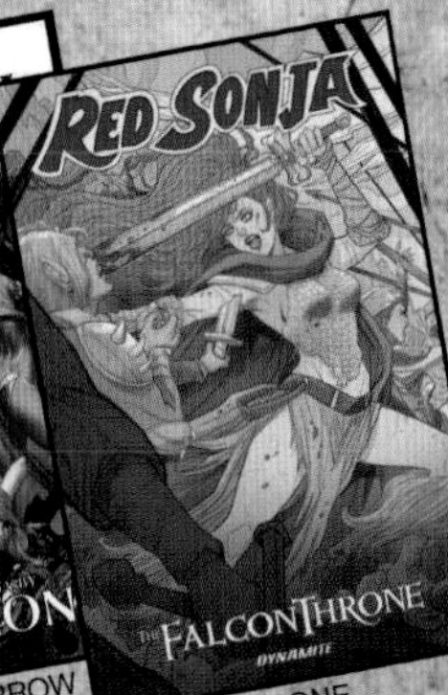
RED SONJA
THE FALCON THRONE
DYNAMITE
FALCON THRONE
9781524101152

Online at **www.DYNAMITE.com**
Instragram **/Dynamitecomics**
On Twitter **@Dynamitecomics**
On Facebook **/Dynamitecomics**
On Tumblr **dynamitecomics.tumblr.com**
On YouTube **/Dynamitecomics**

DYNAMITE®

THE SHE-DEVIL WITH A SWORD TAKES MANHATTAN!

RED SONJA
WORLDS AWAY: VOLUME 1
AMY CHU
CARLOS GOMEZ
WORLDS AWAY
VOLUME 1
DYNAMITE

"SLICK STORYTELLING AND STRONG VISUALS MAKE THIS BOOK A WINNER IN ANY TIME. ABSOLUTELY RECOMMENDED."
SciFi Pulse

"RED SONJA JUST MAY BE ONE OF THE STRONGEST PROPERTIES DYNAMITE IS PRODUCING. THIS IS A GREAT JUMPING ON POINT."
All-Comic

"DYNAMITE HAS A SURE-FIRE HIT HERE AND WITH A CREATIVE TEAM OF AMY CHU AND CARLOS GOMEZ AT THE HELM THERE IS NO TELLING JUST HOW AMAZING THIS IS GOING TO GET."
Outright Geekery

Written by **AMY CHU** (Poison Ivy, Kiss)
Drawn by **CARLOS GOMEZ** (The Dresden Files)

TRADE PAPERBACK AVAILABLE NOW

Also available: **VOLUME 2: BACK ROADS**

DYNAMITE
www.dynamite.com
/dynamitecomics
@dynamitecomics

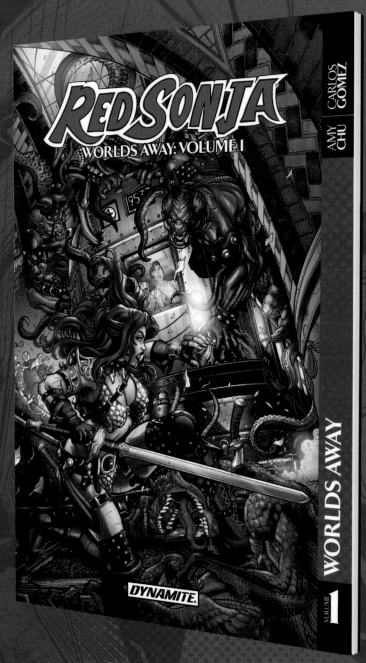